32 BASIC Programs for the TRS-80 (Level II) Computer

32 BASIC Programs for the TRS-80 (Level II) Computer

Tom Rugg and Phil Feldman

dilithium Press
Portland, Oregon

ISBN: 0-918398-27-4
Library of Congress catalog card number: 79-56399

Printed in the United States of America.

dilithium Press
P.O. Box 92
Forest Grove, Oregon 97116

TRS-80 refers to the Radio Shack microcomputer and is a registered trademark of Tandy Corporation, Fort Worth, Texas.

Acknowledgements

Our thanks to the following for their help and encouragement: Our wives and families, John Craig, Merl and Patti Miller, Asenatha McCauley, Herb Furth, Freddie, Wayne Green, and Knute Johnson.

AN IMPORTANT NOTE

The publisher and authors have made every effort to assure that the computer programs and programming information in this publication are accurate and complete. However, this publication is prepared for general readership, and neither the publisher nor the authors have any knowledge about or ability to control any third party's use of the programs and programming information. There is no warranty or representation by either the publisher or the authors that the programs or programming information in this book will enable the reader or user to achieve any particular result.

Preface

You have bought yourself a Radio Shack TRS-80 computer with Level II BASIC (or maybe you just have access to one at school or work). You will soon find that the most frequent question you are asked goes something like this: "Oh, you got a computer, eh? Uh . . . what are you going to do with it?"

Your answer, of course, depends on your own particular situation. Maybe you got it for mathematical work, or for your business, or for home usage, or to enable you to learn more about computers. Maybe you got it for a teaching/learning tool or for playing games.

Even if you got the computer specifically for only one of these reasons, you should not neglect the others. The computer is such a powerful tool that it can be used in many different ways. If it is not being used for its "intended" function right now, why not make use of it in some other way?

The TRS-80 is so small and portable that you can, say, take it home from work over the weekend and let the kids play educational games. They will have fun *and* learn a lot. After they go to bed, you can use it to help plan your personal finances. Or, you can let your guests at a party try to outsmart the TRS-80 (or each other) at some fascinating games. The possibilities go on and on.

All these things can be done with the TRS-80, but the TRS-80 cannot do any of them without the key ingredient—a computer program. People with little or no exposure to computers may be in for a surprise when they learn this. A computer without a program is like a car without a driver. It just sits there.

So you ask, "Where can I get some programs to do the things I want my computer to do?" Glad you asked. There are several alternatives.

1. Hire a computer programmer. If you have a big budget, this is the way to go. Good programmers are expensive and hard to find (and you will not know for sure if they're really good until after the job is finished). Writing a couple of programs that are moderately complex will probably cost you more than you paid for the TRS-80 itself.

2. Learn to program yourself. This is a nice alternative, but it takes time. There are lots of programming books available — some are good, some not so good. You can take courses at local colleges. If you can afford the time and you have a fair amount of common sense and inner drive, this is a good solution.

3. Buy the programs you want. This is cheaper than hiring your own programmer because all the buyers share the cost of writing the programs. You still will not find it very cheap, especially if you want to accumulate several dozen programs. Each program might cost anywhere from a few dollars to several hundred dollars. The main problem is that you cannot be sure how good the programs are, and, since they are generalized for all possible buyers, you may not be able to easily modify them to do exactly what *you* want. Also, they have to be written in a computer language that *your* computer understands. Even if you find a program written in the BASIC language, you will soon learn that the TRS-80's BASIC is not the same as other versions. Variations between versions of the same language typically result in the program not working.

This book gives you the chance to take the third alternative at the lowest possible cost. If you divide the cost of the book by the number of programs in it (use your computer if you like), you will find that the cost per program is amazingly low. Even if there are only a few programs in the book that will be useful to you, the cost is pretty hard to beat.

Just as important is the fact that these programs are written specifically for your TRS-80. If you type them in exactly as shown, they will work! No changes are needed. In addition, we show you exactly what to change in order to make some simple modifications that may suit your taste or needs. Plus, if you have learned a little about BASIC, you can go even further and follow the suggestions about more extensive changes that can be made. This approach was used to try to make every program useful to you, whether you are a total beginner or an old hand with computers.

But enough of the sales pitch. Our main point is that we feel a computer is an incredibly flexible machine, and it is a shame to put it to only one or two limited uses and let it sit idle the rest of the time. We are giving you a pretty wide range of things to do with your TRS-80, and we are really only scratching the surface.

So open your eyes and your mind. Play a mental game against the computer (WARI, JOT). Evaluate your next financial decision (LOAN, DECIDE). Expand your vocabulary or improve your reading speed (VOCAB, TACHIST). Solve mathematical equations (DIFFEQN, SIMEQN).

But please, don't leave your TRS-80 asleep in the corner too much. Give it some exercise.

How to Use This Book

Each chapter of this book presents a computer program that runs on a 16K Radio Shack TRS-80 (Level II) computer. Most will also run on a 4K TRS-80 with Level II (see Appendix 1). Each chapter is made up of eight sections that serve the following functions:

1. **Purpose**: Explains what the program does and why you might want to use it.
2. **How To Use It**: Gives the details of what happens when you run the program. Explains your options and the meanings of any responses you might give. Provides details of any limitations of the program or errors that might occur.
3. **Sample Run**: Shows you what you will see on the screen when you run the program.
4. **Program Listing**: Provides a "listing" (or "print-out") of the BASIC program. These are the instructions to the computer that you must provide so it will know what to do. You must type them in extremely carefully for correct results.
5. **Easy Changes**: Shows you some very simple changes you can make to the program to cause it to work differently, if you wish. You do not have to understand how to program to make these changes.
6. **Main Routines**: Explains the general logic of the program, in case you want to figure out how it works. Gives the BASIC line numbers and a brief explanation of what each major portion of the program accomplishes.
7. **Main Variables**: Explains what each of the key variables in the program is used for, in case you want to figure out how it works.

8. **Suggested Projects:** Provides a few ideas for major changes you might want to make to the program. To try any of these, you will need to understand BASIC and use the information provided in the previous two sections (Main Routines and Main Variables).

To use any of these programs on your TRS-80 computer, you need only use the first four sections. The last four sections are there to give you supplementary information if you want to tinker with the program.

RECOMMENDED PROCEDURE

Here is our recommendation of how to try any of the programs in this book:

1. Read through the documentation that came with the TRS-80 to learn the fundamentals of communication with the computer. This will teach you how to turn the computer on, enter a program, correct mistakes, run a program, etc.
2. Pick a chapter and read Section 1 ("Purpose") to see if the program sounds interesting or useful to you. If not, move on to the next chapter until you find one that is. If you are a beginner you might want to try one of the short "Miscellaneous Programs" first.
3. Read Sections 2 and 3 of the chapter ("How To Use It" and "Sample Run") to learn the details of what the program does.
4. Enter the NEW command to eliminate any existing program that might already be in your TRS-80's memory. Using Section 4 of the chapter ("Program Listing"), carefully enter the program into the TRS-80. Be particularly careful to get all the punctuation characters right (i.e., commas, semicolons, colons, quotation marks, etc.).
5. **After the entire program is entered into the TRS-80's memory, use the LIST command to display what you have entered so you can double check for typographical errors, omitted lines, etc.** Don't mistake a semicolon for a colon, or an alphabetic I or O for a numeric 1 or 0 (zero). Take a minute to note the differences in these characters before you begin.
6. Before trying to RUN the program, use the CSAVE command to save the program temporarily on cassette. This could prevent a lot of wasted effort in case something goes wrong (power failure, computer malfunction, etc.).

7. Now RUN the program. Is the same thing happening that is shown in the Sample Run? If so, accept our congratulations and go on to step 9. If not, stay cool and go to step 8.

8. If you got a SYNTAX ERROR in a line, LIST that line and look at it closely. Something is not right. Maybe you interchanged a colon and a semicolon. Maybe you typed a numeric 1 or 0 instead of an alphabetic I or O. Maybe you misspelled a word or omitted one. Keep looking until you find it, then correct the error and go back to step 7.

   If you got some other kind of error message, consult the TRS-80 documentation for an explanation. Keep in mind that the error might not be in the line that is pointed to by the error message. It is not unusual for the mistake to be in a line immediately preceding the error message line. Another possibility is that one or more lines were omitted entirely. In any event, fix the problem and go back to step 7.

   If there are no error messages, but the program is not doing the same thing as the Sample Run, there are two possibilities. First, maybe the program isn't *supposed* to do exactly the same thing. Some of the programs are designed to do unpredictable things to avoid repetition (primarily the game programs and graphic displays). They should be doing the same *types* of things as the Sample Run, however.

   The second possibility is that you made a typing error that did not cause an error message to be displayed, but simply changed the meaning of one or more lines in the program. These are a little tricky to find, but you can usually narrow it down to the general area of the problem by noting the point at which the error takes place. Is the first thing displayed correct? If so, the error is probably after the PRINT statement that caused the first thing to be displayed. Look for the same types of things mentioned before. Make the corrections and go back to step 7.

9. Continue running the program, trying to duplicate the Sample Run. If you find a variation that cannot be accounted for in the "How To Use It" section of the chapter, go to step 8. Otherwise, if it seems to be running properly, CSAVE the program on cassette and check it with CLOAD?.

10. Read Section 5 of the chapter ("Easy Changes"). Try any of the changes that look interesting. If you think the changed version is better. CSAVE it on cassette, too. You will probably

want to give it a slightly different title in the first REM statement to avoid future confusion.

A NOTE ON THE PROGRAM LISTINGS

A line on the screen of the TRS-80 is 64 characters wide. The
printer that was used to create the Program Listing section of
each chapter prints lines up to 80 characters long. For best
reproduction in this book, it is preferable that each published
line be no longer than 59 characters. This combination of facts
might cause you a little confusion when you are copying the
programs into your TRS-80. Here's the way it works.

Wherever there is a line in a program that is longer than 59
characters, it has been divided into two lines that are each no
more than 59 characters. You can recognize this easily because
the second part has no line number at the left-hand side. This
division is only for the purpose of printing the book. You should
think of a divided line like this as one long line and enter it
into your TRS-80 as a single line. Where possible, this division
is made in such a way that the first part of the line ends with
a colon so you can notice it more easily.

Don't be fooled by the fact that the cursor on your TRS-80
jumps down to the next line after you enter the 64th character
—it's just one long line until you press **ENTER**.

Contents

Section 3—GAME PROGRAMS

Section 4—GRAPHICS DISPLAY PROGRAMS

Section 5—MATHEMATICS PROGRAMS

Section 6—MISCELLANEOUS PROGRAMS

Short programs that do interesting things.

Section 1
Applications Programs

INTRODUCTION TO APPLICATIONS PROGRAMS

Good practical applications are certainly a prime use of personal computers. There are a myriad of ways the TRS-80 can help us to do useful work. Here are six programs for use around the home or business.

Financial considerations are always important. LOAN will calculate interest, payment schedules etc. for mortgages, car loans, or any such business loan. Do you ever have trouble balancing your checkbook(s)? CHECKBOOK will enable you to rectify your monthly statements and help you find the cause of any errors.

Fuel usage is a constant concern for those of us who drive. MILEAGE will determine and keep track of a motor vehicle's general operating efficiency.

The tedium of analyzing questionnaires and examinations can be greatly relieved with the aid of your computer. In particular, teachers and market researchers should find QUEST/EXAM useful.

Often we are faced with difficult decisions. DECIDE transforms the TRS-80 into a trusty advisor. Help will be at hand for any decision involving the selection of one alternative from several choices.

Before anything else, you might want to consult BIORHYTHM each day. Some major airlines, and other industries, are placing credence on biorhythm theory. If you agree, or "just in case," simply turn on your TRS-80 and load this program.

BIORHYTHM

PURPOSE

Did you ever have one of those days when nothing seemed to go right? All of us seem to have days when we are clumsy, feel depressed, or just cannot seem to force ourselves to concentrate as well as usual. Sometimes we know why this occurs. It may result from the onset of a cold or because of an argument with a relative. Sometimes, however, we find no such reason. Why can't we perform up to par on some of those days when nothing is known to be wrong?

Biorhythm theory says that all of us have cycles, beginning with the moment of birth, that influence our physical, emotional, and intellectual states. We will not go into a lot of detail about how biorhythm theory was developed (your local library probably has some books about this if you want to find out more), but we will summarize how it supposedly affects you.

The physical cycle is twenty-three days long. For the first 11½ days, you are in the positive half of the cycle. This means you should have a feeling of physical well-being, strength, and endurance. During the second 11½ days, you are in the negative half of the cycle. This results in less endurance and a tendency toward a general feeling of fatigue.

The emotional cycle lasts for twenty-eight days. During the positive half (the first fourteen days), you should feel more cheerful, optimistic, and cooperative. During the negative half, you will tend to be more moody, pessimistic, and irritable.

The third cycle is the intellectual cycle, which lasts for thirty-three days. The first half is a period in which you should have greater success in learning new material and pursuing creative, intellectual activities. During the second half, you are supposedly better off reviewing old material rather than attempting to learn difficult new concepts.

The ups and downs of these cycles are relative to each individual. For example, if you are a very self-controlled, unemotional person to begin with, your emotional highs and lows may not be very noticeable. Similarly, your physical and intellectual fluctuations depend upon your physical condition and intellectual capacity.

The day that any of these three cycles changes from the plus side to the minus side (or vice versa) is called a "critical day." Biorhythm theory says that you are more accident-prone on critical days in your physical or emotional cycles. Critical days in the intellectual cycle aren't considered as dangerous, but if they coincide with a critical day in one of the other cycles, the potential problem can increase. As you might expect, a triple critical day is one on which you are recommended to be especially careful.

Please note that there is quite a bit of controversy about biorhythms. Most scientists feel that there is not nearly enough evidence to conclude that biorhythms can tell you anything meaningful. Others believe that biorhythm cycles exist, but that they are not as simple and inflexible as the 23, 28, and 33 day cycles mentioned here.

Whether biorhythms are good, bad, true, false, or anything else is not our concern here. We are just presenting the idea to you as an interesting theory that you can investigate with the help of your TRS-80 computer.

HOW TO USE IT

The program first asks for the birth date of the person whose biorhythm cycles are to be charted. You provide the month and day as you might expect. For the year, you only need to enter the last two digits if it is between 1900 and 1999. Otherwise, enter all four digits.

Next the program asks you for the start date for the biorhythm chart. Enter it in the same way. Of course, this date cannot be earlier than the birth date.

After a delay of about a second, the program clears the screen and begins plotting the biorhythm chart, one day at a time. The left side of the screen displays the date, while the right side displays the chart. The left half of the chart is the "down" (negative) side of each cycle. The right half is the "up" (positive) side. The center line shows the critical days when you are at a zero point (neither positive or negative).

Each of the three curves is plotted with an identifying letter— P for physical, E for emotional, and I for intellectual. When the curves cross, an asterisk is displayed instead of either of the two (or three) letters.

Twelve days of the chart are displayed on one screen, and then the program waits for you to press a key. If you press the E key, the current chart ends and the program starts over again. If you press the **SPACE** key (or any other key except **BREAK** or **SHIFT**), the program clears the screen and displays the next twelve days of the chart.

The program will allow you to enter dates from the year 100 A.D. and on. We make no guarantees about any extreme future dates, however, such as entering a year greater than 3000. We sincerely hope that these limitations do not prove to be too confining for you.

SAMPLE RUN

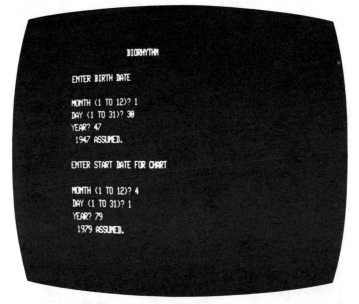

The operator enters his or her birth date and the date for the beginning of the chart

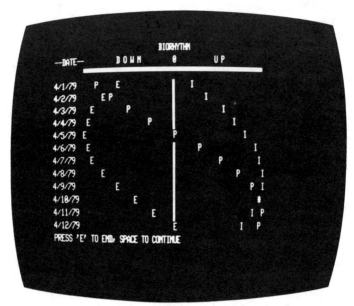

The program responds with the first 12 days of the operator's biorhythm chart, then waits for a key to be pressed.

PROGRAM LISTING

```
100 REM: BIORHYTHM
110 REM: COPYRIGHT 1979 BY TOM RUGG AND PHIL FELDMAN
120 CLEAR 200:DEFINT K,L:DEFDBL B,J,M-Z
130 L=0:T=25:P=3.1415926535:CLS
140 PRINT TAB(15);"BIORHYTHM":PRINT
150 PRINT"ENTER BIRTH DATE"
160 GOSUB 500
170 GOSUB 600
180 JB=JD
190 PRINT:PRINT"ENTER START DATE FOR CHART"
200 GOSUB 500
210 GOSUB 600
220 JC=JD
230 IF JC>=JB THEN 270
240 PRINT"CHART DATE CAN'T BE EARLIER THAN"
250 PRINT"BIRTH DATE.  TRY AGAIN."
260 GOTO 150
270 FOR K=1 TO 1000:NEXT
280 GOSUB 700
300 N=JC-JB
```

```
310 V=23:GOSUB 800:GOSUB 850
320 V=28:GOSUB 800:GOSUB 850
330 V=33:GOSUB 800:GOSUB 850
340 GOSUB 1000
350 PRINT C$;TAB(8);L$
360 JC=JC+1:L=L+1:IF L<12 THEN 300
370 PRINT"PRESS 'E' TO END, SPACE TO CONTINUE";
380 R$=INKEY$:IF R$="" THEN 380
390 IF R$="E" THEN 120
400 L=0:GOTO 280
500 PRINT
505 INPUT"MONTH (1 TO 12)";M
510 M=INT(M):IF M<1 OR M>12 THEN 505
520 INPUT"DAY (1 TO 31)";D
530 D=INT(D):IF D<1 OR D>31 THEN 520
540 INPUT"YEAR";Y
550 Y=INT(Y):IF Y<0 THEN 540
560 IF Y>99 THEN 580
570 Y=Y+1900:PRINT Y;"ASSUMED."
580 RETURN
600 W=FIX((M-14)/12)
610 JD=INT(1461*(Y+4800+W)/4)
620 B=FIX(367*(M-2-W*12)/12)
640 JD=JD+B
650 B=INT(INT(3*(Y+4900+W)/100)/4)
660 JD=JD+D-32075-B
670 RETURN
700 CLS
710 PRINT TAB(29);"BIORHYTHM"
720 PRINT"--DATE--";TAB(17);
730 PRINT"D O W N";TAB(33);"0";TAB(45);"U P"
740 PRINT TAB(8);
750 FOR K=1 TO T+T+1:PRINT CHR$(131);:NEXT:PRINT:RETURN
800 W=INT(N/V):R=N-(W*V)
810 RETURN
850 IF V<>23 THEN 900
860 L$=CHR$(32):FOR K=1 TO 5:L$=L$+L$:NEXT
870 L$=L$+LEFT$(L$,19)
880 L$=LEFT$(L$,T)+CHR$(149)+RIGHT$(L$,T)
890 IF V=23 THEN C$="P"
900 IF V=28 THEN C$="E"
910 IF V=33 THEN C$="I"
920 W=R/V:W=W*2*P
930 W=T*SIN(W):W=W+T+1.5
940 W=INT(W):A$=MID$(L$,W,1)
950 IF A$="P" OR A$="E" OR A$="*" THEN C$="*"
```

```
955 IF W=1 THEN 980
957 IF W=T+T+1 THEN 990
960 L$=LEFT$(L$,W-1)+C$+RIGHT$(L$,T+T+1-W)
970 RETURN
980 L$=C$+RIGHT$(L$,T+T):RETURN
990 L$=LEFT$(L$,T+T)+C$:RETURN
1000 W=JC+68569:R=INT(4*W/146097)
1010 W=W-INT((146097*R+3)/4)
1020 Y=INT(4000*(W+1)/1461001)
1030 W=W-INT(1461*Y/4)+31
1040 M=INT(80*W/2447)
1050 D=W-INT(2447*M/80)
1060 W=INT(M/11):M=M+2-12*W
1070 Y=100*(R-49)+Y+W
1080 A$=STR$(M):W=LEN(A$)-1
1090 C$=MID$(A$,2,W)+"/"
1100 A$=STR$(D):W=LEN(A$)-1
1110 C$=C$+MID$(A$,2,W)+"/"
1120 A$=STR$(Y):W=LEN(A$)-1
1130 C$=C$+MID$(A$,W,2)
1140 RETURN
```

EASY CHANGES

1. Want to see the number of days between any two dates? Insert this line:

    305 PRINT "DAYS ="; N: END

   Then enter the earlier date as the birth date, and the later date as the start date for the chart. This will cause the program to display the difference in days and then end.
2. To alter the number of days of the chart shown on each screen, alter the 12 in line 360.

MAIN ROUTINES

120 - 140   Initializes variables. Displays titles.
150 - 180   Asks for birth date and converts to Julian date format (i.e., the number of days since January 1, 4713 B.C.
190 - 220   Asks for start date for chart and converts to Julian date format.
230 - 260   Checks that chart date is not sooner than birth date.

270	Delays about one second before displaying chart.
280	Displays heading at top of screen.
300	Determines number of days between birth date and current chart date.
310 - 330	Plots points in L$ string for each of the three cycles.
340	Converts Julian date back into month-day-year format.
350	Displays one line on the chart.
360 - 400	Adds one to chart date. Checks to see if the screen is full.
500 - 580	Subroutine to ask operator for month, day, and year. Edits replies.
600 - 670	Subroutine to convert month, day, and year into Julian date format.
700 - 750	Subroutine to clear screen and display headings.
800 - 810	Subroutine to calculate remainder R of N/V.
850 - 990	Subroutine to plot a point in L$ based on V and R.
1000 -1140	Subroutine to convert Julian date JC back into month-day-year format.

MAIN VARIABLES

L	Counter of number of lines on screen.
T	Number of characters on one side of the center of the chart.
P	Pi.
JB	Birth date in Julian format.
JD	Julian date calculated in subroutine.
JC	Chart start date in Julian format.
K	Loop and work variable.
N	Number of days between birth and current chart date.
V	Number of days in present biorhythm cycle (23, 28, or 33).
C$	String with date in month/day/year format.
L$	String with one line of the biorhythm chart.
R$	Reply from operator after screen fills up.
M	Month (1 - 12)
D	Day (1 - 31)
Y	Year (100 or greater)

W, B   Work variables.
R   Remainder of N/V (number of days into cycle).
A$ Work variable.

SUGGESTED PROJECTS

Investigate the biorhythms of some famous historical or athletic personalities. For example, are track and field athletes usually in the positive side of the physical cycle on the days that they set world records? Where was Lincoln in his emotional and intellectual cycles when he wrote "The Gettysburg Address"? Do a significant percentage of accidents befall people on critical days?

CHECKBOOK

PURPOSE

Many people consider the monthly ritual of balancing the checkbook to be an irritating and error-prone activity. Some people get confused and simply give up after the first try, while others give up the first time they cannot reconcile the bank statement with the checkbook. Fortunately, you have an advantage—your computer. This program takes you through the necessary steps to balance your checkbook, doing the arithmetic for you, of course.

HOW TO USE IT

The program starts off by giving you instructions about how to verify that the amount of each check and deposit are the same on the statement as they are in your checkbook. Sometimes the bank will make an error in reading the amount that you wrote on a check (especially if your handwriting is not too clear), and sometimes you will copy the amount incorrectly into your checkbook. While you are comparing these figures, make a check mark in your checkbook next to each check and deposit listed on the statement. A good system is to alternate the marks you use each month (maybe an "x" one month and a check mark the next) so you can easily see which checks and deposits came through on which statement.

Next, the program asks for the ending balance shown on the bank statement. You are then asked for the *check number* (not the amount) of the most recent check shown on the statement.

This will generally be the highest numbered check the bank has processed, unless you like to write checks out of sequence. Your account balance after this most recent check will be reconciled with the statement balance, so that is what the program asks for next—your checkbook balance after the most recent check.

The program must compensate for any differences between what your checkbook has in it prior to the most recent check and what the statement has on it. First, if you have any deposits that are not shown on the statement before the most recent check, you must enter them. Generally, there are none, so you just enter "END."

Next you have to enter the amounts of any checks that have not yet "cleared" the bank and that are prior to the most recent check. Look in your checkbook for any checks that do not have your check mark next to them. Remember that some of these could be several months old.

Next you enter the amount of any service charges or debit memos that are on the statement, but which have not been shown in your checkbook prior to the most recent check. Typically, this is just a monthly service charge, but there might also be charges for printing new checks for you or some other adjustment that takes money away from you. Credit memos (which give money back to you) are not entered until later. Be sure to make an entry in your checkbook for any of these adjustments so that next month's statement will balance.

Finally, you are asked for any recent deposits or credit memos that were *not* entered in your checkbook prior to the most recent check, but that *are* listed on the bank statement. It is not unusual to have one or two of these, since deposits are generally processed by banks sooner than checks.

Now comes the moment of truth. The program tells you whether or not you are in balance and displays the totals. If so, pack things up until next month's statement arrives.

If not, you have to figure out what is wrong. You have seven options of what to do next which allow you to review the numbers you entered in case of a typing error. If you find an error, go back to the beginning and try again. Of course, if it is a simple error that precisely accounts for the amount by which you are out of balance, there is no need to go through the whole thing again.

If you entered everything correctly, the most likely cause of the out of balance condition is an arithmetic error in your checkbook. Look for errors in your addition and subtraction, with subtraction being the most likely culprit. This is especially likely if the amount of the error is a nice even number like one dollar or ten cents.

Another common error is accidentially adding the amount of a check in your checkbook instead of subtracting it. If you did this, your error will be twice the amount of the check (which makes it easy to find).

If this still does not explain the error, check to be sure you subtracted *last* month's service charge when you balanced your checkbook with the previous statement. And, of course, if you did not balance your checkbook last month, you cannot expect it to come out right this month.

The program has limitations of how many entries you can make in each category (checks outstanding, deposits outstanding, etc.), but these can be changed easily. See "Easy Changes" below.

<u>NOTE: SEE DISCLAIMER IN FRONT PART OF BOOK.</u>

SAMPLE RUN

```
              CHECKBOOK BALANCER

FIRST, COMPARE THE BANK STATEMENT
WITH YOUR CHECKBOOK.
MAKE SURE THE STATEMENT AND THE
CHECKBOOK SHOW THE SAME FIGURES
FOR EACH CHECK AND DEPOSIT.

MAKE A MARK IN THE CHECKBOOK NEXT TO
EACH CHECK AND DEPOSIT LISTED
ON THE STATEMENT.

WHAT'S THE ENDING BALANCE SHOWN
ON THE STATEMENT?
? 520.16
```

NOW FIND THE MOST RECENT CHECK THAT
IS SHOWN ON THE BANK STATEMENT.
WHAT IS THE CHECK NUMBER OF THIS CHECK?
? <u>1652</u>

WHAT BALANCE DOES YOUR CHECKBOOK
SHOW AFTER CHECK NO. 1652
? <u>48Ø.12</u>

ENTER THE AMOUNT OF EACH DEPOSIT
THAT IS SHOWN IN YOUR CHECKBOOK
PRIOR TO CHECK NO. 1652
BUT IS NOT ON THE STATEMENT.
WHEN NO MORE, SAY 'END'
? <u>END</u>

TOTAL = Ø

NOW ENTER THE AMOUNTS OF ANY CHECKS
THAT ARE IN YOUR CHECKBOOK PRIOR
TO CHECK 1652 BUT THAT
HAVE NOT BEEN SHOWN ON A BANK
STATEMENT YET.

WHEN NO MORE, SAY 'END'
? <u>35.Ø4</u>
? <u>1Ø</u>
? <u>END</u>

TOTAL = 45.Ø4

NOW ENTER THE AMOUNTS OF ANY
SERVICE CHARGES OR DEBIT MEMOS.

WHEN NO MORE, SAY 'END'
? <u>2.35</u>
? <u>2.65</u>
? <u>END</u>

TOTAL = 5

ENTER THE AMOUNT OF EACH DEPOSIT
THAT IS SHOWN IN YOUR CHECKBOOK
AFTER CHECK NO. 1652 THAT IS
ALSO LISTED ON THE STATEMENT.

WHEN NO MORE, SAY 'END'
? <u>END</u>

TOTAL = Ø

CONGRATULATIONS! IT BALANCES.

STATEMENT BALANCE + DEPOSITS OUTSTANDING
+ SERVICE CHARGES = 525.16

CHECKBOOK BALANCE + CHECKS OUTSTANDING
+ RECENT DEPOSITS = 525.16

DIFFERENCE = Ø

PRESS ANY KEY TO CONTINUE

NEXT ACTION:
  1 - LIST CHECKS OUTSTANDING
  2 - LIST DEPOSITS OUTSTANDING
  3 - LIST SERVICE CHARGES
  4 - START OVER
  5 - END PROGRAM
  6 - DISPLAY BALANCING INFO
  7 - LIST DEPOSITS AFTER LAST CHECK
? <u>5</u>

PROGRAM LISTING

```
100 REM: CHECKBOOK
110 REM: COPYRIGHT 1979 BY TOM RUGG AND PHIL FELDMAN
120 CLEAR 50:DEFDBL C,D,S,R,T,W:CLS
130 PRINT TAB(9);"CHECKBOOK BALANCER"
140 PRINT
150 MC=50:MD=50:MS=50:MR=50
160 DIM C(MC),D(MD),S(MS),R(MR)
170 TC=0:TD=0:TS=0:TR=0:NC=0:ND=0:NS=0:NR=0
180 E$="ERROR.  RE-ENTER, PLEASE."
190 PRINT"FIRST, COMPARE YOUR BANK STATEMENT"
200 PRINT"WITH YOUR CHECKBOOK."
220 PRINT"MAKE SURE THE STATEMENT AND THE"
230 PRINT"CHECKBOOK SHOW THE SAME FIGURES"
240 PRINT"FOR EACH CHECK AND DEPOSIT."
250 PRINT:PRINT"MAKE A MARK IN THE CHECKBOOK NEXT TO"
260 PRINT"EACH CHECK AND DEPOSIT LISTED"
270 PRINT"ON THE STATEMENT.":PRINT
```

```
280 PRINT"WHAT'S THE ENDING BALANCE SHOWN"
290 PRINT"ON THE STATEMENT?":INPUT SB
300 PRINT:PRINT"NOW FIND THE MOST RECENT CHECK THAT"
310 PRINT"IS SHOWN ON THE BANK STATEMENT."
330 PRINT"WHAT IS THE CHECK NUMBER OF THIS CHECK?"
340 INPUT LC
350 IF LC=INT(LC) THEN 380
360 PRINT"NO, NOT THE AMOUNT OF THE CHECK."
370 GOTO 300
380 PRINT
390 PRINT"WHAT BALANCE DOES YOUR CHECKBOOK"
400 PRINT"SHOW AFTER CHECK NO.";LC
410 INPUT CB
420 PRINT
430 PRINT"ENTER THE AMOUNT OF EACH DEPOSIT"
440 PRINT"THAT IS SHOWN IN YOUR CHECKBOOK"
450 PRINT"PRIOR TO CHECK NO.";LC
460 PRINT"BUT IS NOT ON THE STATEMENT."
470 A$="WHEN NO MORE, SAY 'END'":PRINT A$
480 INPUT R$
490 IF R$="END" THEN 545
500 IF VAL(R$)>0 THEN 520
510 PRINT E$:GOTO 470
520 ND=ND+1:D(ND)=VAL(R$):TD=TD+D(ND)
530 IF ND<MD THEN 480
540 L$="NO MORE ROOM.":PRINT:PRINT L$
545 PRINT:PRINT"TOTAL =";TD:PRINT
550 PRINT"NOW ENTER THE AMOUNTS OF ANY CHECKS"
560 PRINT"THAT ARE IN THE CHECKBOOK PRIOR"
570 PRINT"TO CHECK";LC;"BUT THAT"
580 PRINT"HAVE NOT BEEN SHOWN ON A BANK"
590 PRINT"STATEMENT YET."
600 PRINT:PRINT A$
610 INPUT R$
620 IF R$="END" THEN 690
630 IF VAL(R$)>0 THEN 660
640 PRINT:PRINT E$
650 GOTO 600
660 NC=NC+1:C(NC)=VAL(R$):TC=TC+C(NC)
670 IF NC<MC THEN 610
680 PRINT:PRINT L$:PRINT
690 PRINT:PRINT"TOTAL =";TC:PRINT
700 PRINT"NOW ENTER THE AMOUNTS OF ANY"
710 PRINT"SERVICE CHARGES OR DEBIT MEMOS."
720 PRINT:PRINT A$
```

```
730 INPUT R$
740 IF R$="END" THEN 800
750 IF VAL(R$)>0 THEN 770
760 PRINT:PRINT E$:GOTO 720
770 NS=NS+1:S(NS)=VAL(R$):TS=TS+S(NS)
780 IF NS<MS THEN 730
790 PRINT:PRINT L$:PRINT
800 PRINT:PRINT"TOTAL =";TS:PRINT
805 GOSUB 2000
810 W=SB+TD+TS-CB-TC-TR:W=ABS(W)
815 IF W<.001 THEN W=0 ELSE GOTO 840
820 PRINT"CONGRATULATIONS!  IT BALANCES."
830 GOTO 850
840 PRINT"SORRY.  IT'S OUT OF BALANCE."
850 PRINT
860 PRINT"STATEMENT BALANCE + DEPOSITS OUTSTANDING"
870 PRINT"+ SERVICE CHARGES =";SB+TD+TS
880 PRINT
890 PRINT"CHECKBOOK BALANCE + CHECKS OUTSTANDING"
900 PRINT"+ RECENT DEPOSITS =";CB+TC+TR
910 PRINT
920 PRINT"DIFFERENCE =";W
925 PRINT:PRINT"PRESS ANY KEY TO CONTINUE"
930 IF INKEY$="" THEN 930
935 PRINT
940 PRINT"NEXT ACTION:"
950 PRINT" 1 - LIST CHECKS OUTSTANDING"
960 PRINT" 2 - LIST DEPOSITS OUTSTANDING"
970 PRINT" 3 - LIST SERVICE CHARGES"
980 PRINT" 4 - START OVER"
990 PRINT" 5 - END PROGRAM"
1000 PRINT" 6 - DISPLAY BALANCING INFO"
1010 PRINT" 7 - LIST DEPOSITS AFTER LAST CHECK"
1020 INPUT R$:R=VAL(R$)
1030 IF R<1 OR R>7 THEN 1050
1040 ON R GOTO 1100,1200,1300,1400,1500,850,1700
1050 PRINT:PRINT E$:GOTO 935
1100 PRINT:PRINT"CHECKS OUTSTANDING"
1110 FOR J=1 TO NC
1120 PRINT C(J):NEXT
1130 GOTO 925
1200 PRINT:PRINT"DEPOSITS OUTSTANDING"
1210 FOR J=1 TO ND
1220 PRINT D(J):NEXT
1230 GOTO 925
```

```
1300 PRINT:PRINT"SERVICE CHARGES"
1310 FOR J=1 TO NS
1320 PRINT S(J):NEXT
1330 GOTO 925
1400 GOTO 120
1500 END
1700 PRINT:PRINT"RECENT DEPOSITS"
1710 FOR J=1 TO NR
1720 PRINT R(J):NEXT
1730 GOTO 925
2000 PRINT
2010 PRINT"ENTER THE AMOUNT OF EACH DEPOSIT"
2020 PRINT"THAT IS SHOWN IN YOUR CHECKBOOK"
2030 PRINT"AFTER CHECK NO.";LC;"THAT IS"
2040 PRINT"ALSO LISTED IN THE STATEMENT."
2050 PRINT:PRINT A$
2060 INPUT R$
2070 IF R$="END" THEN 2130
2080 IF VAL(R$)>0 THEN 2100
2090 PRINT:PRINT E$:GOTO 2050
2100 NR=NR+1:R(NR)=VAL(R$):TR=TR+R(NR)
2110 IF NR<MR THEN 2060
2120 PRINT:PRINT L$
2130 PRINT:PRINT"TOTAL =";TR:PRINT
2140 RETURN
```

EASY CHANGES

Change the limitations of how many entries you can make in each category. Line 150 establishes these limits. If you have more than 50 checks outstanding at some time, change the value of MC to 100, for example. The other three variables can also be changed if you anticipate needing more than 50 entries. They are: the number of deposits outstanding (MD), the number of service charges and debit memos (MS), and the number of recent deposits and credit memos (MR).

MAIN ROUTINES

120 - 290	Initializes variables and displays first instructions.
300 - 370	Gets most recent check number.
380 - 410	Gets checkbook balance after most recent check number.
420 - 545	Gets outstanding deposits.

550 - 690	Gets outstanding checks.
700 - 800	Gets service charges and debit memos.
805	Gets recent deposits and credit memos.
810 - 920	Does balancing calculation. Displays it.
925 - 1050	Asks for next action. Goes to appropriate subroutine.
1100 - 1130	Subroutine to display checks outstanding.
1200 - 1230	Subroutine to display deposits outstanding.
1300 - 1330	Subroutine to display service charges and debit memos.
1400	Restarts program.
1500	Ends the program.
1700 - 1730	Subroutine to display recent deposits.
2000 - 2140	Subroutine to get recent deposits.

MAIN VARIABLES

MC	Maximum number of checks outstanding.
MD	Maximum number of deposits outstanding.
MS	Maximum number of service charges, debit memos.
MR	Maximum number of recent deposits, credit memos.
C	Array for checks outstanding.
D	Array for deposits outstanding.
S	Array for service charges and debit memos.
R	Array for recent deposits and credit memos.
TC	Total of checks outstanding.
TD	Total of deposits outstanding.
TS	Total of service charges and debit memos.
TR	Total of recent deposits and credit memos.
NC	Number of checks outstanding.
ND	Number of deposits outstanding.
NS	Number of service charges and debit memos.
NR	Number of recent deposits and credit memos.
E$	Error message.
SB	Statement balance.
LC	Number of last check on statement.
CB	Checkbook balance after last check on statement.
R$	Reply from operator.
W	Amount by which checkbook is out of balance.
R	Numeric value of reply for next action.

A$	Message showing how to indicate no more data.
L$	Message indicating no more room for data.
J	Loop variable.

SUGGESTED PROJECTS

1. Add more informative messages and a more complete introduction to make the program a tutorial for someone who has
   never balanced a checkbook before.
2. Allow the operator to modify any entries that have been
   discovered to be in error. This could be done by adding
   another option to the "NEXT ACTION" list, which would
   then ask the operator which category to change. This would
   allow the operator to correct an error without having to
   re-enter everything from the beginning.
3. If the checkbook is out of balance, have the program do an
   analysis (as suggested in the "How To Use It" section) and
   suggest the most likely errors that might have caused the condition.
4. Allow the operator to find arithmetic errors in the checkbook. Ask for the starting balance, then ask for each check or
   deposit amount. Add or subtract, depending on which type
   the operator indicates. Display the new balance after each
   entry so the operator can compare with the checkbook entry.

DECIDE

PURPOSE

"Decisions, decisions!" How many times have you uttered this lament when confronted by a difficult choice? Wouldn't a trusty advisor be helpful on such occasions? Well, you now have one—your TRS-80 computer of course.

This program can help you make decisions involving the selection of one alternative from several choices. It works by prying relevant information from you and then organizing it in a meaningful, quantitiative manner. Your best choice will be indicated and all of the possibilities given a relative rating.

You can use the program for a wide variety of decisions. It can help with things like choosing the best stereo system, saying yes or no to a job or business offer, or selecting the best course of action for the future. Everything is personalized to your individual decision.

HOW TO USE IT

The first thing the program does is ask you to categorize the decision at hand into one of these three categories:
1) Choosing an item (or thing),
2) Choosing a course of action, or
3) Making a yes or no decision.
You simply press **1**, **2**, or **3** to indicate which type of decision is facing you. (It is not necessary to hit the **ENTER** key.) If you are choosing an item, you will be asked what type of item it is.

If the decision is either of the first two types, you must next enter a list of all the possibilities under consideration. A question mark will prompt you for each one. When the list is complete, type "END" in response to the last question mark. You must, of course, enter at least two possibilities. (We hope you don't have trouble making decisions from only one possibility!) After the list is finished, it will be re-displayed so that you can verify that it is correct. If not, you must re-enter it.

Now you must think of the different factors that are important to you in making your decision. For example, location, cost, and quality of education might govern the decision of which college to attend. For a refrigerator purchase, the factors might be things like price, size, reliability, and warranty. In any case, you will be prompted for your list with a succession of question marks. Each factor is to be entered one at a time with the word "END" used to terminate the list. When complete, the list will be re-displayed. You must now decide which single factor is the most important and input its number. (You can enter 0 if you wish to change the list of factors.)

The program now asks you to rate the importance of each of the other factors relative to the most important one. This is done by first assigning a value of 10 to the main factor. Then you must assign a value from 0 - 10 to each of the other factors. These numbers reflect your assessment of each factor's relative importance as compared to the main one. A value of 10 means it is just as important; lesser values indicate how much less importance you place on it.

Now you must rate the decision possibilities with respect to each of the importance factors. Each importance factor will be treated separately. Considering *only* that importance factor, you must rate how each decision possibility stacks up. The program first assigns a value of 10 to one of the decision possibilities. Then you must assign a relative number (lower, higher, or equal to 10) to each of the other decision possibilities.

An example might alleviate possible confusion here. Suppose you are trying to decide whether to get a dog, cat, or canary for a pet. Affection is one of your importance factors. The program assigns a value of 10 to the cat. Considering *only* affection, you might assign a value of 20 to the dog and 6.5 to the canary. This means *you* consider a dog twice as affectionate as a cat but a canary only about two thirds as affectionate as a cat. (No slighting of bird lovers is intended here, of course. Your actual ratings may be entirely different.)

Armed with all this information, the program will now determine which choice seems best for you. The various possibilities are listed in order of ranking. Alongside each one is a relative rating with the best choice being normalized to a value of 100.

Of course, DECIDE should not be used as a substitute for good, clear thinking. However, it can often provide valuable insights. You might find one alternative coming out surprisingly low or high. A trend may become obvious when the program is re-run with improved data. At least, it may help you think about decisions systematically and honestly.

SAMPLE RUN

```
                    DECIDE

     I CAN HELP YOU MAKE A DECISION. ALL I
NEED TO DO IS ASK SOME QUESTIONS AND THEN
ANALYZE THE INFORMATION YOU GIVE.


     ---------------------------------------


WHICH OF THESE BEST DESCRIBES THE TYPE OF
DECISION FACING YOU?

     1) CHOOSING AN ITEM FROM VARIOUS
        ALTERNATIVES.
     2) CHOOSING A COURSE OF ACTION FROM
        VARIOUS ALTERNATIVES.
     3) MAKING A 'YES' OR 'NO' DECISION.

WHICH ONE (1, 2, OR 3)? 1

WHAT TYPE OF ITEM MUST YOU DECIDE UPON
? VACATION

     I NEED TO HAVE A LIST OF EACH
VACATION UNDER CONSIDERATION.

     INPUT THEM ONE AT A TIME IN RESPONSE
TO EACH QUESTION MARK. THE ORDER IN WHICH
YOU INPUT THEM HAS NO SPECIAL SIGNIFICANCE.
```

    TYPE THE WORD 'END' TO INDICATE THAT
THE WHOLE LIST HAS BEEN ENTERED.

? MOUNTAIN CAMPING
? AFRICAN SAFARI
? TRIP TO WASHINGTON D.C.
? END

O.K. HERE'S THE LIST YOU'VE GIVEN ME:

    1) MOUNTAIN CAMPING
    2) AFRICAN SAFARI
    3) TRIP TO WASHINGTON D.C.

IS THIS LIST CORRECT (Y OR N) ? YES

    NOW, THINK OF THE DIFFERENT FACTORS
THAT ARE IMPORTANT TO YOU IN CHOOSING
THE BEST VACATION.

    INPUT THEM ONE AT A TIME IN RESPONSE
TO EACH QUESTION MARK.

    TYPE THE WORD 'END' TO TERMINATE THE
LIST.

? RELAXATION
? AFFORDABILITY
? CHANGE OF PACE
? END

HERE'S THE LIST OF FACTORS YOU GAVE ME:

    1) RELAXATION
    2) AFFORDABILITY
    3) CHANGE OF PACE

    DECIDE WHICH FACTOR ON THE LIST IS THE
MOST IMPORTANT AND INPUT ITS NUMBER.
(TYPE Ø IF THE LIST NEEDS CHANGING.)

? 2

    NOW LET'S SUPPOSE WE HAVE A SCALE OF
IMPORTANCE RANGING FROM Ø-1Ø.

    WE'LL GIVE AFFORDABILITY A
VALUE OF 1Ø SINCE AFFORDABILITY
WAS RATED THE MOST IMPORTANT.

    ON THIS SCALE, WHAT VALUE OF IMPORTANCE
WOULD THE OTHER FACTORS HAVE?

RELAXATION
? 5.5

CHANGE OF PACE
? 9

    EACH VACATION MUST NOW BE COMPARED WITH
RESPECT TO EACH IMPORTANCE FACTOR.
    WE'LL CONSIDER EACH FACTOR SEPARATELY
AND THEN RATE EACH VACATION IN TERMS
OF THAT FACTOR ONLY.

    LET'S GIVE MOUNTAIN CAMPING
A VALUE OF 1Ø ON EVERY SCALE.
    THEN EVERY OTHER VACATION
WILL BE ASSIGNED A VALUE HIGHER OR LOWER
THAN 1Ø. THIS VALUE DEPENDS ON HOW MUCH
YOU THINK IT IS BETTER OR WORSE THAN
MOUNTAIN CAMPING.
᙭᙭᙭᙭᙭᙭᙭᙭᙭ (HIT ANY KEY TO CONTINUE)
(A key is pressed)

    CONSIDERING ONLY RELAXATION AND
ASSIGNING 1Ø TO MOUNTAIN CAMPING ;
WHAT VALUE WOULD YOU ASSIGN TO
AFRICAN SAFARI? 3
TRIP TO WASHINGTON D.C.? 9

    CONSIDERING ONLY AFFORDABILITY AND
ASSIGNING 1Ø TO MOUNTAIN CAMPING ;
WHAT VALUE WOULD YOU ASSIGN TO
AFRICAN SAFARI? 1
TRIP TO WASHINGTON D.C.? 8

    CONSIDERING ONLY CHANGE OF PACE AND
ASSIGNING 1Ø TO MOUNTAIN CAMPING ;

WHAT VALUE WOULD YOU ASSIGN TO
AFRICAN SAFARI? 6Ø
TRIP TO WASHINGTON D.C.? 25

TRIP TO WASHINGTON D.C. COMES OUT BEST
BUT IT'S VERY CLOSE.
- - - - HERE IS THE FINAL LIST IN ORDER - - - -
TRIP TO WASHINGTON D.C. HAS BEEN
GIVEN A VALUE OF 1ØØ AND THE OTHERS RATED
ACCORDINGLY.

  1ØØ   TRIP TO WASHINGTON D.C.
  98.6587   MOUNTAIN CAMPING
  78.8376   AFRICAN SAFARI

PROGRAM LISTING

```
100 REM: DECIDE
110 REM: COPYRIGHT 1979 BY PHIL FELDMAN AND TOM RUGG
150 CLEAR 500
160 MD=10
170 DIM L$(MD),F$(MD),V(MD),C(MD,MD),D(MD),Z(MD)
180 E$="END"
200 GOSUB 2000
210 PRINT"   I CAN HELP YOU MAKE A DECISION.
    ALL I NEED TO DO IS ASK"
220 PRINT"SOME QUESTIONS AND THEN ANALYZE THE
    INFORMATION YOU GIVE."
230 PRINT:PRINT TAB(8);STRING$(44,"-"):PRINT
240 PRINT"WHICH OF THESE BEST DESCRIBES THE
    TYPE OF DECISION FACING YOU?"
250 PRINT:PRINT"  1) CHOOSING AN ITEM FROM VARIOUS
    ALTERNATIVES."
260 PRINT"  2) CHOOSING A COURSE OF ACTION FROM
    VARIOUS ALTERNATIVES."
270 PRINT"  3) MAKING A 'YES' OR 'NO' DECISION."
280 PRINT:PRINT"WHICH ONE (1, 2, OR 3)?";
290 R$=INKEY$:IF R$="" THEN 290
300 T=VAL(R$):IF T<1 OR T>3 THEN 290
350 PRINT T:GOSUB 2000
400 FOR J=1 TO 9:R$=INKEY$:NEXT:ON T GOTO 410,440,470
410 PRINT"WHAT TYPE OF ITEM MUST YOU DECIDE UPON"
420 INPUT T$:GOTO 500
440 T$="COURSE OF ACTION":GOTO 500
470 T$="'YES' OR 'NO'"
480 NI=2:L$(1)="DECIDING YES":L$(2)="DECIDING NO"
```

```
490 GOTO 750
500 GOSUB 2000:NI=0
510 PRINT"   I NEED TO HAVE A LIST OF EACH"
520 PRINT T$;" UNDER CONSIDERATION.":PRINT
530 PRINT"   INPUT THEM ONE AT A TIME IN RESPONSE TO
    EACH QUESTION MARK."
540 PRINT"THE ORDER IN WHICH YOU INPUT THEM HAS
    NO SPECIAL SIGNIFICANCE."
550 PRINT:PRINT"   TYPE THE WORD ";E$;" TO INDICATE
    THAT THE WHOLE LIST"
560 PRINT"HAS BEEN ENTERED.":PRINT
580 IF NI>=MD THEN PRINT"-- LIST FULL --":GOTO 620
590 NI=NI+1:INPUT L$(NI)
600 IF L$(NI)<>E$ THEN 580
610 NI=NI-1
620 IF NI>=2 THEN 650
630 PRINT:PRINT"YOU MUST HAVE AT LEAST 2 CHOICES !":
    PRINT
640 PRINT"TRY AGAIN":GOSUB 2100:GOTO 500
650 GOSUB 2000:
    PRINT"O.K. HERE'S THE LIST YOU'VE GIVEN ME:":PRINT
660 FOR J=1 TO NI:
    PRINT"  ";J;CHR$(24);") ";L$(J):NEXT:PRINT
670 FOR J=1 TO 9:R$=INKEY$:NEXT:
    PRINT"IS THIS LIST CORRECT (Y OR N) ? ";
680 R$=INKEY$:IF R$="" THEN 680
690 IF R$="Y" THEN PRINT"YES":GOTO 750
700 IF R$="N" THEN PRINT"NO"
710 IF R$="N" THEN PRINT:
    PRINT"THE LIST MUST BE RE-ENTERED"
720 IF R$="N" THEN GOSUB 2100:GOSUB 500
730 GOTO 680
750 GOSUB 2000:FOR J=1 TO 9:R$=INKEY$:NEXT
760 PRINT"   NOW, THINK OF THE DIFFERENT FACTORS"
770 IF T<3 THEN
    PRINT"THAT ARE IMPORTANT TO YOU IN CHOOSING"
780 IF T<3 THEN PRINT"THE BEST ";T$;"."
790 IF T=3 THEN
    PRINT"THAT ARE IMPORTANT TO YOU IN DECIDING ";T$;"."
800 PRINT:PRINT"   INPUT THEM ONE AT A TIME IN
    RESPONSE TO EACH"
810 PRINT"QUESTION MARK.":PRINT
820 PRINT"   TYPE THE WORD ";E$;" TO
    TERMINATE THE LIST."
830 PRINT:NF=0
835 IF NF>=MD THEN PRINT"-- LIST FULL --":PRINT:GOTO 870
```

```
840 NF=NF+1:INPUT F$(NF)
850 IF F$(NF)<>E$ THEN 835
860 NF=NF-1:PRINT
870 IF NF<1 THEN PRINT"YOU MUST HAVE AT
    LEAST ONE ! -- REDO IT"
880 IF NF<1 THEN GOSUB 2100:GOTO 750
890 GOSUB 2000:
    PRINT"HERE'S THE LIST OF FACTORS YOU GAVE ME:":PRINT
900 FOR J=1 TO NF:
    PRINT" ";J;CHR$(24);") ";F$(J):NEXT:PRINT
910 PRINT"  DECIDE WHICH FACTOR ON THE LIST IS THE
    MOST IMPORTANT"
920 PRINT"AND INPUT ITS NUMBER. (TYPE 0 IF THE
    LIST NEEDS CHANGING.)"
930 PRINT
940 INPUT A:A=INT(A):IF A=0 THEN 750
950 IF A>NF OR A<0 THEN 890
1000 GOSUB 2000:IF NF=1 THEN 1200
1010 PRINT"  NOW LET'S SUPPOSE WE HAVE A SCALE OF
     IMPORTANCE"
1020 PRINT"RANGING FROM 0-10."
1030 PRINT:PRINT"  WE'LL GIVE ";F$(A);" A"
1040 PRINT"VALUE OF 10 SINCE ";F$(A)
1050 PRINT"WAS RATED THE MOST IMPORTANT.":PRINT
1060 PRINT"  ON THIS SCALE, WHAT VALUE OF IMPORTANCE"
1070 PRINT"WOULD THE OTHER FACTORS HAVE?"
1080 FOR J=1 TO NF:IF J=A THEN 1110
1090 PRINT:PRINT F$(J):INPUT V(J)
1100 IF V(J)<0 OR V(J)>10 THEN
     PRINT"  IMPOSSIBLE VALUE - TRY AGAIN":GOTO 1090
1110 NEXT
1200 V(A)=10:Q=0:FOR J=1 TO NF:Q=Q+V(J):NEXT:
     FOR J=1 TO NF
1210 V(J)=V(J)/Q:NEXT:GOSUB 2000
1220 IF T<>3 THEN PRINT"   EACH ";T$;
1230 IF T=3 THEN
     PRINT"   DECIDING 'YES' OR DECIDING 'NO' ";
1240 PRINT" MUST NOW"
1250 PRINT"BE COMPARED WITH RESPECT TO
     EACH IMPORTANCE FACTOR."
1260 PRINT"   WE'LL CONSIDER EACH FACTOR SEPARATELY
     AND THEN RATE"
1270 IF T<>3 THEN PRINT"EACH ";T$;" IN TERMS"
1280 IF T=3 THEN
     PRINT"DECIDING 'YES' OR DECIDING 'NO' IN TERMS"
1290 PRINT"OF THAT FACTOR ONLY.":PRINT
```

```
1300 PRINT"    LET'S GIVE ";L$(1)
1310 PRINT"A VALUE OF 10 ON EVERY SCALE."
1320 IF T<>3 THEN PRINT"      THEN EVERY OTHER ";T$
1330 IF T=3 THEN PRINT"      THEN DECIDING 'NO'"
1340 PRINT"WILL BE ASSIGNED A VALUE HIGHER OR
     LOWER THAN 10.  THIS"
1350 PRINT"VALUE DEPENDS ON HOW MUCH YOU THINK IT IS
     BETTER OR WORSE"
1360 PRINT"THAN ";L$(1);"."
1370 PRINT" ********* (HIT ANY KEY TO CONTINUE)"
1380 R$=INKEY$:IF R$="" THEN 1380
1390 FOR J=1 TO NF
1400 PRINT TAB(8);STRING$(25,"-")
1410 PRINT"    CONSIDERING ONLY "F$(J);" AND"
1420 PRINT"ASSIGNING 10 TO ";L$(1);" ;"
1430 PRINT"WHAT VALUE WOULD YOU ASSIGN TO"
1440 FOR K=2 TO NI
1450 PRINT L$(K);:INPUT C(K,J):IF C(K,J)>=0 THEN 1470
1460 PRINT"  -- NEGATIVE VALUES NOT LEGAL --":GOTO 1450
1470 NEXT:PRINT:C(1,J)=10:NEXT
1500 FOR J=1 TO NF:Q=0:FOR K=1 TO NI
1510 Q=Q+C(K,J):NEXT:FOR K=1 TO NI
1520 C(K,J)=C(K,J)/Q:NEXT:NEXT
1530 FOR K=1 TO NI:D(K)=0:FOR J=1 TO NF
1540 D(K)=D(K)+C(K,J)*V(J):NEXT:NEXT
1550 MX=0:FOR K=1 TO NI
1560 IF D(K)>MX THEN MX=D(K)
1570 NEXT:FOR K=1 TO NI:D(K)=D(K)*100/MX:NEXT
1600 FOR K=1 TO NI:Z(K)=K:NEXT:NM=NI-1
1610 FOR K=1 TO NI:FOR J=1 TO NM:N1=Z(J):N2=Z(J+1):
     IF D(N1)>D(N2) THEN 1630
1620 Z(J+1)=N1:Z(J)=N2
1630 NEXT:NEXT:J1=Z(1):J2=Z(2):DF=D(J1)-D(J2):
     GOSUB 2000
1700 PRINT L$(J1);
1710 PRINT" COMES OUT BEST"
1720 IF DF<5 THEN PRINT"BUT IT'S VERY CLOSE.":GOTO 1800
1730 IF DF<10 THEN PRINT"BUT IT'S FAIRLY CLOSE.":
     GOTO 1800
1740 IF DF<20 THEN PRINT"BY A FAIR AMOUNT.":GOTO 1800
1750 PRINT"QUITE DECISIVELY."
1800 PRINT"- - - - HERE IS THE FINAL LIST IN
     ORDER  - - - -"
1810 PRINT L$(J1);" HAS BEEN"
1820 PRINT"GIVEN A VALUE OF 100 AND THE
     OTHERS RATED ACCORDINGLY."
```

```
1840 PRINT"   ";STRING$(30,"-")
1850 FOR J=1 TO NI:Q=Z(J):PRINT D(Q),L$(Q):NEXT
1860 END
2000 FOR J=1 TO 400:NEXT
2010 CLS:PRINT TAB(26);"DECIDE":PRINT:RETURN
2100 FOR J=1 TO 1500:NEXT:RETURN
```

EASY CHANGES

1. The word "END" is used to flag the termination of various input lists. If you wish to use something else (because of conflicts with items on the list), change the definition of E$ in line 180. For example, to use the word "DONE," change line 180 to

180 E$="DONE"

2. Line 2100 contains a timing delay used regularly in the program. If things seem to change too fast, you can make the number 1500 larger. Try

2100 FOR J=1 TO 3000:NEXT:RETURN

3. The program can currently accept up to ten decision alternatives and/or ten importance factors. If you need more, increase the value of MD in line 160. Thus, to use 15 values, line 160 should be

160 MD = 15

MAIN ROUTINES

150 - 180	Initializes and dimensions variables.
200 - 350	Determines category of decision.
400 - 490	Gets or sets T$.
500 - 730	Gets list of possible alternatives from user.
750 - 950	Gets list of importance factors from user.
1000 - 1110	User rates each importance factor.
1200 - 1470	User rates the decision alternatives with respect to each importance factor.
1500 - 1570	Evaluates the various alternatives.
1600 - 1630	Sorts alternatives into their relative ranking.
1700 - 1860	Displays results.
2000 - 2010	Subroutine to clear screen and display header.
2100	Time wasting subroutine.

MAIN VARIABLES

MD	Maximum number of decision alternatives.
NI	Number of decision alternatives.
L$	String array of the decision alternatives.
NF	Number of importance factors.
F$	String array of the importance factors.
V	Array of the relative values of each importance factor.
A	Index number of most important factor.
C	Array of relative values of each alternative with respect to each importance factor.
T	Decision category (1=item, 2=course of action, 3=yes or no).
T$	String name of decision category.
E$	String to signal the end of an input data list.
J,K	Loop indices.
R$	User reply string.
Q,N1,N2	Work variables.
D	Array of each alternative's value.
MX	Maximum value of all alternatives.
DF	Rating difference between best two alternatives.
Z	Array of the relative rankings of each alternative.

SUGGESTED PROJECTS

1. Allow the user to review his numerical input and modify it if desired.
2. Insights into a decision can often be gained by a sensitivity analysis. This involves running the program a number of times for the same decision. Each time, one input value is changed (usually the one you are least confident about). By seeing how the results change, you can determine which factors are the most important. Currently, this requires a complete re-running of the program each time. Modify the program to allow a change of input after the regular output is produced. Then recalculate the results based on the new values. (Note that many input arrays are clobbered once all the input is given. This modification will require saving the original input in new arrays so that it can be reviewed later.)

LOAN

PURPOSE

One of the most frustrating things about borrowing money from a bank (or credit union or Savings and Loan) is that it's not easy to fully evaluate your options. When you are borrowing from a credit union to buy a new car, you might have the choice of a thirty-six or a forty-eight month repayment period. When buying a house, you can sometimes get a slightly lower interest rate for your loan if you can come up with a larger down payment. Which option is best for you? How will the monthly payment be affected? Will there be much difference in how fast the principal of the loan decreases? How much of each payment will be for interest, which is tax-deductible?

You need to know the answers to all these questions to make the best decision. This program gives you the information you need.

HOW TO USE IT

The program first asks you the size of the loan you are considering. Only whole dollar amounts are allowed—no pennies. Loans of ten million dollars or more are rejected (you can afford to hire an investment counselor if you want to borrow that much). Then you are asked the yearly interest rate for the loan. Enter this number as a percentage, such as "10.8". Next, you are asked to give the period of the loan in months. For a five year loan, enter 60. For a thirty year mortgage, enter 360. The program then displays this information for you and calculates the monthly payment that will cause the loan to be paid off with equal payments each month over the life of the loan.

At this point you have four options. First, you can show a monthly analysis. This displays a month-by-month breakdown, showing the state of the loan after each payment. The four columns of data shown for each month are the payment number (or month number) of the loan, the remaining balance of the loan after that payment, the amount of that payment that was interest, and the accumulated interest paid to date. Twelve lines of data are displayed on the screen, and then you can either press the **T** key to get the final totals for the loan, or any other key to get the data for the next twelve months of the loan.

The second option is overriding the monthly payment. It is a common practice with second mortgage loans to make smaller monthly payments each month with a large "balloon" payment as the final payment. You can use this second option to try various monthly payments to see how they affect that big payment at the end. After overriding the monthly payment, you will want to use the first option next to get a monthly analysis and final totals using the new monthly payment.

The third option is to simply start over. You will generally use this option if you are just comparing what the different monthly payments would be for different loan possibilities.

The fourth option ends the program.

By the way, there is a chance that the monthly payment calculated by your lender will differ from the one calculated here by a penny or two. We like to think that this is because we are making a more accurate calculation.

NOTE: SEE DISCLAIMER IN FRONT PART OF BOOK

SAMPLE RUN

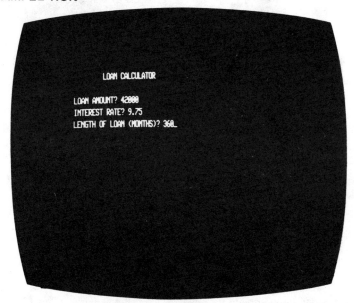

```
        LOAN CALCULATOR

LOAN AMOUNT? 42000
INTEREST RATE? 9.75
LENGTH OF LOAN (MONTHS)? 360_
```

The operator enters the three necessary pieces of information about his or her loan.

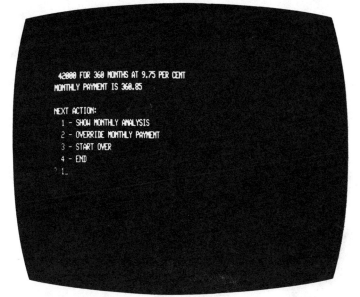

```
42000 FOR 360 MONTHS AT 9.75 PER CENT
MONTHLY PAYMENT IS 360.85

NEXT ACTION:
  1 - SHOW MONTHLY ANALYSIS
  2 - OVERRIDE MONTHLY PAYMENT
  3 - START OVER
  4 - END
? 1_
```

The program responds with the monthly payment that will pay off the loan with equal payments over its life, then asks the operator what to do next. The operator asks for the monthly analysis.

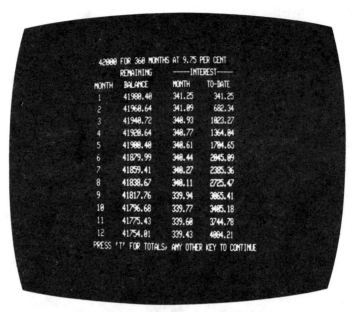

The program responds with information about the first twelve months of the loan, then waits.

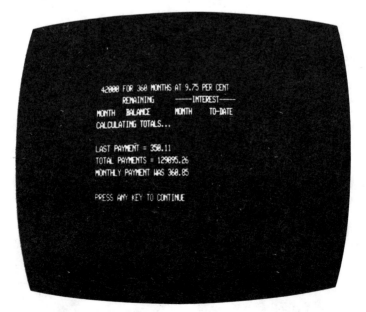

The operator presses "T", and after a few seconds the program displays totalling information about the loan.

PROGRAM LISTING

```
100 REM: LOAN CALCULATOR
110 REM: COPYRIGHT 1979 BY TOM RUGG AND PHIL FELDMAN
120 CLEAR 50:CLS:DEFINT J,L,N:DEFDBL A-F,M,P-Z
130 PRINT TAB(8);"LOAN CALCULATOR"
140 PRINT
150 INPUT"LOAN AMOUNT";A
155 GOSUB 1000:IF A=0 THEN 150
160 INPUT"INTEREST RATE";R
170 INPUT"LENGTH OF LOAN (MONTHS)";N
180 R=ABS(R):M=R/1200
190 GOSUB 800
200 W=(1+M)↑N
210 P=(A*M*W)/(W-1)
220 P=INT(P*100+.99):P=P/100
230 PRINT"MONTHLY PAYMENT IS";P
240 FP=P:PRINT
250 PRINT"NEXT ACTION:"
270 PRINT"  1 - SHOW MONTHLY ANALYSIS"
280 PRINT"  2 - OVERRIDE MONTHLY PAYMENT"
290 PRINT"  3 - START OVER"
300 PRINT"  4 - END"
310 INPUT C
320 ON C GOTO 440,400,120,370
330 PRINT"CHOICES ARE 1, 2, 3, AND 4"
340 GOTO 250
370 END
400 PRINT:INPUT"MONTHLY PAYMENT";P
410 GOTO 240
440 GOSUB 450:GOTO 510
450 GOSUB 800
460 PRINT TAB(7);"REMAINING";TAB(22);
470 PRINT"-----INTEREST-----"
480 PRINT"MONTH    BALANCE";TAB(22);
490 PRINT"MONTH       TO-DATE"
500 RETURN
510 B=A*100:TT=0:TP=0:L=0:P=P*100:R$=""
520 FOR J=1 TO N
530 T=M*B
540 T=INT(T+.5)
550 IF J=N THEN P=B+T
560 TP=TP+P:B=B-P+T:TT=TT+T
565 IF B<0 THEN GOSUB 2000
570 IF R$="T" THEN 660
580 PB=B/100
```

```
590 PT=T/100
600 T2=TT/100
610 PRINT J;TAB(5);
615 PRINT USING"#########.##-";PB;PT;T2
617 IF B=0 THEN J=N:GOTO 630
620 L=L+1:IF L<12 THEN 660
630 PRINT"PRESS 'T' FOR TOTALS, ANY OTHER
    KEY TO CONTINUE";
640 R$=INKEY$:IF R$="" THEN 640
650 L=0:GOSUB 450:
    IF R$="T" THEN PRINT"CALCULATING TOTALS..."
660 NEXT
670 PRINT:PRINT"LAST PAYMENT =";P/100
680 PRINT"TOTAL PAYMENTS =";TP/100
690 PRINT"MONTHLY PAYMENT WAS";FP
710 PRINT:PRINT"PRESS ANY KEY TO CONTINUE"
720 R$=INKEY$:IF R$="" THEN 720
730 P=FP:GOTO 240
800 CLS
810 PRINT A;"FOR";N;"MONTHS AT";R;"PER CENT"
830 RETURN
1000 A=ABS(A):A=INT(A)
1010 IF A<10000000 THEN RETURN
1020 PRINT"TOO LARGE"
1030 A=0:RETURN
2000 P=P+B:TP=TP+B:B=0
2010 RETURN
```

EASY CHANGES

1. The number of lines of data that are displayed on each screen
   when getting a monthly analysis can be changed by altering
   the constant 12 in statement 620.
2. To include the monthly payment in the heading at the top of
   each screen of the monthly analysis, insert the following line:

   815 IF FP<>0 THEN PRINT"MONTHLY PAYMENT IS";FP

MAIN ROUTINES

120 - 170	Displays title. Gets loan information.
200 - 230	Calculates and displays monthly payment.
250 - 370	Asks for next action. Goes to corresponding routine.

400 - 410	Gets override for monthly payment.
440 - 730	Calculates and displays monthly analysis.
800 - 830	Subroutine to clear screen and display data about the loan at the top.
1000 - 1030	Edits loan amount (size and whole dollar).
2000 - 2010	Subroutine to handle early payoff of loan.

MAIN VARIABLES

A	Amount of loan.
R	Interest rate (percentage).
N	Length of loan (number of months).
M	Monthly interest rate (not percentage).
W	Work variable.
P	Monthly payment (times 100).
FP	First monthly payment.
C	Choice of next action.
B	Remaining balance of loan (times 100).
TT	Total interest to date (times 100).
TP	Total payments to date.
L	Number of lines of data on screen.
R$	Reply from operator at keyboard.
J	Work variable for loops.
T	Monthly interest.
PB	Remaining balance to be displayed (two decimal places).
PT	Monthly interest to be displayed (two decimal places).
T2	Total interest to be displayed (two decimal places).

SUGGESTED PROJECTS

1. Display a more comprehensive analysis of the loan along with the final totals. Show the ratio of total payments to the amount of the loan (TP divided by A), for example.
2. Modify the program to show an analysis of resulting monthly payments for a range of interest rates and/or loan lengths near those provided by the operator. For example, if an interest rate of 9.5 percent was entered, display the monthly payments for 8.5, 9, 9.5, 10, and 10.5 percent.

MILEAGE

PURPOSE

For many of us, automobile operating efficiency is a continual concern. This program can help by keeping track of gasoline consumption, miles driven, and fuel mileage for a motor vehicle. It allows reading and writing data files with the cassette unit. Thus, a master data file may be retained and updated. The program computes mileage (miles per gallon or MPG) obtained after each gasoline fill-up. A running log of all information is maintained. This enables trends in vehicle operation efficiency to be easily checked.

HOW TO USE IT

The program requests the following data from the operator as a record of each gasoline fill-up: date, odometer reading, and number of gallons purchased. The most useful results will be obtained if entries are chronological and complete, with each entry representing a full gasoline fill-up.

In order to use the cassette features, the operator must be able to position the tape correctly for both reading and writing. The simplest way to do this is to only record files at the beginning of a tape. One tape could certainly be used this way, with each file writing over the previous one. However, we suggest alternating between two physical tapes. This will insure a reasonably up-to-date back-up tape in case of any failure. A special cassette control technique allows the recorder to be operational when necessary. Thus, you will be able to fast forward or rewind the cassette to reach any desired tape location.

The program operates from a central command mode. The operator requests branching to any one of five available subroutines. When a subroutine completes execution, control returns to the command mode for any additional requests. A brief description of each subroutine now follows:

1) READ OLD MASTER FILE

This reads previously stored data from the cassette. Any data already in memory is deleted. During the read, the name of the data file and the total number of records read are displayed.

2) INPUT FROM TERMINAL

This allows data records to be entered directly from the terminal. This mode is used to provide additional information after a cassette read and to enter data for the first time. The program will prompt the operator for the required information and then let him verify that it was entered correctly. A response of "F" to the verification request signals that no more data is to be entered.

3) WRITE NEW MASTER FILE

This command causes the current data to be written on cassette. The program requests a name for the file. When later read, this name will be displayed, allowing verification of the correct data file.

4) DISPLAY MILEAGE DATA

This subroutine computes mileage (miles per gallon) from the available data. It formats all information and displays it in tabular form. When data fills the screen, the user is prompted to hit any key to continue the listing. When all data is displayed, hitting any key will re-enter command mode.

5) TERMINATE PROGRAM

Ends execution and returns the computer to BASIC.

SAMPLE RUN

                              MILEAGE

COMMAND LIST
    1 - READ OLD MASTER FILE FROM CASSETTE
    2 - INPUT DATA FROM THE TERMINAL
    3 - WRITE NEW MASTER FILE TO CASSETTE
    4 - DISPLAY MILEAGE DATA
    5 - TERMINATE PROGRAM

ENTER COMMAND BY NUMBER? <u>2</u>

ENTER THE FOLLOWING DATA AS REQUESTED
- DATE (E.G. 1/3Ø/79)
- ODOMETER READING (MILES)
- # GALLONS BOUGHT

DATE? <u>9/28/78</u>
ODOMETER? <u>51Ø51.1</u>
GALLONS? <u>14.6</u>

    INPUT   DATE: 9/28/78
    CHECK   ODOMETER: 51Ø51.1
                GALLONS: 14.6

       - IS INPUT OK ? -

(Y=YES, N=NO, F=YES AND FINISHED)? <u>Y</u>

DATE?

           :
           :

      (10 more entries are input)

           :
           :

(Y=YES, N=NO, F=YES AND FINISHED)? <u>F</u>

    (the five commands are listed again)

ENTER COMMAND BY NUMBER? <u>4</u>

DATE	ODOMETER	GALLONS	MPG
9/28/78	51Ø51.1	14.6	Ø
1Ø/6/78	51299.7	13.8	18.Ø143
1Ø/17/78	51553.8	13.1	19.3971
1Ø/29/78	51798	13.7	17.8248
11/5/78	52Ø41.9	13.3	18.3382
11/15/78	523Ø4.9	14	18.7857
11/26/78	5257Ø.8	13.7	19.4Ø89
12/1/78	52842.5	14.6	18.6Ø95
12/9/78	53Ø48.4	11.8	17.449
12/15/78	53359.7	14.7	21.1769
12/23/78	536Ø1.2	13.3	18.1579

HIT ANY KEY FOR COMMAND MODE

(a key is pressed)

(the five commands are listed again)

ENTER COMMAND BY NUMBER? 3

1) THE CASSETTE KEYS ARE NOW OPERATIONAL.
2) POSITION THE CASSETTE TAPE FOR WRITING.
3) PRESS THE CASSETTE STOP KEY.
4) HOLD DOWN THE KEYBOARD'S ENTER KEY.

(the above is duly done)

5) PRESS THE RECORD AND PLAY KEYS ON
   CASSETTE UNIT.

(the above is done)

NAME FOR FILE? VOLVO78
WRITING FILE: VOLVO78
  RECORDS # 1 2 3 4 5 6 7 8 9 1Ø 11

6) PRESS THE CASSETTE STOP KEY.
7) PRESS THE KEYBOARD'S ENTER KEY.

_____

(a subsequent run)

ENTER COMMAND BY NUMBER? 1

1) THE CASSETTE KEYS ARE NOW OPERATIONAL.
2) POSITION THE CASSETTE TAPE FOR READING.
3) PRESS THE CASSETTE STOP KEY.
4) HOLD DOWN THE KEYBOARD'S ENTER KEY.

(the above is duly done)

5) PRESS THE PLAY KEY ON CASSETTE UNIT.
6) PRESS THE KEYBOARD'S ENTER KEY.
    (the above is done)

READING FILE: VOLVO 78
  READING RECORDS # 1 2 3 4 5 6 7 8 9 1Ø 11
  11   DATA RECORDS READ

7) PRESS THE CASSETTE STOP KEY.
8) PRESS THE KEYBOARD'S ENTER KEY.
(the above is done to return to command mode)

ENTER COMMAND BY NUMBER? <u>5</u>
READY

PROGRAM LISTING

```
100 REM: MILEAGE
110 REM: COPYRIGHT 1979 BY PHIL FELDMAN AND TOM RUGG
120 CLEAR 200
130 MW=15:MR=20:N=0
140 DIM D$(MR),D(MR),G(MR),M(MR):B$=""
150 CLS:R=0:PRINT TAB(25);"MILEAGE":PRINT:
    PRINT"COMMAND LIST"
160 PRINT" 1 - READ OLD MASTER FILE FROM CASSETTE"
170 PRINT" 2 - INPUT DATA FROM THE TERMINAL"
180 PRINT" 3 - WRITE NEW MASTER FILE TO CASSETTE"
190 PRINT" 4 - DISPLAY MILEAGE DATA"
200 PRINT" 5 - TERMINATE PROGRAM":PRINT
210 INPUT" ENTER COMMAND BY NUMBER";R:
    IF R<1 OR R>5 THEN 150
220 ON R GOSUB 700,300,500,600,800:GOTO 150
300 IF N=MR THEN 470
310 PRINT:PRINT"ENTER THE FOLLOWING DATA AS REQUESTED"
320 PRINT" - DATE (E.G. 1/30/79)"
330 PRINT" - ODOMETER READING (MILES)"
340 PRINT" - # GALLONS BOUGHT"
350 N=N+1:PRINT:INPUT"DATE";R$:R$=LEFT$(R$,8):D$(N)=R$
360 INPUT"ODOMETER";R:D(N)=R:IF R<0 THEN 360
370 INPUT"# GALLONS";R:G(N)=R:IF R<0 THEN 370
380 PRINT:PRINT TAB(3);"INPUT    DATE: ";D$(N)
390 PRINT TAB(3);"CHECK    ODOMETER:";D(N):
    PRINT TAB(13);"GALLONS:";G(N)
400 PRINT:PRINT"         - IS INPUT OK ? -":PRINT
410 INPUT" (Y=YES, N=NO, F=YES AND FINISHED)";R$:
    R$=LEFT$(R$,1)
420 IF R$="N" THEN N=N-1:PRINT:PRINT" REDO LAST DATA":
    GOTO 350
430 IF R$="F" THEN RETURN
440 IF R$<>"Y" THEN 400
450 IF N=MR THEN 470
460 GOTO 350
470 PRINT:PRINT"*** NO MORE DATA ALLOWED":GOSUB 920:
    RETURN
500 IF N<1 THEN PRINT:PRINT"*** NO DATA TO WRITE":
    GOSUB 920:RETURN
510 R$="WRITING":GOSUB 850:PRINT
```

```
520 PRINT"5) PRESS THE RECORD AND PLAY KEYS ON
    CASSETTE UNIT."
530 INPUT"NAME FOR FILE";T$:K=N:IF N>MW THEN K=MW
540 PRINT#-1,T$:PRINT#-1,K:K=1:L=N
550 IF N>MW THEN K=N-MW+1:
    PRINT" - ONLY LAST";MW;"VALUES WILL BE WRITTEN"
560 PRINT"WRITING FILE: ";T$:PRINT"  RECORDS # ";
570 FOR J=K TO L:PRINT#-1,D$(J),D(J),G(J):PRINT J;:NEXT
580 PRINT:PRINT:PRINT"6) PRESS THE CASSETTE STOP KEY."
590 PRINT"7) PRESS THE KEYBOARD'S ENTER KEY.":
    GOSUB 960:RETURN
600 IF N<=1 THEN PRINT:PRINT"*** NOT ENOUGH DATA":
    GOSUB 920:RETURN
610 M(1)=0:FOR J=2 TO N:
    IF G(J)=0 OR G(J-1)=0 THEN M(J)=0:GOTO 640
620 R=(D(J)-D(J-1))/G(J):IF R<0 THEN R=0
630 M(J)=R
640 NEXT:K=-10:L=0
650 K=K+11:L=L+11:IF L>N THEN L=N
660 CLS:PRINT"DATE","ODOMETER","GALLONS","MPG"
670 FOR J=K TO L:PRINT D$(J),D(J),G(J),M(J):NEXT:PRINT
680 IF L=N THEN PRINT"HIT ANY KEY FOR COMMAND MODE":
    GOSUB 960:RETURN
690 PRINT"HIT ANY KEY TO CONTINUE":GOSUB 960:GOTO 650
700 R$="READING":GOSUB 850
710 PRINT:PRINT"5) PRESS THE PLAY KEY ON CASSETTE UNIT."
720 PRINT"6) PRESS THE KEYBOARD'S ENTER KEY.":GOSUB 960
730 INPUT#-1,T$:PRINT"READING FILE: ";T$:INPUT#-1,N
740 IF N>MR THEN PRINT"*** TOO MANY FILES ON TAPE":END
750 PRINT"  READING RECORDS # ";
760 FOR J=1 TO N:INPUT#-1,D$(J),D(J),G(J):PRINT J;:
    NEXT:PRINT
770 PRINT N;" DATA RECORDS READ"
780 PRINT:PRINT"7) PRESS THE CASSETTE STOP KEY."
790 PRINT"8) PRESS THE KEYBOARD'S ENTER KEY.":
    GOSUB 960:RETURN
800 END
850 PRINT:PRINT"1) THE CASSETTE KEYS ARE NOW OPERATIONAL."
860 PRINT"2) POSITION THE CASSETTE TAPE FOR ";R$;"."
870 PRINT"3) PRESS THE CASSETTE STOP KEY."
880 PRINT"4) HOLD DOWN THE KEYBOARD'S ENTER KEY."
890 PRINT#-1,B$:R$=INKEY$:IF R$=B$ THEN 890
900 RETURN
920 FOR Q=1 TO 1000:NEXT:RETURN
960 R$=INKEY$:IF R$=B$ THEN 960
970 RETURN
```

EASY CHANGES

1. Changing the value of MR in line 130 alters the maximum number of data records that the program allows. You may need to make MR smaller if you are running out of memory, or larger to accomodate additional data. The current value of twenty is appropriate for a TRS-80 with 4K of memory. For typical data (such as in the sample run), a 16K TRS-80 will allow well over 500 data records. To adjust MR, simply change its value in line 130 from its current value of 20 to whatever you choose. If you increase the value of MR, you should also change the argument of the CLEAR in line 120. Make this argument ten times the value used for MR in line 130.
2. Currently, the program will write a maximum of fifteen data records during the cassette write operation. This number can be altered by changing the value of MW in line 130 from its value of fifteen to whatever you choose. Only the most recent MW records will be written to tape if MW is less than the number of available records when a cassette write is issued. If the number of available records is less than MW, then all the records will be written. The value of MW should not be larger than the value of MR.
3. If you do not care about seeing the dates, they can be removed easily. This saves a little typing on data entry and also allows more data records in a given amount of memory. To remove this feature, delete line 320 entirely and change line 350 to read

        350 N=N+1:PRINT:D$(N)="- - - - -"

MAIN ROUTINES

120 - 140	Dimensioning and variable initialization
150 - 220	Command mode. Displays available subroutines.
300 - 470	Accepts terminal input.
500 - 590	Writes data to the cassette unit.
600 - 690	Calculates mileage and displays all information.
700 - 790	Reads data from the cassette unit.
800	Terminates execution.
850 - 900	Displays messages for cassette operation.
920	Delay loop.
960 - 970	Tests for operator response.

MAIN VARIABLES

MW	Maximum number of data records to write.
MR	Maximum number of data records in memory.
N	Current number of data records in memory.
D$	Array of dates.
D	Array of odometer readings.
G	Array of gallons per fill-up.
M	Array of mileage per fill-up.
R	Command mode input.
R$	Temporary string variable, holds operator's input.
T$	Data file name used in reading or writing with cassette.
B$	Null string.
J	Work variable, loop index.
K,L	Loop bounds.

SUGGESTED PROJECTS

1. Calculate and print the average MPG over the whole data file. The total miles driven is $D(N) - D(1)$. The total gallons used is the sum of $G(J)$ for $J=2$ to N. This calculation can be done at the end of the DISPLAY MILEAGE subroutine. Programming should be done between lines 670 and 680.

2. Allow the user the option to write to cassette only the entries since a certain date. Ask which date and search the D$ array for it. Then set MW to the appropriate number of records to write. These changes are to be made between lines 500 and 510 at the beginning of the subroutine to write on cassette.

3. Add a new command option to verify a data file just written to cassette. It would read the tape and compare it to the data already in memory.

4. Add an option to do statistical calculations over a given subset of the data. The operator inputs a beginning and ending date. He is then shown things like average MPG, total miles driven, total gallons purchased, etc.; all computed only over the range requested.

5. Write a subroutine to graphically display MPG. A bar graph might work well.

6. Add a new parameter in each data record—the cost of each fill-up. Then compute things like the total cost of gasoline, miles/dollar, etc.

QUEST/EXAM

PURPOSE

If you've ever had to analyze the results of a questionnaire, or grade a multiple-choice examination, you know what a tedious and time-consuming process it can be. This is particularly true if you need to accumulate statistics for each question showing how many people responded with each possible answer.

With this program, you provide the data, and the computer does the work.

HOW TO USE IT

First, enter the number of questions on the questionnaire or exam. The maximum is 50. Then enter the number of choices per question. This is an integer from 2 through 9. Each answer will be a digit from one to this number or left blank.

Next enter the maximum number of entries (exam papers) that you are going to analyze. Be sure to enter a number at least as large as the number of papers that you will be evaluating.

Finally, you are asked if you want to input names for each entry. This is especially useful when grading exams, to enable you to re-check later to verify that you entered the proper data for each student.

At this point, the program asks you for the answer key. If you are scoring an exam, provide the correct answers. The program displays "guide numbers" to help you keep track of which answers you are providing. If you are analyzing a questionnaire, you have no answer key, so just press the **ENTER** key.

Now the program asks you to begin providing the answers for each entry. Again, guide numbers are displayed above the area where you are to enter the data so you can more easily provide the proper answer for the proper question number. If no answer was given for a particular question, leave a blank space. However, if either the first or the last question was left blank, you will have to enclose the entire string of answers within quotation marks. This will cause a small problem in keeping your alignment straight with the guide numbers, but you'll get used to it. See below for an alternate way to do this.

If you make a mistake when entering the data, the program will tell you and ask you to re-enter it. This is most commonly caused by either failing to enter the correct number of answers or entering an invalid character instead of an acceptable answer number. Remember that each answer must be either a blank or a number from one to the number of choices you allowed per question.

By the way, you can avoid entering blanks for unanswered questions. Suppose you have a maximum of 5 possible answers per question. Simply tell the program there are 6 choices per question. Then, when a question is unanswered, you can enter a 6 instead of leaving it blank.

If you specified that you wanted names for each entry, the program asks you for the name after you have entered the answer key. Do not use commas in the name unless you enclose the entire name in quotation marks.

If you provided an answer key, the program displays the number and percentage correct after each entry before going on to ask for the next one. When you have no more entries, press the **ENTER** key instead of entering a string of answers.

At this point, the program displays five options from which you choose your next action. Here are brief explanations. You can experiment to verify how they work.

Option one lets you analyze each question, to see how many people responded with each answer. The percentage of people who responded with each answer is also shown. In the case of an exam, the right answer is indicated with the word "RIGHT."

Option two allows you to go back and provide more entries. This allows you to pause after entering part of the data, do some analysis of what you have entered so far, and then go back and continue entering data.

Option three lets you review what you have entered, including the answer key. This permits you to check for duplicate, omitted, or erroneous entries.

Option four starts the program over at the beginning again, and option five ends the program.

SAMPLE RUN

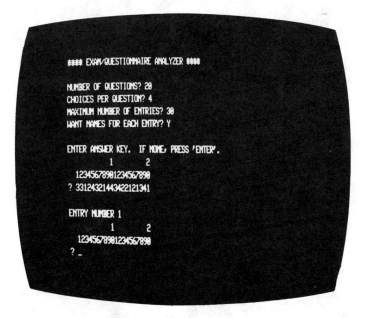

The operator provides the required information about the examination being scored. The program waits for the data from the first examination paper.

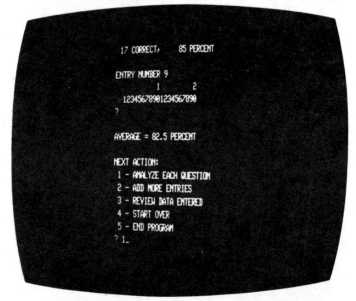

```
             1        2
     12345678901234567890
   ? 33124321443422121341

   ENTRY NUMBER 1
             1        2
     12345678901234567890
   ? 33223321443421121341
   NAME FOR ENTRY NUMBER 1
   ? J ANDERSON
    17 CORRECT,      85 PERCENT

   ENTRY NUMBER 2
             1        2
     12345678901234567890
   ? _
```

The answers are entered for the first student, followed by the student's
name. The program responds with the number and percentage correct.

```
    17 CORRECT,      85 PERCENT

   ENTRY NUMBER 9
             1        2
     12345678901234567890
   ?

   AVERAGE = 82.5 PERCENT

   NEXT ACTION:
    1 - ANALYZE EACH QUESTION
    2 - ADD MORE ENTRIES
    3 - REVIEW DATA ENTERED
    4 - START OVER
    5 - END PROGRAM
   ? 1_
```

Later, instead of providing data for a ninth student, the operator presses
the ENTER key, indicating no more entries. The program displays the
overall percentage correct, and displays a "menu" of choices of actions.
The operator picks number one.

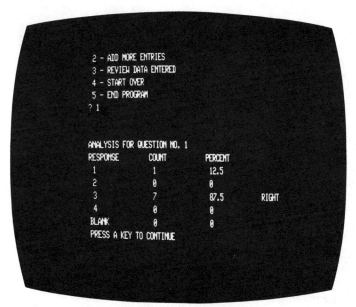

```
2 - ADD MORE ENTRIES
3 - REVIEW DATA ENTERED
4 - START OVER
5 - END PROGRAM
? 1


ANALYSIS FOR QUESTION NO. 1
RESPONSE        COUNT       PERCENT
1               1           12.5
2               0           0
3               7           87.5          RIGHT
4               0           0
BLANK           0           0
PRESS A KEY TO CONTINUE
```

The program provides an analysis of the responses for question number one, then waits for a key to be pressed. Note that seven students answered with number 3, the correct answer.

```
5 - END PROGRAM
? 3
                1          2
      12345678901234567890

3312432144342212134114-ANSWER KEY
3322332144342112134114-NO. 1 J ANDERSON
3322432144342212134114-NO. 2 J CRANE
3321442234342212233114-NO. 3 R FORBES
3321431134342112323114-NO. 4 M SARGENT
3312432144342212134114-NO. 5 R PRIMO
3312432244342232134114-NO. 6 A DIPIRRO
1312422143342212134414-NO. 7 K VANFLEET
3312432134342412234114-NO. 8 A BERMAN
PRESS A KEY TO CONTINUE
```

Later, the operator asks for option number 3, which lists the data entered for each of the students.

PROGRAM LISTING

```
100 REM: QUESTIONNAIRE/EXAM ANALYZER
110 REM: COPYRIGHT 1979 BY TOM RUGG AND PHIL FELDMAN
120 CLEAR 700:CLS:DEFINT C-W
130 PRINT"**** EXAM/QUESTIONNAIRE ANALYZER ****":PRINT
140 E$="*** ERROR. RE-ENTER. ***":
    P$="PRESS A KEY TO CONTINUE"
150 INPUT"NUMBER OF QUESTIONS";Q
160 IF Q<1 OR Q>50 THEN 150
170 INPUT"CHOICES PER QUESTION";C
180 IF C<2 OR C>9 THEN 170 ELSE DIM C(C)
190 INPUT"MAXIMUM NUMBER OF ENTRIES";N
200 IF N<1 THEN 190 ELSE DIM Q$(N)
210 INPUT"WANT NAMES FOR EACH ENTRY";R$
220 R$=LEFT$(R$,1):IF R$="N" THEN 250
230 IF R$<>"Y" THEN 210
240 DIM N$(N)
250 PRINT:
    PRINT"ENTER ANSWER KEY.  IF NONE, PRESS 'ENTER'."
260 GOSUB 900:A$="":C$=RIGHT$(STR$(C),1)
310 INPUT A$:IF LEN(A$)=0 THEN A$="":GOTO 340
320 IF LEN(A$)<>Q THEN PRINT E$:GOTO 250
330 T$=A$:GOSUB 850:IF T$="B" THEN PRINT E$:GOTO 250
340 K=1
350 R=0:PRINT:PRINT"ENTRY NUMBER";K
360 GOSUB 900
370 INPUT Q$(K):W=LEN(Q$(K))
380 IF W=0 THEN 500
390 IF W<>Q THEN PRINT E$:GOTO 350
400 T$=Q$(K):GOSUB 850:IF T$="B" THEN PRINT E$:GOTO 350
410 IF R$="N" THEN 430 ELSE
    PRINT"NAME FOR ENTRY NUMBER";K
420 INPUT N$(K):IF LEN(N$(K))=0 THEN N$(K)=""
430 IF A$="" THEN 480
440 FOR J=1 TO Q
450 IF MID$(A$,J,1)=MID$(Q$(K),J,1) THEN R=R+1
460 NEXT
470 TR=TR+R:PRINT R;"CORRECT,",R*100/Q;"PERCENT"
480 K=K+1:IF K<=N THEN 350
500 K=K-1:IF A$="" THEN 520
510 PRINT:PRINT"AVERAGE =";TR*100/(Q*K);"PERCENT"
520 GOTO 960
530 PRINT:FOR J=1 TO Q
540 R=0:PRINT:PRINT"ANALYSIS FOR QUESTION NO.";J
545 PRINT"RESPONSE","COUNT","PERCENT"
```

```
550 FOR L=0 TO C:C(L)=0:NEXT:M=0
560 FOR L=1 TO K:T$=MID$(Q$(L),J,1)
570 W=VAL(T$)
580 C(W)=C(W)+1
600 NEXT L
620 FOR L=1 TO C:PRINT L,C(L),C(L)*100/K,
630 IF A$="" THEN PRINT:GOTO 660
640 T$=RIGHT$(STR$(L),1)
650 IF T$=MID$(A$,J,1) THEN PRINT"RIGHT" ELSE PRINT
660 NEXT:PRINT"BLANK",C(0),C(0)*100/K
670 PRINT P$
680 IF INKEY$="" THEN 680
690 NEXT J:GOTO 960
700 L=0:GOSUB 900:PRINT:IF A$="" THEN 720
710 PRINT TAB(2);A$;"--ANSWER KEY"
720 FOR J=1 TO K
730 PRINT TAB(2);Q$(J);"--NO.";J;
740 IF R$="N" THEN PRINT:ELSE PRINT N$(J)
750 L=L+1:IF L<10 THEN 780
760 L=0:PRINT P$
770 IF INKEY$="" THEN 770
780 NEXT:PRINT P$
790 IF INKEY$="" THEN 790 ELSE 960
850 FOR J=1 TO LEN(T$):IF MID$(T$,J,1)=" " THEN 870
860 IF MID$(T$,J,1)<"1" OR MID$(T$,J,1)>C$ THEN 880
870 NEXT:RETURN
880 T$="B":RETURN
900 W=Q/10:IF W<1 THEN 920
910 FOR J=1 TO W:PRINT TAB(J*10);J;:NEXT:PRINT
920 PRINT TAB(2);
930 FOR J=1 TO Q:T$=STR$(J):PRINT MID$(T$,LEN(T$),1);
940 NEXT:PRINT:RETURN
960 PRINT:PRINT"NEXT ACTION:"
970 PRINT" 1 - ANALYZE EACH QUESTION"
980 PRINT" 2 - ADD MORE ENTRIES"
990 PRINT" 3 - REVIEW DATA ENTERED"
1000 PRINT" 4 - START OVER"
1010 PRINT" 5 - END PROGRAM"
1050 INPUT T$:IF T$<"1" OR T$>"5" THEN 1070
1060 ON VAL(T$) GOTO 530,480,700,120,1100
1070 PRINT E$:GOTO 960
1100 END
```

EASY CHANGES

1. This program will run in a 4K TRS-80 if a limited amount of data is entered. The limit is about 20 questions, five choices per question, 30 entries, and no names for each entry. To take advantage of a 16K computer, change the 700 in line 120 to be 8000. This way, there's easily room for 50 questions, nine choices per question, 100 entries, with names for each entry.

MAIN ROUTINES

120 - 140	Initializes variables.
150 - 240	Performs initialization dialog. Selects options. Allocates arrays.
250 - 320	Gets answer key (if any) from operator.
330	Checks legality of answer key.
350 - 400	Gets exam data for Kth entry.
410 - 420	Gets name for Kth entry, if applicable.
430 - 470	Scores Kth exam, if applicable.
500 - 510	Displays average score, if an exam.
530 - 690	Analyzes responses to each question.
700 - 790	Displays data entered.
850 - 880	Subroutine to check legality of input data.
900 - 940	Subroutine to display guide numbers over input data area.
960 - 1100	Displays choices for next action. Gets response and goes to appropriate routine.

MAIN VARIABLES

E$	Error message
P$	Message about pressing a key to continue.
Q	Number of questions (1 - 50).
C	Number of choices per question (2 - 9).
C	Array for tallying number of people responding with each choice.
N	Maximum number of entries.
Q$	Array of N strings of entries.
R$	Set to N if no names for each entry, or Y otherwise.
N$	Array of Q names (if R$ is Y).

A$	Answer key string (null if not an exam).
C$	String value of highest legal answer choice.
K	Counter of number of exams scored.
R	Number of questions answered right (if exam).
W	Work variable.
J, L, M	Loop variables.
TR	Total right for all entries.
T$	Temporary work string variable.

SUGGESTED PROJECTS

1. Add an option to change the answer key after the data for the exams is entered. This would be useful in case a mistake was found when reviewing the data.
2. Add an option to allow the operator to re-score each of the exams after all are entered, in case some were overlooked at the time of entry.
3. Combine some of the capabilities of the STATS program with this one.

Section 2

Educational Programs

INTRODUCTION TO EDUCATION PROGRAMS

Education is one area where computers are certain to have more and more impact. Though a computer cannot completely replace a human teacher, the machine does have certain advantages. It is ready anytime you are, allows you to go at your own pace, handles rote drill effortlessly, and is devoid of any personality conflicts.

With a good software library, the TRS-80 can be a valuable learning center in the school or at home. Here are six programs to get you started.

Mathematics is certainly a "natural" subject for computers. NUMBERS is designed for pre-school children. While familiarizing youngsters with computers, it provides an entertaining way for them to learn numbers and elementary counting. ARITHMETIC is aimed at older, grade school students. It provides drill in various kinds of math problems. The child can adjust the difficulty factors, allowing the program to be useful for several years.

By no means is the TRS-80 restricted to mathematical disciplines. We include two programs designed to improve your word skills. VOCAB will help you expand your vocabulary. TACHIST turns the TRS-80 into a reading clinic, helping you to improve your reading speed.

Do you have trouble familiarizing yourself with the increasingly prevalent metric system? METRIC is the answer.

Need help learning a certain subject? FLASHCARD allows you to create your own "computer flashcards." Then you can drill yourself until you get it right.

ARITHMETIC

PURPOSE

ARITHMETIC provides mathematics drills for grade school children. The student can request problems in addition, subtraction, or multiplication from the program. Also, he or she may ask that the problems be easy, medium, or hard. The program should be useful to a child over an extended period of time. He can progress naturally to a harder category of problems when he begins to regularly perform well at one level. The difficulty and types of problems encompass those normally encountered by school children between the ages of six and ten.

The problems are constructed randomly within the constraints imposed by the degree of difficulty selected. This gives the student fresh practice each time the program is used. After entering answers, he is told whether he was right or wrong. The correct answers are also displayed.

HOW TO USE IT

To begin, the student must indicate what type of problem he wishes to do. The program requests an input of 1, 2, or 3 to indicate addition, subtraction, or multiplication, respectively. It then asks whether easy, medium, or hard problems are desired. Again an input of 1, 2, or 3 is required.

Now the screen will clear and four problems of the desired type will be displayed. The user now begins to enter his answers to each problem.

A question mark is used to prompt the user for each digit of the answer, one digit at a time. This is done moving right to left, the way arithmetic problems are naturally solved.

To start each problem, the question mark will appear in the spot for the rightmost (or units column) digit of the answer. When the key for a digit from 0 - 9 is pressed, that digit will replace the question mark on the screen. The question mark moves to the immediate left waiting for a digit for the "tens" column.

Digits are entered in this right to left manner until the complete answer has been input. Then the **ENTER** key must be pressed. This will end the answer to the current problem and move the question mark to begin the answer for the next question.

If the **ENTER** key is pressed to begin a problem, an answer of zero is assumed intended. No problems created by this program have answers of more than three digits. If a four-digit answer is given, the program will accept the answer, but then go immediately to the next problem. Answers to the problems are never negative.

The program will display the correct answers to the four problems on the screen after the student has entered his four answers. The message "RIGHT!" or "WRONG!" will also be displayed below each problem.

Then the message "HIT ANY KEY TO CONTINUE" will be displayed. After the key is pressed, a new set of four problems of the same type will be presented.

This continues until twenty problems have been worked. The program then shows what the student's performance has been. This is expressed as the number of problems solved correctly and also as the percentage of problems solved correctly.

The program then asks whether or not the student would like to do more problems. Simply hit "Y" or "N" to answer this question.

SAMPLE RUN

The operator chooses to do hard addition problems.

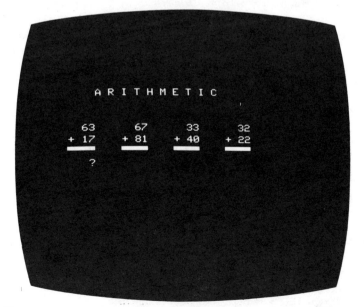

The initial set of 4 problems is presented. With a question mark, the program prompts the operator for the answer to the first problem.

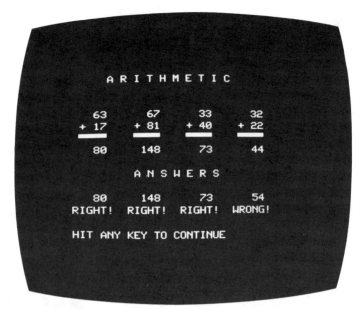

The operator has entered his or her four answers. The program displays the correct answers and indicates whether or not each problem was solved correctly. The program waits for the operator to hit any key in order to continue with the next set of four problems.

PROGRAM LISTING

```
100 REM: ARITHMETIC
110 REM: COPYRIGHT 1979 BY PHIL FELDMAN AND TOM RUGG
140 CLEAR 50:DIM A(4),B(4),C(4),G(4)
150 ND=0
160 NP=20
170 RANDOM
200 GOSUB 910:PRINT:PRINT"WHAT TYPE PROBLEM SHALL WE DO?"
210 PRINT" 1 - ADDITION"
220 PRINT" 2 - SUBTRACTION"
230 PRINT" 3 - MULTIPLICATION"
240 PRINT"WHICH TYPE (1, 2, OR 3) ?";
250 R$=INKEY$:T=VAL(R$):IF T<1 OR T>3 THEN 250
260 PRINT CHR$(24);"-";T:GOSUB 1300
270 PRINT STRING$(32,"=");:PRINT"WHAT KIND SHALL WE DO?"
280 PRINT" 1 - EASY PROBLEMS"
290 PRINT" 2 - MEDIUM PROBLEMS"
300 PRINT" 3 - HARD PROBLEMS"
310 PRINT"WHAT KIND (1, 2, OR 3) ?";
320 R$=INKEY$:D=VAL(R$):IF D<1 OR D>3 THEN 320
```

```
330 PRINT CHR$(24);"-";D
350 ON D GOTO 360,370,400
360 GOSUB 940:GOSUB 920:GOSUB 930:GOTO 420
370 GOSUB 940:GOSUB 930
380 IF T=3 THEN GOSUB 960:GOSUB 920:GOTO 420
390 IF T<>3 THEN GOSUB 950:GOSUB 920:GOTO 420
400 GOSUB 950:GOSUB 920:GOSUB 930
410 IF T=3 THEN GOSUB 940:GOSUB 930
420 IF T<>2 THEN 450
430 FOR J=1 TO 4:IF B(J)>C(J) THEN R=C(J):C(J)=B(J):
    B(J)=R
440 NEXT
450 GOSUB 1000:GOSUB 910
600 FOR J=1 TO 4:GOSUB 1100:NEXT
610 FOR K=1 TO 4:P=378+K*16:GOSUB 800:G(K)=N:NEXT
620 PRINT@532,"A N S W E R S";
630 FOR J=1 TO 4:P=626+J*16:GOSUB 1400:NEXT
640 FOR J=1 TO 4:P=690+J*16
650 IF A(J)<>G(J) THEN PRINT@P,"WRONG!";:GOTO 670
660 PRINT@P,"RIGHT!";:NR=NR+1
670 NEXT:FOR K=1 TO 9:R$=INKEY$:NEXT
680 PRINT@834,"HIT ANY KEY TO CONTINUE";
690 R$=INKEY$:IF R$="" THEN 690
700 FOR J=1 TO 10:R$=INKEY$:NEXT
710 ND=ND+4:IF ND<NP THEN GOSUB 910:GOTO 350
720 GOSUB 1500
730 PRINT:PRINT"WANT MORE PROBLEMS (Y OR N) ?"
740 R$=INKEY$:IF R$="" THEN 740
750 IF R$="Y" THEN GOTO 140
760 IF R$="N" THEN CLS:END
770 GOTO 740
800 N=0:M=1:FOR J=1 TO 10:R$=INKEY$:NEXT
810 PRINT@P,"?";
820 R$=INKEY$:IF R$="" THEN 820
830 A=ASC(R$):IF A=13 AND M=1 THEN PRINT@P,"0";:RETURN
840 IF A=13 THEN PRINT@P,CHR$(32);:RETURN
850 V=VAL(R$):IF V=0 AND A<>48 THEN 820
860 PN=48+V:PRINT@P,CHR$(PN);:N=N+M*V:M=M*10
870 IF M>1000 THEN RETURN
880 P=P-2:GOTO 810
910 CLS:PRINT CHR$(23);TAB(6);"A R I T H M E T I C";:
    RETURN
920 FOR K=1 TO 4:C(K)=L+RND(H-L+1)-1:NEXT:RETURN
930 FOR K=1 TO 4:B(K)=L+RND(H-L+1)-1:NEXT:RETURN
940 H=9:L=0:RETURN
```

```
950 H=99:L=0:RETURN
960 H=25:L=1:RETURN
1000 ON T GOTO 1010,1020,1030
1010 FOR J=1 TO 4:A(J)=B(J)+C(J):NEXT:RETURN
1020 FOR J=1 TO 4:A(J)=C(J)-B(J):NEXT:RETURN
1030 FOR J=1 TO 4:A(J)=C(J)*B(J):NEXT:RETURN
1100 B$="":IF C(J)<10 THEN B$=CHR$(32)
1110 P=182+J*16:PRINT@P,B$;C(J);:P=244+J*16:PRINT@P,C$;
1120 B$="":IF B(J)<10 THEN B$=CHR$(32)
1130 P=246+J*16:PRINT@P,B$;B(J);
1140 P=308+J*16:PRINT@P,STRING$(4,131);
1150 RETURN
1300 ON T GOTO 1310,1320,1330
1310 C$="+":RETURN
1320 C$="-":RETURN
1330 C$="X":RETURN
1400 B$=CHR$(32):IF A(J)>999 THEN PRINT@P,A(J);:RETURN
1410 IF A(J)>99 THEN PRINT@P,B$;A(J);:RETURN
1420 IF A(J)>9 THEN PRINT@P,B$;B$;A(J);:RETURN
1430 PRINT@P,B$;B$;B$;A(J);:RETURN
1500 GOSUB 910:PRINT
1510 PRINT"YOU GOT";NR;"RIGHT"
1520 PRINT"OUT OF";NP;"PROBLEMS"
1530 P=NR/NP*100
1540 PRINT:PRINT"THAT'S";P;" PERCENT CORRECT":RETURN
```

EASY CHANGES

1. The program currently does twenty problems per session. You can change this number by altering the variable NP in line 160. For example,

    160 NP=12

    will cause the program to do only twelve problems per session. The value of NP should be kept a positive multiple of four.

2. Zero is currently allowed as a possible problem operand. If you do not wish to allow this, change lines 940 and 950 to read as follows:

    940 H=9:L=1:RETURN

    950 H=99:L=1:RETURN

MAIN ROUTINES

140 - 170	Initializes constants.
200 - 330	Asks operator for type of problems desired.
350 - 450	Sets A, B, C arrays, clears screen.
600 - 770	Mainline routine—displays problems, gets operator's answers, displays correct answers and user's performance.
800 - 880	Subroutine to get and display user's answers.
910	Subroutine to clear screen and display title.
920 - 930	Subroutine to set B, C arrays.
940 - 960	Subroutine to set L, H.
1000 - 1030	Subroutine to calculate A array from B, C arrays.
1100 - 1150	Subroutine to display problems.
1300 - 1330	Subroutine to set C$.
1400 - 1430	Subroutine to display the correct answers.
1500 - 1540	Subroutine to display operator's performance.

MAIN VARIABLES

NP	Number of problems to do in the session.
ND	Number of problems done.
NR	Number of correct answers given.
C,B,A	Arrays of top operand, bottom operand, and correct answer to each problem.
N	Operator's answer to current problem.
G	Array of operator's answers.
T	Type of problems requested (1=addition, 2=subtraction, 3=multiplication).
D	Kind of problem requested (1=easy, 2=medium, 3=hard).
H,L	Highest, lowest integers to allow as problem operands.
M	Answer column being worked on.
R$	Operator's input character.
V	Value of R$.
A	Ascii value of R$.
PN	CHR$ argument.
B$	Character spacing string.
C$	Operation symbol string.

R	Work variable.
J,K	Loop indices.
P	Screen position, also percentage correct.

SUGGESTED PROJECTS

1. Keep track of problems missed and repeat them quickly for additional practice.
2. No negative operands or answers are currently allowed. Rewrite the problem generation routines and the operator's answer routines to allow the possibility of negative answers.
3. The answers are now restricted to three-digit numbers. However, the program will work fine for four-digit numbers if the operands of the problems were allowed to be large enough. Dig into the routines at lines 350 - 450 and 940 - 960. See how they work and then modify them to allow possible four-digit answers.
4. The operator cannot currently correct any mistakes he makes while typing in his answers. Modify the program to allow him to do so.
5. Modify the program to allow problems in division.

FLASHCARD

PURPOSE

There are certain things that the human mind is capable of learning only through repetition. Not many people can remember the multiplication tables after their first exposure, for example. The same applies to learning the vocabulary of a foreign language, the capital cities of the fifty states, or famous dates in history. The best way to learn them is to simply review them over and over until you have them memorized.

A common technique for doing this involves the use of flashcards. You write one half of the two related pieces of information on one side of a card, and the other half on the other side. After creating a set of these cards, you can drill yourself on them over and over until you always remember what's on the other side of each card.

But why waste precious natural resources by using cards? Use your computer instead. This program lets you create flashcards, drill using them, and save them on cassette tape for later review.

HOW TO USE IT

The program gives you seven options. The first time you run it, you'll want to enter new flashcards, so you should reply with number 1.

To create the cards, the program asks you for each side of each flashcard, one at a time. First enter side one of the first card, and so on. As you enter the data, be careful not to use any commas or colons unless the entire expression is enclosed in quotes. Also, be careful not to enter such a long stream of data that it goes to the next line on the screen. This can cause confusion due to spacing differences during drill.

At any time, you can enter the keyword "*BACK" to correct an erroneous entry. This causes the program to back up and ask you for the previous entry again.

As the program is currently written, you must enter at least five flashcards, and no more than twelve. We will show you how to change these limits in the "Easy Changes" section.

When you have entered all the flashcards you want, enter "*END" instead of side one of the next card. This puts the program back into "command" mode to ask you what to do next. If you want to quiz yourself on the cards you just entered, respond with the number 4.

The program flashes one side of one card on the screen for you. Both are chosen at random—the side and the card. Your job is to respond with the other side. If you enter it correctly, the program says "RIGHT!" If not, it tells you the correct response. In either event, the program continues by picking another side and card at random. This continues until you respond with "*END", which tells the program you do not want to drill any more. It will then tell you how many you got right out of the number you attempted, as well as the percentage, and then return to command mode.

During the drill sequence, by the way, the program will not repeat a card that was used in the previous four questions (i.e., one less than the minimum number of cards you can enter).

To save a set of flashcards on cassette, use option number 3. The program will tell you to put the cassette into position and then enter a name for the file. You should give it a good descriptive name in order to remember what kind of flashcards they are in the future. Be sure to write the name on the cassette, too. After the flashcards have been copied to the cassette, the program will say "DONE" and return to the command mode.

The other commands are easily understood, so we will just explain them briefly. A little experimentation will show you how they work.

Command number 5 lets you verify that the set of flashcards just saved on tape are okay. You do not have to enter the name of the file—the same name is used that was used to save the file.

Command number 2 is used to load a flashcard tape that has been previously saved. The program asks for the name of the file, so it can scan the cassette until it finds the one you asked for. If you don't know the name of the file, enter any name; the program will show you the name it finds, as well as side one of all the file's flashcards.

Command number 6 allows you to add more flashcards to those currently in memory.

Command number 7 ends the program.

SAMPLE RUN

```
        FLASHCARD  PROGRAM
LIMIT  IS  12  CARDS
----OPTIONS----
  1 - ENTER NEW FLASHCARDS
  2 - LOAD A FLASHCARD TAPE
  3 - SAVE CURRENT SET ON TAPE
  4 - DRILL ON CURRENT SET
  5 - VERIFY FLASHCARDS ON TAPE
  6 - ADD TO CURRENT CARDS
  7 - END PROGRAM
  ? 1

SIDE ONE OF CARD NO. 1
? THE PEN
SIDE TWO
? LA PLUMA

SIDE ONE OF CARD NO. 2
? THE DOOR
SIDE TWO
? LA PUERTA

SIDE ONE OF CARD NO. 3
? THE SCHOOL
SIDE TWO
? LA ESCUELA

SIDE ONE OF CARD NO. 4
? THE FLOOR
SIDE TWO
? EL SUELO
```

```
SIDE ONE OF CARD NO. 5
? THE STORE
SIDE TWO
? LA TIENDRA

SIDE ONE OF CARD NO. 6
? *END

----OPTIONS----

  1 - ENTER NEW FLASHCARDS
  2 - LOAD A FLASHCARD TAPE
  3 - SAVE CURRENT SET ON TAPE
  4 - DRILL ON CURRENT SET
  5 - VERIFY FLASHCARDS ON TAPE
  6 - ADD TO CURRENT CARDS
  7 - END PROGRAM
? 4

TELL ME WHAT'S ON THE
OTHER SIDE OF EACH CARD AS I SHOW IT.

THE DOOR
? LA PUERTA

RIGHT!

LA PLUMA
? THE PEN

RIGHT!

THE FLOOR
? LA ESCUELA

NO, THE CORRECT RESPONSE IS
EL SUELO

THE SCHOOL
? LA ESCUELA

RIGHT!

LA TIENDRA
? *END
```

3 RIGHT OUT OF 4
75 PER CENT

PROGRAM LISTING

```
100 REM: FLASHCARD
110 REM: COPYRIGHT 1979 BY TOM RUGG AND PHIL FELDMAN
120 CLEAR 240:DEFINT A-Z:N=-1
130 L=12:M=5
140 DIM F$(L),B$(L),P(M-1)
150 RANDOM:CLS:E$="** ERROR ** "
160 W$="** PRESS 'STOP' KEY ON RECORDER **"
170 PRINT"FLASHCARD PROGRAM"
180 PRINT:PRINT"LIMIT IS";L;"CARDS.":GOTO 2000
190 K=1:W=0:C=0:PRINT
200 F$(K)="":PRINT"SIDE ONE OF CARD NO.";K:INPUT F$(K)
205 IF LEN(F$(K))=0 THEN PRINT E$:GOTO 200
210 IF LEFT$(F$(K),4)="*END" THEN 280
220 IF LEFT$(F$(K),5)<>"*BACK" THEN 230
222 K=K-1:IF K<1 THEN K=1
225 PRINT:PRINT"BACKING UP":GOTO 200
230 B$(K)="":PRINT"SIDE TWO":INPUT B$(K)
235 IF LEN(B$(K))=0 THEN PRINT E$:GOTO 230
240 IF LEFT$(B$(K),5)="*BACK" THEN 225
250 PRINT
260 K=K+1:IF K<=L THEN 200
270 PRINT"THAT'S THE";L;"CARD LIMIT."
280 PRINT:K=K-1:GOTO 2000
290 IF K>=M THEN 310
300 PRINT E$;" MINIMUM IS";M;"CARDS.":GOTO 2000
310 PRINT:PRINT"TELL ME WHAT'S ON THE"
320 PRINT"OTHER SIDE OF EACH CARD AS I SHOW IT."
330 PRINT
340 R=RND(K):FOR J=0 TO M-2:IF P(J)=R THEN 340
390 NEXT:J=RND(2):IF J=2 THEN 420
400 PRINT F$(R):C$=B$(R):GOTO 430
420 PRINT B$(R):C$=F$(R)
430 R$="":INPUT R$
440 IF LEFT$(R$,4)="*END" THEN 600
450 PRINT
460 IF R$=C$ THEN 500
470 PRINT"NO, THE CORRECT RESPONSE IS"
480 PRINT C$
490 W=W+1:GOTO 520
500 PRINT"RIGHT!"
```

```
510 C=C+1
520 FOR J=1 TO M-2:P(J-1)=P(J):NEXT:P(M-2)=R:PRINT
560 GOTO 340
600 GOSUB 1500:GOTO 2000
700 IF K<1 THEN 1800
710 GOSUB 1600
720 PRINT"PRESS 'RECORD' AND 'PLAY' BUTTONS, THEN"
730 PRINT"PROVIDE NAME FOR FILE WHEN READY.":INPUT N$
735 PRINT"WRITING ";N$
740 PRINT#N,N$:PRINT#N,STR$(K):FOR J=1 TO K
750 PRINT#N,F$(J),B$(J)
760 PRINT J;:NEXT
770 PRINT#N,"*END"
790 PRINT:PRINT"DONE"
800 PRINT W$
810 GOTO 2000
900 E=0:GOSUB 1600
910 PRINT"PRESS 'PLAY', THEN PRESS ANY KEY."
920 R$=INKEY$:IF R$="" THEN 920
930 PRINT"SEARCHING FOR ";N$
935 INPUT#N,R$:IF R$=N$ THEN 950
940 PRINT"FOUND ";R$:
    IF R$="*END" THEN 930 ELSE GOTO 935
950 PRINT:PRINT"FOUND ";N$:INPUT#N,R$
960 IF VAL(R$)<>K THEN E=1:PRINT E$;" BAD COUNT":
    GOTO 1020
970 FOR J=1 TO K:INPUT#N,R$,T$
975 PRINT R$:PRINT T$
980 IF R$<>F$(J) OR T$<>B$(J) THEN E=1
990 NEXT
1010 PRINT:PRINT"DONE"
1020 IF E=0 THEN PRINT"O.K.":PRINT W$:GOTO 2000
1030 PRINT"NO GOOD":PRINT W$:GOTO 2000
1150 INPUT"NAME OF TAPE FILE";N$
1160 GOSUB 1600:PRINT"PRESS 'PLAY',"
1170 PRINT"THEN PRESS ANY KEY."
1180 R$=INKEY$:IF R$="" THEN 1180
1185 PRINT"SEARCHING FOR ";N$
1190 INPUT#N,R$:IF R$<>N$ THEN PRINT R$:GOTO 1190
1200 PRINT:PRINT"FOUND ";N$:PRINT
1210 INPUT#N,R$:K=VAL(R$):IF K=0 THEN 1030
1220 IF K<=L THEN 1250 ELSE PRINT E$
1230 PRINT"FILE HAS";K;"CARDS.  PROGRAM LIMITED TO";L
1240 GOTO 2000
1250 FOR J=1 TO K
```

```
1260 INPUT#N,F$(J),B$(J)
1270 PRINT F$(J):PRINT B$(J)
1280 NEXT
1290 INPUT#N,R$:IF R$<>"*END" THEN 1030
1300 PRINT:PRINT"LOADED";K;"CARDS."
1310 PRINT W$:GOTO 2000
1500 PRINT:IF C+W=0 THEN RETURN
1510 PRINT C;"RIGHT OUT OF";C+W
1520 PRINT C*100/(C+W);"PERCENT"
1530 PRINT:RETURN
1600 PRINT
1610 PRINT"HOLD A KEY DOWN AFTER CASSETTE IS
     IN POSITION."
1620 PRINT
1630 IF INKEY$<>"" THEN RETURN
1640 PRINT#N,"X":GOTO 1630
1800 PRINT:PRINT E$;" NO CARDS YET."
1810 GOTO 2000
2000 R$="":PRINT:PRINT"----OPTIONS----"
2010 PRINT" 1 - ENTER NEW FLASHCARDS"
2020 PRINT" 2 - LOAD A FLASHCARD TAPE"
2030 PRINT" 3 - SAVE CURRENT SET ON TAPE"
2040 PRINT" 4 - DRILL ON CURRENT SET"
2050 PRINT" 5 - VERIFY FLASHCARDS ON TAPE"
2060 PRINT" 6 - ADD TO CURRENT CARDS"
2070 PRINT" 7 - END PROGRAM"
2080 INPUT R$:IF VAL(R$)<1 OR VAL(R$)>7 THEN 2100
2090 ON VAL(R$) GOTO 190,1150,700,290,900,260,2140
2100 PRINT:PRINT E$:GOTO 2000
2140 END
```

EASY CHANGES

1. Change the limits of the number of flashcards that can be
   entered by altering line 130. L is the upper limit and M is the
   minimum. The current upper limit of twelve will fit in a
   TRS-80 with 4K of memory if each side of each flashcard
   averages no more than about twelve to fifteen characters
   in length. In a 16K TRS-80, you can make L as large as about
   four hundred for flashcards this size. You will also need to
   change line 120 to CLEAR 8000 or so (instead of 240). Do
   not make M much larger than about ten or so, or you will
   slow down the program and use more memory than you
   might want.

2. If you want to use some keywords other than "*END" and "*BACK", substitute whatever you like in lines 210, 220, 240, and 440. Be sure you use expressions that are the same length as these two, however, If not, you will also need to change the last number just before each occurrence of the expression to correspond with the length.
3. To cause the program to always display side one of the flashcards (and ask you to respond with side two), change this line:

390 NEXT

To cause it to always display side two, change it this way:

390 NEXT:GOTO 420

4. To eliminate the "echoing" on the screen of a tape file being verified, remove line 975. To do the same for a tape being loaded, remove line 1270.

MAIN ROUTINES

130 - 180	Initializes variables. Creates arrays. Displays title and options.
190 - 280	Accepts flashcards entered by operator.
290 - 600	Drills operator on flashcards in memory.
700 - 810	Saves flashcards on cassette file.
900 - 1030	Verifies that flashcards on cassette tape are the same as those in memory.
1150 - 1310	Loads flashcards from cassette file into memory.
1500 - 1530	Subroutine to display number right and attempted during drill.
1600 - 1640	Subroutine to free cassette recorder until a key is held down.
1800 - 1810	Displays error message if operator tries to save flashcards on cassette before any are entered.
2000 - 2140	Displays options and analyzes response. Branches to appropriate routine.

MAIN VARIABLES

N	Cassette number for cassette files.
L	Upper limit of number of flashcards that can be entered.
M	Minimum number of flashcards that can be entered.

R	Subscript of random flashcard chosen during drill.
K	Number of flashcards entered.
W	Number of wrong responses.
C	Number of correct responses.
F$	Array containing front side of flashcards (side 1).
B$	Array containing back side of flashcards (side 2).
P	Array containing subscripts of $M-1$ previous flashcards during drill.
J	Loop and subscript variable.
C$	The correct response during drill.
R$	Response from operator. Also temporary string variable.
N$	Name of cassette file.
E	Error flag—set to 1 if error occurs on cassette.
T$	Temporary string variable.

SUGGESTED PROJECTS

1. Modify the program for use in a classroom environment. You might want to allow only command 2 to be used (to load a cassette tape), and then immediately go into "drill" mode for some fixed number of questions (maybe 20 or 50).

METRIC

PURPOSE

In case you don't realize it, we live in a metric world. The United States is one of the last holdouts, but that is changing rapidly. So if you're still inching along or watching those pounds, it's time to convert.

METRIC is an instructional program designed to familiarize you with the metric system. It operates in a quiz format; the program randomly forms questions from its data resources. You are then asked to compare two quantities—one in our old English units and one in the corresponding metric units. When you are wrong, the exact conversion and the rule governing it are given.

The two quantities to compare are usually within 50% of each other. Thus, you are constantly comparing an "English" quantity and a metric one which are in the same ball park. This has the effect of providing you some insight by sheer familiarity with the questions.

HOW TO USE IT

The first thing the program does is ask you how many questions you would like to do for the session. Any value of one or higher is acceptable.

The sample run shows how each question is formulated. A quantity in English units is compared with one in metric units. Either one may appear first in the question. Each quantity will have an integral value. The relating word ("longer," "hotter," "heavier," etc.) indicates what type of quantities are being compared.

There are three possible replies to each question. Pressing **Y** or **N** means that you think the answer is yes or no, respectively. Pressing any other key indicates that you have no idea as to the correct answer.

If you answer the question correctly, you will be duly congratulated and the program will proceed to the next question. A wrong answer or a response of "no idea," however, will generate some diagnostic information. The first value used in the question will be shown converted to its exact equivalent in the corresponding units. Also, the rule governing the situation will be displayed. At the end of any question, the program will request that you hit any key to proceed to the next question.

The program will continue generating the requested number of questions. Before ending, it will show you how many correct answers you gave and your percentage correct.

SAMPLE RUN

```
            A METRIC QUIZ
HOW MANY QUESTIONS SHALL WE DO? 3

QUESTION 1 OF 3

IS 48 MILES LONGER THAN
    92 KILOMETERS ? ("N" key pressed)

YOU SAY 'NO' AND YOU'RE RIGHT - VERY GOOD!

**** HIT ANY KEY TO CONTINUE ***

QUESTION 2 OF 3

IS 73 DEGREES FAHRENHEIT HOTTER THAN
    22 DEGREES CENTIGRADE ? ("Y" key pressed)

YOU SAY 'YES' AND YOU'RE RIGHT - VERY GOOD!

**** HIT ANY KEY TO CONTINUE ***

QUESTION 3 OF 3

IS 79 KILOGRAMS HEAVIER THAN
    152 POUNDS ? ("N" key pressed)

YOU SAY 'NO' BUT YOU'RE WRONG
```

```
 --------------------

 79 KILOGRAMS EQUALS
 174.166 POUNDS

---- THE RULE IS ----

 1 KILOGRAM EQUALS
 2.20463 POUNDS

*** HIT ANY KEY TO CONTINUE ***

YOU GOT 2 RIGHT OUT OF 3 QUESTIONS

PERCENTAGE CORRECT = 66.6667
```

PROGRAM LISTING

```
100 REM: METRIC
110 REM: COPYRIGHT 1979 BY PHIL FELDMAN AND TOM RUGG
150 CLEAR 50:B$=CHR$(32):RANDOM:DEFINT J,N
160 DIM ES$(30),MS$(30),R$(30),C(30),EP$(30),MP$(30)
200 GOSUB 400:GOSUB 450
210 INPUT"HOW MANY QUESTIONS SHALL WE DO";NQ
220 IF NQ<1 THEN 210
230 FOR J=1 TO NQ:GOSUB 600:GOSUB 900:NEXT:GOSUB 450
240 PRINT"YOU GOT";NR;"RIGHT OUT OF";NQ;"QUESTIONS"
250 PRINT:P=100*NR/NQ:PRINT"PERCENTAGE CORRECT =";P
260 END
400 RESTORE:ND=0
410 ND=ND+1
420 READ ES$(ND),MS$(ND),R$(ND),C(ND),EP$(ND),MP$(ND)
430 IF ES$(ND)<>"XXX" THEN 410 ELSE ND=ND-1:RETURN
450 CLS:PRINT,"A METRIC QUIZ":PRINT:RETURN
600 N=RND(ND):F=0:IF RND(0)>0.5 THEN F=1
610 V1=RND(98)+1:V3=V1*C(N):IF F=1 THEN V3=V1/C(N)
620 IF N=1 THEN V3=(V1-32)/1.8:
    IF F=1 THEN V3=(V1*1.8)+32
630 V2=INT(V3*(0.5+RND(0))+0.5):T=0:IF V2<V3 THEN T=1
640 GOSUB 450:PRINT"QUESTION";J;"OF";NQ:PRINT
650 IF F=0 THEN
    PRINT"IS";V1;EP$(N);B$;R$(N);" THAN" ELSE 670
660 PRINT B$;B$;V2;MP$(N);" ?":GOTO 690
670 PRINT"IS";V1;MP$(N);B$;R$(N);" THAN"
680 PRINT B$;B$;V2;EP$(N);" ?"
690 Q$="":Q$=INKEY$:IF Q$="" THEN 690
700 IF Q$="Y" THEN PRINT:PRINT"YOU SAY 'YES'";:R=1:
    GOTO 730
```

```
710 IF Q$="N" THEN PRINT:PRINT"YOU SAY 'NO'";:R=0:
    GOTO 730
720 PRINT:PRINT"YOU HAVE NO IDEA":R=2
730 X=T-R:IF R=2 THEN GOSUB 800:GOTO 760
740 IF X<>0 THEN PRINT" BUT YOU'RE WRONG":GOSUB 800:
    GOTO 760
750 PRINT" AND YOU'RE RIGHT - VERY GOOD!":NR=NR+1
760 RETURN
800 PRINT STRING$(35,"-")
810 IF F=0 THEN PRINT V1;EP$(N);" EQUALS":
    PRINT V3;MP$(N)
820 IF F=1 THEN PRINT V1;MP$(N);" EQUALS":
    PRINT V3;EP$(N)
830 PRINT"------------ THE RULE IS -----------"
840 IF F=1 THEN IF N=1 THEN 860 ELSE 880 ELSE IF
    N>1 THEN 870
850 PRINT" DEG.C = (DEG.F - 32)/1.8":RETURN
860 PRINT" DEG.F = (DEG.C * 1.8) + 32":RETURN
870 PRINT" 1 ";ES$(N);" EQUALS":PRINT C(N);MP$(N):
    RETURN
880 Q=INT(1.E5/C(N))/1.E5
890 PRINT" 1 ";MS$(N);" EQUALS":PRINT Q;EP$(N):RETURN
900 PRINT:PRINT"**** HIT ANY KEY TO CONTINUE ****"
910 Q$="":Q$=INKEY$:IF Q$="" THEN 910
920 RETURN
1000 DATA DEGREE FAHRENHEIT,DEGREE CENTIGRADE,
     HOTTER,0.5
1010 DATA DEGREES FAHRENHEIT,DEGREES CENTIGRADE
1020 DATA MILE PER HOUR,KILOMETER PER HOUR,FASTER,
     1.60935
1030 DATA MILES PER HOUR,KILOMETERS PER HOUR
1040 DATA FOOT,METER,LONGER,0.3048
1050 DATA FEET,METERS
1060 DATA MILE,KILOMETER,LONGER,1.60935
1070 DATA MILES,KILOMETERS
1080 DATA INCH,CENTIMETER,LONGER,2.54
1090 DATA INCHES,CENTIMETERS
1100 DATA GALLON,LITRE,MORE,3.78533
1110 DATA GALLONS,LITRES
1120 DATA POUND,KILOGRAM,HEAVIER,0.45359
1130 DATA POUNDS,KILOGRAMS
1999 DATA XXX,XXX,XXX,0,XXX,XXX
```

EASY CHANGES

1. To have the program always ask a fixed number of questions, change line 210 to set NQ to the desired value. For example:

$$210 \ NQ=10$$

will cause the program to do 10 questions.
2. There are currently seven conversions built into the program:

N	Type	English Unit	Metric Unit
1	temperature	degrees F.	degrees C.
2	speed	miles/hour	kilometers/hour
3	length	feet	meters
4	length	miles	kilometers
5	length	inches	centimeters
6	volume	gallons	litres
7	weight	pounds	kilograms

If you wish to be quizzed on only one type of question, set N to this value by adding line 605. Thus,

$$605 \ N=4$$

will cause the program to only produce questions comparing miles and kilometers. To add additional data to the program, see the first "Suggested Project."
3. You can easily have the questions posed in one "direction" only. To go only from English to metric units add

$$607 \ \ F=0$$

while to go from metric to English units use

$$607 \ \ F=1$$

4. You might want the converted value and governing rule to be displayed even when the correct answer is given. This is accomplished by adding line 755 as follows:

$$755 \ \ GOSUB \ 800$$

MAIN ROUTINES

150 - 160	Dimensions and initializes variables.
200 - 260	Mainline routine, drives other routines.

400 - 430	Reads and initializes data.
450	Displays header.
600 - 760	Forms and asks questions. Processes user's reply.
800 - 890	Displays exact conversion and governing rule.
900 - 920	Waits for user to hit any key.
1000 - 1999	Data statements.

MAIN VARIABLES

ND	Number of conversions in the data.
ES\$,EP\$	String arrays of English units' names (singular, plural).
MS\$,MP\$	String arrays of metric units' names (singular, plural).
R\$	String array of the relation descriptors.
C	Array of the conversion factors.
Q	Work variable.
B\$	String constant of one blank character.
J	Current question number.
NR	Number of questions answered right.
P	Percentage answered right.
NQ	Number of questions in session.
N	Index number of current question in the data list.
F	Flag on question "direction" (0=English to metric; 1=metric to English).
V1,V2	Numeric values on left, right sides of the question.
V3	The correct value of the right hand side.
T	Flag on the question's correct answer (1=true; 0=false).
Q\$	User reply string.
R	User reply flag (0=no; 1=yes; 2=no idea).
X	User's result (0 if correct answer was given).

SUGGESTED PROJECTS

1. Each built-in conversion requires six elements of data in this order:

Element	Data Description
1	English unit (singular)
2	Metric unit (singular)
3	Relation descriptor (e.g., "hotter," "faster," etc.)

4	Conversion factor (from English to metric)
5	English unit (plural)
6	Metric unit (plural)

Each of these elements, except the fourth, is a string. The data statements in the listing should make clear how the information is to be provided. You can add new data to the program with appropriate data statements in this format. New data should be added after the current data, i.e. just before line 1999. Line 1999 is a special data statement to trigger the end of all data to the program. The program is dimensioned up to thirty entries while only seven are currently used. (Note: this format allows only conversions where one unit is a direct multiple of the other. Temperature, which does not fit this rule, is handled as a special case throughout the program.)

2. Convert the program to handle units conversion questions of any type.
3. Keep track of the questions asked and which ones were missed. Then do not ask the same questions too soon if they have been answered correctly. However, do re-ask those questions missed for additional practice.

NUMBERS

PURPOSE

This is an educational program for pre-school children. After a few weeks of watching Sesame Street on television, most three and four year old children will learn how to count from one to ten. The NUMBERS program allows these children to practice their numbers and have fun at the same time.

HOW TO USE IT

We know a child who learned how to type CLOAD and RUN to get this program started before she turned three, but you'll probably have to help your child with this for a while. The program asks the question, "WHAT NUMBER COMES AFTER n?", where n is a number from one to nine. Even if the child can't read yet, he or she will soon learn to look for the number at the end of the line. The child should respond with the appropriate number, and then press the **ENTER** key.

If the answer is correct, the program displays the message "THAT'S RIGHT!", pauses for a couple of seconds, and then clears the screen and displays three geometric shapes. In the upper left of the screen a square is drawn. In the lower center, a triangle is drawn. Then as asterisk (or a snowflake, perhaps?) is drawn in the upper right portion of the screen. After about a five second delay, the program clears the screen and asks another question. The same number is never asked twice in a row. The size of the three figures is chosen at random each time.

If the child provides the wrong answer, a message indicates the error and the same question is asked again.

The program keeps on going until you hit the **BREAK** key. Remember that most children have a pretty short attention span, so please do not force your child to continue after his or her interest diminishes. Keep each session short and fun. This way, it will always be a treat to "play" with the computer.

SAMPLE RUN

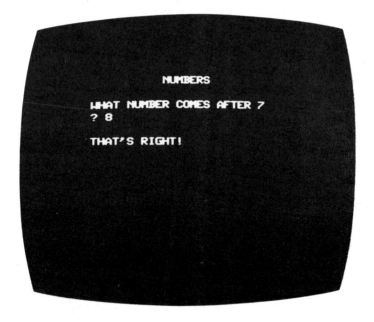

The program asks what number comes after 7, and waits for a response. The operator says "8", and the program acknowledges that the answer is correct.

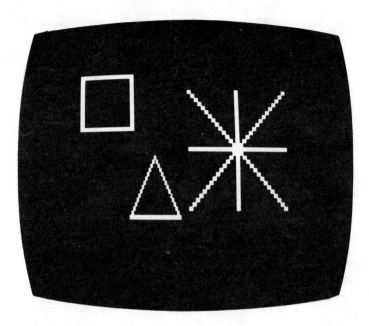

Because of the correct response, the program draws three geometric figures.

PROGRAM LISTING

```
100 REM: NUMBERS
110 REM: COPYRIGHT 1979 BY TOM RUGG AND PHIL FELDMAN
120 CLEAR 50:DEFINT A-Z
130 M=9:E=10:TS=20
140 RANDOM:CLS
150 PRINT CHR$(23)
160 PRINT TAB(10);"NUMBERS"
170 R=RND(M):IF R=P THEN 170
180 PRINT
190 PRINT"WHAT NUMBER COMES AFTER";R
200 INPUT R$
210 PRINT
220 IF VAL(R$)=R+1 THEN 300
230 PRINT"NO, THAT'S NOT IT.  TRY AGAIN."
240 GOTO 180
300 PRINT"THAT'S RIGHT!"
310 FOR X=1 TO 1000:NEXT
320 P=R:CLS
330 E=RND(15)+5
400 Y=1:FOR X=1 TO 2*E:SET(X,Y):NEXT
```

```
410 X=2*E:FOR Y=1 TO E:SET(X,Y):SET(X+1,Y):NEXT
420 Y=E:FOR X=2*E TO 1 STEP -1:SET(X,Y):NEXT
430 X=1:FOR Y=E TO 1 STEP -1:SET(X,Y):SET(X+1,Y):NEXT
450 FOR J=1 TO E
460 Y=TS+J:X=TS+Y:SET(X,Y):NEXT
470 FOR J=1 TO E
480 Y=TS+J:X=TS+TS-J+2:SET(X,Y):NEXT
490 Y=TS+E+1:FOR X=TS+TS-E+1 TO TS+TS+E+1
500 SET(X,Y):NEXT
520 A=90:B=19:IF E>17 THEN E=17
530 FOR J=1 TO E
540 X=A+J+J:Y=B+J:SET(X-1,Y):SET(X,Y)
550 Y=B-J:SET(X,Y):SET(X-1,Y)
560 Y=B:SET(X,Y):SET(X-1,Y)
570 X=A:SET(X,Y):SET(X-1,Y)
580 Y=B+J:SET(X,Y):SET(X-1,Y)
590 Y=B-J:SET(X-1,Y):SET(X,Y)
600 X=A-J-J:SET(X-1,Y):SET(X,Y)
610 Y=B:SET(X-1,Y):SET(X,Y)
620 Y=B+J:SET(X-1,Y):SET(X,Y)
630 NEXT
800 FOR J=1 TO 2000:NEXT
810 CLS:PRINT CHR$(23)
820 GOTO 170
```

EASY CHANGES

1. Change the range of numbers that the program asks by altering the value of M in line 120. For a beginner, use a value of 3 for M instead of 9. Later, increase the value of M to 5, and then 8.
2. Alter the delay after "THAT'S RIGHT!" is displayed by altering the value of 1000 in statement 310. Double it to double the time delay, etc. The same can be done with the 2000 in line 800 to alter the delay after the figures are drawn.
3. To avoid randomness in the size of the figures that are drawn, replace line 330 with

330 E=15

Instead of 15, you can use any integer from 3 to 26.

4. To slowly increase the size of the figures from small to large as correct answers are given (and the reverse for incorrect answers), do the following:
   a. Replace the 10 in line 130 with a 3.
   b. Insert this line

   225 E=E−3: IF E < 3 THEN E=3

   c. Replace line 330 with the following:

   330 E=E+3: IF E > 20 THEN E=20

MAIN ROUTINES

120 - 160	Initializes variables. Clears screen.
170	Picks random integer from 1 to M.
180 - 240	Asks question. Gets answer. Determines if right or wrong.
310	Delays about 1½ seconds.
320 - 430	Draws a square.
450 - 500	Draws a triangle.
520 - 630	Draws an asterisk.
800	Delays about 5 seconds.
810 - 820	Clears screen. Goes back to ask next question.

MAIN VARIABLES

M	Maximum number that will be asked.
E	Edge length of geometric figures.
R	Random integer in range from 1 to M.
P	Previous number that was asked.
R$	Reply given by operator.
X,Y	Coordinates in CRT display.
TS	Triangle's starting location (top).
A,B	X,Y coordinate values.
J	Subscript variable.

SUGGESTED PROJECTS

1. Modify the program to ask the next letter of the alphabet. Use the ASC and CHR$ functions in picking a random letter from A to Y, and to check whether the response is correct or not.
2. Ask each number from 1 to M once (in a random sequence). At the end of the sequence, repeat those that were missed.
3. Add different shapes to the graphics display that is done after a correct answer. Try an octagon, a diamond, and a rectangle. Or, combine this program with one of the graphics display programs.

TACHIST

PURPOSE

This program turns your computer into a tachistoscope (tah-KISS-tah-scope). A tachistoscope is used in reading classes to improve reading habits and, as a result, improve reading speed. The program displays a word or phrase on the screen for a fraction of a second, then asks you what it was. With a little practice, you will find that you can read phrases that are displayed for shorter and shorter time periods.

HOW TO USE IT

The program starts off by displaying a brief introduction and waiting for you to press any key (except the **BREAK** key or shift keys, of course). After you press a key, the screen is blanked out except for two horizontal dash lines in the upper left-hand corner. After two and a half seconds, a phrase is flashed on the screen between the two lines. Then the screen is blanked again, and you are asked what the phrase was.

If you respond correctly, the next phrase is displayed for a shorter time period (half as long). If you respond incorrectly, the program shows you the correct phrase, and the next phrase is displayed for a longer period of time (twice as long).

The fastest the computer can display a phrase and erase it is about .02 seconds (one-fiftieth). See if you can reach the top speed and still continue to read the phrases correctly.

A great deal of research has been done to determine how people read and what they should do to read both faster and with better comprehension. We will not try to explain it all (see the bibliography), but a couple of things are worth mentioning.

To read fast, you should not read one word at a time. Instead, you should learn to quickly read an entire phrase at once. By looking at a point in the center of the phrase (and slightly above it), your eyes can see the whole phrase *without* the necessity of scanning it from left to right, word by word. Because the tachistoscope flashes an entire phrase on the screen at once, it forces you to look at a single point and absorb the whole phrase, rather than scanning left to right, word by word.

If you can incorporate this technique into your reading and increase the width of the phrases you absorb, your reading speed can increase dramatically.

SAMPLE RUN

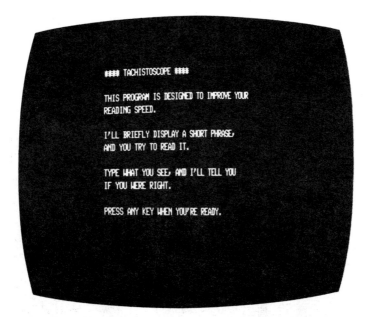

The program displays an introduction, then waits.

The program clears the screen and displays two parallel lines in the upper left corner of the screen for a couple of seconds.

The program flashes a short phrase (chosen at random) between the two lines for a fraction of a second, then clears the screen.

The program asks what the phrase was. The operator responds correctly. The program acknowledges the correct response, and indicates that the next phrase will be shown for half as long.

PROGRAM LISTING

```
100 REM: TACHISTOSCOPE
110 REM: COPYRIGHT 1979 BY TOM RUGG AND PHIL FELDMAN
120 CLEAR 50:DEFINT A-Z
130 T=128
140 L=50
150 DIM T$(L)
160 C=0
170 READ R$
180 IF R$="XXX" THEN 250
190 C=C+1
200 IF C>L THEN PRINT"TOO MANY DATA STATEMENTS":END
210 T$(C)=R$
220 GOTO 170
250 RANDOM
260 CLS
270 PRINT"**** TACHISTOSCOPE ****"
280 PRINT
290 PRINT"THIS PROGRAM IS DESIGNED TO IMPROVE YOUR"
300 PRINT"READING SPEED."
```

```
310 PRINT
320 PRINT"I'LL BRIEFLY DISPLAY A SHORT PHRASE,"
330 PRINT"AND YOU TRY TO READ IT."
340 PRINT
350 PRINT"TYPE WHAT YOU SEE, AND I'LL TELL YOU"
360 PRINT"IF YOU WERE RIGHT."
370 PRINT
410 PRINT"PRESS ANY KEY WHEN YOU'RE READY."
420 R$=INKEY$:IF R$="" THEN 420
430 R=RND(C)
440 IF R=P1 OR R=P2 OR R=P3 THEN 430
450 IF R=P4 OR R=P5 THEN 430
460 GOSUB 840:FOR K=1 TO 1500:NEXT
470 PRINT@64,T$(R);
480 FOR J=1 TO T:NEXT
500 CLS:FOR K=1 TO 500:NEXT
510 PRINT:PRINT:PRINT:PRINT
520 PRINT"WHAT WAS IT?"
530 INPUT R$
550 IF R$<>T$(R) THEN 700
560 PRINT"THAT'S RIGHT!"
570 T=T/2
590 R$="FOR HALF AS LONG."
600 P1=P2:P2=P3:P3=P4:P4=P5:P5=R
610 PRINT
620 IF T<=4 THEN T=4:R$="AT MAXIMUM SPEED."
630 PRINT"THE NEXT ONE WILL BE DISPLAYED ";R$
640 PRINT:GOTO 410
700 PRINT"NO, THAT'S NOT IT.  IT WAS"
710 PRINT"'";T$(R);"'"
720 T=T*2
730 IF T>1600 THEN T=1600:R$="AT THE SAME SPEED.":
    GOTO 630
740 R$="FOR TWICE AS LONG.":GOTO 600
840 CLS:PRINT STRING$(12,"-")
850 PRINT
860 PRINT STRING$(12,"-")
870 RETURN
910 DATA"AT THE TIME"
920 DATA"THE BROWN COW"
930 DATA"LOOK AT THAT"
940 DATA"IN THE HOUSE"
950 DATA"THIS IS MINE"
960 DATA"SHE SAID SO"
970 DATA"THE BABY CRIED"
```

```
980 DATA"TO THE STORE"
990 DATA"READING IS FUN"
1000 DATA"HE GOES FAST"
1010 DATA"IN ALL THINGS"
1020 DATA"GREEN GRASS"
1030 DATA"TWO BIRDS FLY"
1040 DATA"LATE LAST NIGHT"
1050 DATA"THEY ARE HOME"
1060 DATA"ON THE PHONE"
1070 DATA"THROUGH A DOOR"
1080 DATA"WE CAN TRY"
1090 DATA"MY FOOT HURTS"
1100 DATA"HAPPY NEW YEAR"
9999 DATA XXX
```

EASY CHANGES

1. Change the phrases that are displayed by changing the DATA statements that start at line 910. Add more and/or replace those shown with your own phrases or words. Line 140 must specify a number that is at least as large as the number of DATA statements. So, to allow for up to 100 DATA statements, change line 140 to say

140 L=100

Be sure to enter your DATA statements in the same form shown in the program listing. To begin with, you may want to start off with shorter phrases or single words. Later, try longer phrases. Do not alter line 9999, which has to be the last DATA statement. In a 4K TRS-80, you have room for about 60 phrases of the approximate size shown in the program listing. In a 16K TRS-80, you can have several hundred of them. Be sure to have at least 6.

2. To change the length of time the first phrase is displayed, change the value of T in line 120. Double it to double the length of time, etc. Don't make it less than four.

3. To cause all phrases to be displayed for the same length of time, remove lines 570 and 720, and insert these lines:

595 R$="AT THE SAME SPEED"
725 R$="AT THE SAME SPEED":GOTO 600

4. If you want to change the waiting period before the phrase is flashed on the screen, change the 1500 in line 460. To make

the delay five seconds, change it to 3000. To make it one second, change it to 600.

5. To put the program into a sort of flashcard mode, in which the phrases are flashed, but no replies are necessary, insert these three lines:

```
515  GOTO 710
595  R$="AT THE SAME SPEED"
715  GOTO 590
```

This will cause each phrase to be flashed (all for the same length of time), and then displayed again so you can verify what it was.

MAIN ROUTINES

120 - 150	Initializes variables
160 - 220	Reads DATA statements into T$ array.
260 - 370	Displays introduction.
410 - 420	Waits for operator to press a key.
430 - 450	Picks random phrase from T$ array. Ensures no duplication from previous five phrases.
460	Clears screen and displays horizontal lines.
470 - 500	Displays phrase for appropriate length of time.
510 - 530	Asks what the phrase was.
550	Determines if typed phrase matches the phrase displayed.
560 - 640	Shortens time for next phrase if reply was correct. Saves subscript to avoid repetition. Goes back to wait for key to be pressed.
700 - 740	Shows what phrase was. Lengthens time for next phrase. Ensures that time period does not exceed maximum.
840 - 870	Subroutine to display horizontal dash lines.
910 - 9999	DATA statements with phrases to be displayed.

MAIN VARIABLES

T	Time that phrase will be displayed.
J	Loop variable.
L	Limit of number of phrases.
T$	Array of phrases (read into from DATA statements).

C   Count of number of phrases actually read.
R$ Temporary string variable. Also, reply of operator.
R   Work variable. Also, subscript of phrase to be dis-
            played.
P1,P2,   Subscripts of the five previous phrases.
P3,P4,P5
K   Temporary work variable.

SUGGESTED PROJECTS

1. Instead of picking phrases at random, go through the list
   once sequentially. Change line 250 to set R to zero, and line
   430 to add one to R, then check if R is greater than C.
2. Instead of only verifying that the current phrase does not
   duplicate any of the previous five phrases, modify the program to avoid duplication of the previous ten or more.
   Changes will be needed to lines 440, 450, and 600.
3. Keep score of the number of correct and incorrect replies,
   and display the percentage each time. Alternatively, come up
   with a rating based on the percentage correct and the speed
   attained, possibly in conjunction with a difficulty factor for
   the phrases used.
4. Add the capability to the program to also have a mode in
   which it can display a two to seven digit number, chosen at
   random. Have the operator try several of the numbers first
   (maybe five-digit ones) before trying the phrases. The phrases
   will seem easy after doing the numbers.

VOCAB

PURPOSE

Did you ever find yourself at a loss for words? Well, this vocabulary quiz can be used in a self-teaching environment or as reinforcement for classroom instruction to improve your ability to remember the jargon of any subject. It allows you to drill at your own pace, without the worry of ridicule from other students or judgment by an instructor. When you make mistakes, only the computer knows, and it's not telling anyone except you. Modifying the program to substitute a different vocabulary list is very simple, so you can accumulate many different versions of this program, each with a different set of words.

HOW TO USE IT

This program is pretty much self-explanatory from the sample run. After you enter "RUN," it asks you how many questions you would like. If you respond with a number less than five, you will still do five. Otherwise, you will do the number you enter.

Next, you get a series of multiple choice questions. Each question is formatted in one of two ways—either you are given a word and asked to select from a list of definitions, or you are given a definition and asked to select from a list of words. The format is chosen at random. You respond with the number of the choice you think is correct. If you are right, you are told so. If not, you are shown the correct answer. From the second correct answer on, you are shown a status report of the number correct out of the number attempted so far.

Finally, after the last question, you are shown the percentage you got correct, along with a comment on your performance. Then you have the option of going back for another round of questions or stopping.

SAMPLE RUN

RUN

✳✳✳✳ VOCABULARY QUIZ ✳✳✳✳

THIS PROGRAM WILL TEST YOUR KNOWLEDGE
OF SOME USEFUL VOCABULARY WORDS.

HOW MANY QUESTIONS SHALL WE DO? 5

```
    1 -- WHAT WORD MEANS ALL-KNOWING?
         1 -- LACONIC
         2 -- HEDONISTIC
         3 -- OMINOUS
         4 -- CONGENITAL
         5 -- OMNISCIENT

? 5
RIGHT!
    2 -- WHAT DOES PARSIMONIOUS MEAN?
         1 -- INDIFFERENT OR UNINTERESTED
         2 -- KEEN IN JUDGMENT
         3 -- STINGY OR FRUGAL
         4 -- WEAK OR EXHAUSTED
         5 -- OF UNKNOWN OR HIDDEN ORIGIN

? 4
NO, THE ANSWER IS NUMBER 3
```

(... later)

YOU HAVE 3 RIGHT OUT OF 5 QUESTIONS.

THAT'S 60 PERCENT.
NOT BAD, BUT ROOM FOR IMPROVEMENT.

WANT TO TRY AGAIN? NO

CHECK YOU LATER.

PROGRAM LISTING

```
100 REM: VOCABULARY QUIZ
110 REM: COPYRIGHT 1979 BY TOM RUGG AND PHIL FELDMAN
120 CLEAR 50:DEFINT A-Z
300 GOSUB 1000
400 GOSUB 2000
500 GOSUB 3000
600 GOSUB 4000
700 GOSUB 5000
800 GOSUB 6000
900 IF E=0 THEN 500
910 GOTO 300
990 REM
1000 IF E<>0 THEN 1060
1010 CLS
1020 PRINT"**** VOCABULARY QUIZ ****"
1030 PRINT
1040 PRINT"THIS PROGRAM WILL TEST YOUR KNOWLEDGE"
1050 PRINT"OF SOME USEFUL VOCABULARY WORDS."
1060 PRINT
1110 INPUT"HOW MANY QUESTIONS SHALL WE DO";L
1120 IF L>4 THEN 1140
1130 PRINT"THAT'S NOT ENOUGH.  LET'S DO 5.":L=5
1140 IF E<>0 THEN 1200
1150 PRINT
1160 RANDOM
1200 RETURN
2000 IF E<>0 THEN 2200
2010 C=5
2020 D=26
2030 DIM D$(D),E$(D)
2040 DIM P(C)
2050 J=1
2060 READ D$(J)
2070 IF D$(J)="XXX" THEN 2140
2090 READ E$(J)
2100 J=J+1
2110 IF J<=D THEN 2060
2120 PRINT"TOO MANY DATA STATEMENTS."
2130 PRINT"ONLY FIRST";D;"ARE USED."
2140 D=J-1
2200 Q=1
2210 E=0
```

```
2220 Q1=0
2300 RETURN
3000 FOR J=1 TO C
3010 P(J)=0
3020 NEXT
3030 FOR J=1 TO C
3040 P=RND(D)
3045 IF P=P1 OR P=P2 OR P=P3 THEN 3040
3050 FOR K=1 TO J
3060 IF P(K)=P THEN 3040
3070 NEXT K
3080 P(J)=P
3090 NEXT J
3110 A=RND(C)
3200 RETURN
4000 PRINT
4010 M=RND(2)
4020 IF M=2 THEN 4100
4030 PRINT Q;"-- WHAT WORD MEANS ";E$(P(A));"?"
4040 FOR J=1 TO C
4050 PRINT TAB(5);J;"-- ";D$(P(J))
4060 NEXT
4070 GOTO 4210
4100 PRINT Q;"-- WHAT DOES ";D$(P(A));" MEAN?"
4110 FOR J=1 TO C
4120 PRINT TAB(5);J;"-- ";E$(P(J))
4130 NEXT
4210 RETURN
5000 INPUT R
5010 IF R>=1 AND R<=C THEN 5050
5020 PRINT"I NEED A NUMBER FROM 1 TO";C
5030 GOTO 5000
5050 IF R=A THEN 5100
5060 PRINT"NO, THE ANSWER IS NUMBER";A
5070 GOTO 5210
5100 PRINT"RIGHT!"
5110 Q1=Q1+1
5210 IF Q1=1 THEN 5300
5220 PRINT"YOU HAVE";Q1;"RIGHT OUT OF";Q;"QUESTIONS."
5300 P3=P2
5310 P2=P1
5320 P1=P(A)
5330 RETURN
6000 Q=Q+1
6010 IF Q<=L THEN RETURN
```

```
6020 E=1
6030 Q=Q1*100/(Q-1)
6040 IF Q>0 THEN 6070
6050 PRINT"WELL, THAT'S A 'PERFECT' SCORE..."
6060 GOTO 6200
6070 PRINT"THAT'S";Q;"PERCENT."
6080 IF Q>25 THEN 6110
6090 PRINT"CONGRATULATIONS ON AVOIDING A SHUTOUT."
6100 GOTO 6200
6110 IF Q>50 THEN 6140
6120 PRINT"YOU CAN USE SOME MORE PRACTICE."
6130 GOTO 6200
6140 IF Q>75 THEN 6170
6150 PRINT"NOT BAD, BUT ROOM FOR IMPROVEMENT."
6160 GOTO 6200
6170 PRINT"VERY GOOD!"
6180 IF Q>95 THEN PRINT"YOU'RE ALMOST AS SMART AS I AM!"
6200 PRINT
6210 INPUT"WANT TO TRY AGAIN";R$
6220 IF LEFT$(R$,1)<>"N" THEN 6240
6230 PRINT:PRINT"CHECK YOU LATER.":PRINT:END
6240 IF LEFT$(R$,1)<>"Y" THEN 6210
6250 RETURN
7000 REM: ON LINE 2020, D MUST BE AT LEAST ONE GREATER
7005 REM: THAN THE NUMBER OF DIFFERENT WORDS.
7010 DATA ANONYMOUS,"OF UNKNOWN OR HIDDEN ORIGIN"
7020 DATA OMINOUS,"THREATENING OR MENACING"
7030 DATA AFFLUENT,"WEALTHY"
7040 DATA APATHETIC,"INDIFFERENT OR UNINTERESTED"
7050 DATA LACONIC,"TERSE"
7060 DATA INTREPID,"FEARLESS OR COURAGEOUS"
7070 DATA GREGARIOUS,"SOCIAL OR COMPANY-LOVING"
7080 DATA ENERVATED,"WEAK OR EXHAUSTED"
7090 DATA VENERABLE,"WORTHY OF RESPECT OR REVERENCE"
7100 DATA DISPARATE,"DIFFERENT AND DISTINCT"
7110 DATA VIVACIOUS,"LIVELY OR SPIRITED"
7120 DATA ASTUTE,"KEEN IN JUDGMENT"
7130 DATA URSINE,"BEARLIKE"
7140 DATA PARSIMONIOUS,"STINGY OR FRUGAL"
7150 DATA OMNISCIENT,"ALL-KNOWING"
7999 DATA XXX
```

EASY CHANGES

1. Add more DATA statements between lines 7000 and 7999, or replace them all with your own. Be careful not to use two or more words with very similar definitions; the program might select more than one of them as possible answers to the same question. Note that each DATA statement first has the vocabulary word, then a comma, and then the definition or synonym. Be sure there are no commas or colons in the definition (unless you enclose the definition in quotes). If you add more DATA statements, you have to increase the value of D in line 2020 to be at least one greater than the number of words. The number of DATA statements you can have depends on how long each one is and how much user memory your computer has. Using DATA statements that average the same length as these, you can probably have about thirty of them in a 4K TRS-80, or as many as 400 in a 16K model. Be sure to leave statement 7999 as it is—it signals that there are no more DATA statements.
2. To get something other than five choices for each question, change the value of C in line 2010. You might want only three or four choices per question.
3. If you do not want to be given a choice of how many questions are going to be asked, remove lines 1110 through 1140 and insert the following lines:

    1110 PRINT"WE'LL DO TEN QUESTIONS."
    1120 L=10

This will always cause ten questions to be asked. Of course, you can use some number other than ten if you want.

MAIN ROUTINES

120 - 910	Mainline routine. Calls major subroutines.
1000 - 1200	Displays introduction. Initializes RND function. Determines number of questions to be asked.
2000 - 2300	Reads vocabulary words and definitions into arrays. Performs housekeeping.
3000 - 3200	Selects choices for answers and determines which will be the correct one.
4000 - 4210	Determines in which format the question will be asked. Asks it.

5000 - 5330	Accepts answer from operator. Determines if right or wrong. Keeps score. Saves subscripts of last three correct answers.
6000 - 6250	Gives final score. Asks about doing it again.
7000 - 7999	DATA statements with vocabulary words and definitions.

MAIN VARIABLES

E	Set to 1 to avoid repeating introduction after the first round.
L	Limit of number of questions to ask.
R	Work variable. Also used for operator's reply to each question.
C	Number of choices of answers given for each question.
D	At least one greater than number of DATA statements. Used to DIM arrays.
D$	Array of vocabulary words.
E$	Array of definitions.
P	Array for numbers of possible answers to each question.
J	Work variable (subscript for FOR-NEXT loops).
Q	Number of questions asked so far (later used to calculate percent correct).
Q1	Number of questions correct so far.
P	Work variable.
P1,P2,P3	Last three correct answers.
A	Subscript of correct answer in P array.
M	Work variable to decide which way to ask question.
R$	Yes or no reply about doing another round.

SUGGESTED PROJECTS

1. Modify lines 6030 through 6200 to display the final evaluation messages based on a finer breakdown of the percent correct. For example, show one message if 100 percent, another if 95 to 99, another if 90 to 94, etc.
2. Ask the operator's name in the introduction routine, and personalize some of the messages with his/her name.

3. Instead of just checking about the last three questions, be sure that the next question has not been asked in the last eight or ten questions. (Check lines 3045 and 5300 through 5320.)
4. Keep track of which questions the operator misses. Then, after going through the number of questions he/she requested, repeat those that were missed.

Section 3
Game Programs

INTRODUCTION TO GAME PROGRAMS

Almost everyone likes to play games. Computer games are a fun and entertaining use of your TRS-80. Besides providing relaxation and recreation, they have some built-in practical bonuses. They often force you to think strategically, plan ahead, or at least be orderly in your thought processes. They are also a good way to help some friends over their possible "computer phobia." We present a collection of games to fit any game playing mood.

Maybe you desire a challenging all-skill game? Like chess or checkers, WARI involves no luck and considerable thinking. The TRS-80 will be your opponent, and a formidable one indeed.

Perhaps you're in the mood for a game with quick action and mounting excitement. GROAN is a fast-paced dice game involving mostly luck with a dash of skill (or intuition) thrown in. The TRS-80 is ready for your challenge anytime.

JOT is a word game. You and the TRS-80 each take secret words and then try to home in on each other's selection.

Do you like solving puzzles? If so, try DECODE. The computer will choose a secret code and then challenge you to find it.

Graphic electronic arcade games are a prevalent landmark of the late seventies. We include two such games. ROADRACE puts you behind the wheel of a high speed race car. You must steer accurately to stay on course. OBSTACLE lets you and a friend compete in a game of cut and thrust. Each of you must avoid crossing the path laid by the other, and by yourself!

DECODE

PURPOSE

Decode is really more of a puzzle than a game, although you can still compete with your friends to see who can solve the puzzles the fastest. Each time you play, you are presented with a new puzzle to solve.

The object is to figure out the computer's secret code in as few guesses as possible. The program gives you information about the accuracy of each of your guesses. By carefully selecting your guesses to make use of the information you have, you can determine what the secret code must be in a surprisingly small number of guesses. Five or six is usually enough.

The first few times you try, you will probably require quite a few more guesses than that, but with practice, you'll discover that you can learn a lot more from each guess than you originally thought.

HOW TO USE IT

The program starts off by displaying a brief introduction. Here are some more details.

The program selects a secret code for you to figure out. The code is a four digit number that uses only the digits 1 through 6. For example, your TRS-80 might pick 6153 or 2242 as a secret code.

Your object is to guess the code in the fewest possible guesses. After each of your guesses, the program tells you a "black" and a "white" number. The black number indicates the number of digits in your guess that were correct—the digit was correct *and* in the correct position. So, if the secret code is 6153 and your guess is 4143, you will be told that black is 2 (because the 1 and the 3 will have been correct). Of course, you aren't told *which* digits are correct. That is for you to figure out by making use of the information you get from other guesses.

Each of the white numbers indicates a digit in your guess that was correct, but which is in the wrong position. For example, if the secret code is 6153 and your guess is 1434, you will be told that white is 2. The 1 and 3 are correct, but in wrong positions.

The white number is determined by ignoring any digits that accounted for a black number. Also, a single position in the secret code or guess can only account for one black or white number. These facts become significant when the secret code and/or your guess have duplicate digits. For example, if the code is 1234 and your guess is 4444, there is only one black, and no whites. If the code is 2244 and your guess is 4122, there are no blacks and three whites.

This may sound a little tricky, but you will quickly get the hang of it.

At any time during the game, you can ask for a "SUMMARY" by entering an S instead of a guess. This causes the program to clear the screen and display each guess (with the corresponding result) that has occurred so far.

Also, if you get tired of trying and want to give up, you can enter a Q (for "quit") to end your misery and find out the answer. Otherwise, you continue guessing until you get the code right (four black, zero white), or until you have used up the maximum of twelve guesses.

SAMPLE RUN

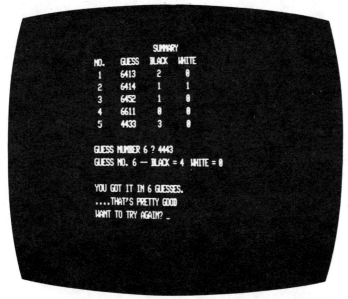

```
#### DECODE ####

FIGURE OUT A 4 POSITION CODE
USING THE DIGITS 1 THROUGH 6

'BLACK' INDICATES A CORRECT DIGIT
IN THE RIGHT POSITION.
'WHITE' INDICATES SOME OTHER CORRECT DIGIT
BUT IN THE WRONG POSITION.

I'VE CHOSEN MY SECRET CODE.
GUESS NUMBER 1 ? 6413
GUESS NO. 1 — BLACK = 2  WHITE = 0
GUESS NUMBER 2 ? _
```

The program displays an introduction, chooses its secret code, and asks for the operator's first guess. After the operator makes a guess, the program responds with a "black" and a "white" number, and asks for the second guess.

```
                  SUMMARY
     NO.    GUESS   BLACK   WHITE
      1     6413      2       0
      2     6414      1       1
      3     6452      1       0
      4     6611      0       0
      5     4433      3       0

GUESS NUMBER 6 ? 4443
GUESS NO. 6 — BLACK = 4  WHITE = 0

YOU GOT IT IN 6 GUESSES.
....THAT'S PRETTY GOOD
WANT TO TRY AGAIN? _
```

Later in the same game, the operator asks for a summary, then makes the guess that turns out to be correct. The program acknowledges that the guess is correct and asks about trying another game.

PROGRAM LISTING

```
100 REM: DECODE
110 REM: COPYRIGHT 1979 BY TOM RUGG AND PHIL FELDMAN
120 CLEAR 100:D=6:P=4:L=12
130 DIM G$(L),G(P),C(P),B(L),W(L)
140 RANDOM
150 GOSUB 1200
170 GOSUB 300:GOSUB 370
180 PRINT"GUESS NUMBER";G;
190 INPUT A$
200 IF LEFT$(A$,1)="S" THEN 500
210 IF LEFT$(A$,1)="Q" THEN 600
220 GOSUB 700
230 GOSUB 800
240 GOSUB 1000
250 IF B(G)=P THEN 2000
260 G$(G)=A$
270 G=G+1:IF G>L THEN 2200
280 GOTO 180
300 G=1:C$=""
310 RETURN
370 FOR J=1 TO P
380 R=RND(D)
390 C$=C$+MID$(STR$(R),2,1)
400 NEXT
410 PRINT"I'VE CHOSEN MY SECRET CODE."
430 RETURN
500 IF G=1 THEN PRINT"NO GUESSES YET":GOTO 180
510 CLS:PRINT,"SUMMARY"
520 PRINT"NO.    GUESS    BLACK    WHITE"
530 FOR J=1 TO G-1
540 PRINTJ;TAB(7);G$(J);TAB(16);B(J);TAB(24);W(J)
560 NEXT:PRINT
570 GOTO 180
600 PRINT
610 PRINT"CAN'T TAKE IT, HUH?"
620 PRINT:PRINT"WELL, MY CODE WAS ";
630 FOR J=1 TO 4
640 PRINT"  .";
650 FOR K=1 TO 900:NEXT
660 NEXT
670 PRINT C$:PRINT
680 GOTO 2090
700 IF LEN(A$)<>P THEN 780
```

```
710 FOR J=1 TO P
720 R=VAL(MID$(A$,J,1))
730 IF R<1 OR R>D THEN 780
740 NEXT
750 RETURN
780 PRINT"ILLEGAL.  TRY AGAIN."
790 GOTO 180
800 B=0:W=0
810 FOR J=1 TO P
820 G(J)=VAL(MID$(A$,J,1))
830 C(J)=VAL(MID$(C$,J,1))
840 IF G(J)=C(J) THEN B=B+1:G(J)=0:C(J)=0
850 NEXT
860 FOR J=1 TO P:IF C(J)=0 THEN 920
870 H=0:FOR K=1 TO P
880 IF C(J)=0 THEN 910
890 IF C(J)<>G(K) THEN 910
900 H=1:G(K)=0:C(J)=0
910 NEXT K:W=W+H
920 NEXT J
930 RETURN
1000 B(G)=B:W(G)=W
1010 PRINT"GUESS NO.";G;"-- BLACK =";B;" WHITE =";W
1020 RETURN
1200 CLS
1210 PRINT"**** DECODE ****"
1220 PRINT
1230 PRINT"FIGURE OUT A";P;"POSITION CODE"
1250 PRINT"USING THE DIGITS 1 THROUGH";D
1260 PRINT
1270 PRINT"'BLACK' INDICATES A CORRECT DIGIT"
1280 PRINT"IN THE RIGHT POSITION."
1300 PRINT"'WHITE' INDICATES SOME OTHER CORRECT DIGIT"
1320 PRINT"BUT IN THE WRONG POSITION."
1330 PRINT
1340 RETURN
2000 PRINT
2010 PRINT"YOU GOT IT IN";G;"GUESSES."
2020 IF G<5 THEN B$="OUTSTANDING!"
2030 IF G=5 OR G=6 THEN B$="PRETTY GOOD"
2040 IF G=7 THEN B$="NOT BAD"
2050 IF G=8 THEN B$="NOT TOO GREAT"
2060 IF G>8 THEN B$="PRETTY BAD"
2070 PRINT"....THAT'S ";B$
2090 INPUT"WANT TO TRY AGAIN";A$
```

```
2100 IF LEFT$(A$,1)="Y" THEN 150
2110 IF LEFT$(A$,1)<>"N" THEN 2090
2120 PRINT:PRINT"COWARD.":PRINT
2130 END
2200 PRINT
2210 PRINT"THAT'S YOUR LIMIT OF";L;"GUESSES."
2220 PRINT"MY CODE WAS ";C$
2240 GOTO 2090
```

EASY CHANGES

1. Modify line 120 to change the complexity of the code and/or the number of guesses you are allowed. For example, the following line would allow fifteen guesses at a five position code using the digits 1 through 8:

120 CLEAR 100: D=8:P=5:L=15

The introduction will automatically reflect the new values for D and P. Be sure that neither D nor P is set greater than 9.

2. To change the program so it will always display the "Summary" information after each guess automatically, replace line 280 with this:

280 GOTO 500

MAIN ROUTINES

120 - 170	Initializes variables. Displays introduction. Chooses secret code.
180 - 240	Gets a guess from operator. Analyzes reply. Displays result.
250	Determines if operator guessed correctly.
260 - 280	Saves guess. Adds one to guess counter. Determines if limit on number of guesses was exceeded.
300 - 310	Subroutine to initialize variables.
370 - 430	Subroutine to choose secret code and inform operator.
500 - 570	Subroutine to display summary of guesses so far.
600 - 680	Subroutine to slowly display secret code when operator quits.
700 - 790	Subroutine to determine if operator's guess was legal.

800 - 930	Subroutine to determine number of black and white responses for the guess.
1000 - 1020	Subroutine to display number of black and white responses for the guess.
1200 - 1340	Subroutine to display title and introduction.
2000 - 2130	Subroutine to analyze operator's performance after correct answer is guessed and ask about playing again.
2200 - 2240	Subroutine to display secret code after operator exceeds limit of number of guesses.

MAIN VARIABLES

D	Number of possible digits in each position of the code (i.e., a digit from 1 to D).
P	Number of positions in the code.
L	Limit of number of guesses that can be made.
G$	Array in which guesses are saved.
G,C	Work arrays in which each guess is analyzed.
B,W	Arrays in which the number of black and white responses is saved for each guess.
R,H	Work variables.
G	Counter of the number of guesses made.
A$	Reply by the operator.
C$	Secret code chosen by the program.
J,K	Loop variables.
B,W	Number of black and white responses for this guess.
B$	String with message about operator's performance.

SUGGESTED PROJECTS

1. Change the analysis at the end of the game to take into account the difficulty of the code as well as the number of guesses it took to figure the code out. A four position code using the digits 1 through 6 has 1296 possibilities, but a five position code using 1 through 8 has 32768 possibilities. Change lines 2020 through 2060 to determine the message to be displayed based on the number of possibilities in the code as well as G.

2. At the beginning of the game, give the operator the option of deciding the complexity of the code. Ask for the number of

positions and the number of digits. Make sure only "reasonable" numbers are used—do not try to create a code with zero positions, for example. Another approach is to ask the operator if he/she wants to play the easy, intermediate, or advanced version. Then set the values of D and P accordingly. Suggestions are:

Easy:	D=3 and P=3
Intermediate:	D=6 and P=4
Advanced:	D=8 and P=5

3. In addition to using the number of guesses to determine how well the operator did, keep track of the amount of time. This will require use of the INKEY$ function instead of the INPUT function in line 190, and a bit of logic to "build" the A$ reply one character at a time. By counting the number of null strings encountered while waiting for keys to be pressed, you can "time" the operator.

GROAN

PURPOSE

Do you like the thrills of fast-paced dice games? If so, GROAN is right up your alley. It is a two-person game with the computer playing directly against you. There is a considerable amount of luck involved. However, the skill of deciding when to pass the dice to your opponent also figures prominently.

The TRS-80 will roll the dice for both players, but don't worry—it will not cheat. (We wouldn't think of stooping to such depths.)

Why is the game called GROAN? You will know soon after playing it.

HOW TO USE IT

The game uses two dice. They are just like regular six-sided dice except for one thing. The die face where the "1" would normally be has a picture of a frowning face instead. The other five faces of each die have the usual numbers two through six on them.

The object is to be the first player to achieve a score agreed upon before the start of the game. Players alternate taking turns. A turn consists of a series of dice rolls (at least one roll, possibly several) subject to the following rules.

As long as no frown appears on either die, the roller builds a running score for this current series of rolls. After each roll with no frown, he has the choice of rolling again or passing the dice to his opponent. If he passes the dice, his score achieved on the current series is added to any previous total he may have had.

But if he rolls and a frown appears, he will be groaning. A frown on only one die cancels any score achieved for the current series of rolls. Any previous score is retained in this case. However, if he rolls a double frown, his entire previous total is wiped out as well as his current total. Thus, he reverts back to a total score of zero—true despair.

The program begins by asking what the winning score should be. Values between 50 and 100 tend to produce the best games, but any positive value is acceptable. Next, a simulated coin toss randomly decides who will get the first roll.

Each dice roll is portrayed with a short graphics display. The dice are shown rolling and then the outcome is displayed pictorially. Before each roll, the TRS-80 indicates whose roll is coming up.

Each roll is followed by a display of the scoreboard. This scoreboard gives all relevant information: score needed to win, both players' scores before the current series of rolls, and the total score for the current series.

If a frown should appear on a die, the scoreboard will indicate the current running total as zero. In addition, the previous total will become zero in the case of the dreaded double frown. In either case, the dice will be passed automatically to the next player.

If a scoring roll results, the roller must decide whether to roll again or to pass the dice. The program has a built-in strategy to decide this for the TRS-80. For you, the question will be asked after the scoreboard is displayed. The two legal replies are P and R. The R means that you wish to roll again. The P means that you choose to pass the dice to the TRS-80. If you should score enough to win, you must still pass the dice to add the current series to your previous total.

The first player to pass the dice with a score greater than or equal to the winning score is the victor. This will surely cause his opponent to GROAN. The computer will acknowledge the winner before signing off.

SAMPLE RUN

The operator has decided to challenge the TRS-80 to a fifty point game of GROAN. The computer wins the coin toss and gets the first dice roll.

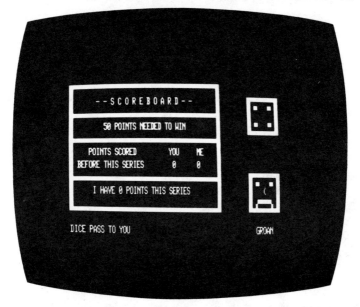

The computer's roll, however, results in a "groan" and a four. This scores no points and the dice pass to the operator.

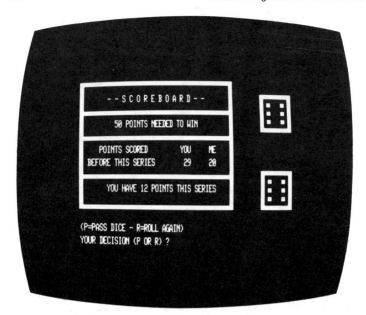

Much later in the same game, the operator rolls a 12 to start a series of rolls. The score was operator-29, TRS-80-20 before the roll. The operator must now decide whether to pass the dice or risk rolling again.

PROGRAM LISTING

```
100 REM: GROAN
110 REM: COPYRIGHT 1979 BY PHIL FELDMAN AND TOM RUGG
120 CLEAR 250:RANDOM:DEFINT W
140 B$=CHR$(191):C$=CHR$(179):L$=CHR$(176):M$=CHR$(140)
150 U$=CHR$(131):N$=CHR$(32):F3$=B$+STRING$(40,140)+B$
160 D1$=B$+STRING$(7,131)+B$:D2$=B$+STRING$(7,32)+B$
170 D3$=B$+STRING$(7,176)+B$:
    E1$=STRING$(4,32)+L$+M$+L$+STRING$(4,32)
180 E2$=N$+L$+M$+U$+N$+N$+N$+U$+M$+L$+N$:
    E3$=U$+M$+L$+STRING$(5,32)+L$+M$+U$
185 E4$=N$+N$+N$+U$+M$+L$+M$+U$+N$+N$+N$
190 F1$=B$+STRING$(40,131)+B$:F2$=B$+STRING$(40,176)+B$
200 CLS:PRINT TAB(25);"G R O A N"
210 PRINT"HOW MUCH NEEDED TO WIN"
220 INPUT"(BETWEEN 50-100 IS BEST) ";W:IF W<=0 THEN 200
230 PRINT:PRINT"LET'S TOSS FOR FIRST ROLL":GOSUB 830
240 PRINT:PRINT"THE COIN IS IN THE AIR AND"
250 Q$="YOU":Q=RND(2):IF Q=2 THEN Q$="I"
260 PRINT TAB(8);:FOR J=1 TO 5:PRINT". ";:GOSUB 830:NEXT
```

```
270 PRINT Q$;" GET FIRST ROLL":GOSUB 840:T=0:
    IF Q=2 THEN 400
300 P$=" YOU":CLS:PRINT TAB(25);"YOU'RE ROLLING":
    GOSUB 830:GOSUB 500
310 T=T+R1+R2:IF F>0 THEN T=0
320 IF F=2 THEN H=0
330 GOSUB 850:IF F>0 THEN PRINT"DICE PASS TO ME":
    GOSUB 840:GOTO 400
340 PRINT"(P=PASS DICE - R=ROLL AGAIN)":
    PRINT"YOUR DECISION (P OR R) ?"
350 Q$=INKEY$:IF Q$="" THEN 350
360 IF Q$="R" THEN 300
370 IF Q$<>"P" THEN 350
380 PRINT:H=H+T:IF H>=W THEN 970
390 T=0:F=1:CLS:GOTO 330
400 T=0:P$="I"
410 CLS:PRINT TAB(26);"I'M ROLLING":GOSUB 830:GOSUB 500
420 T=T+R1+R2:IF F>0 THEN T=0
430 IF F=2 THEN P=0
440 GOSUB 850:IF F>0 THEN PRINT"DICE PASS TO YOU":
    GOSUB 840:T=0:GOTO 300
450 GOSUB 1000:IF X=1 THEN PRINT"I'LL ROLL AGAIN":
    GOSUB 840:GOTO 410
460 PRINT"I'LL STOP WITH THIS":GOSUB 830:P=P+T:
    IF P>=W THEN 970
470 PRINT:PRINT"DICE PASS TO YOU":T=0:GOSUB 840:
    GOTO 300
500 D=266:DL=5:R1=RND(6):R2=RND(6):FOR K=0 TO 40 STEP 8
530 C=D+K:GOSUB 650:C=C+384:GOSUB 650:GOSUB 600:CLS
535 GOSUB 660:C=C-384:GOSUB 660:GOSUB 600:CLS
540 NEXT:C=D+48:GOSUB 650:C=C+384:GOSUB 650
550 C=D+48:R=R1:GOSUB 700
560 C=C+384:R=R2:GOSUB 700:F=0:IF R1=1 THEN F=1:
    GOSUB 800
570 IF R2=1 THEN F=F+1:GOSUB 810
580 IF F=2 THEN GOSUB 820:GOSUB 830
590 RETURN
600 FOR J=1 TO DL:NEXT:RETURN
650 PRINT@C-136,D1$:PRINT@C-72,D2$:PRINT@C-8,D3$:RETURN
660 PRINT@C-197,E1$:PRINT@C-133,E2$:PRINT@C-69,E3$
670 PRINT@C-5,E4$:RETURN
700 ON R GOSUB 710,730,740,750,760,770:RETURN
710 PRINT@C-134,C$;:PRINT@C-130,C$;:PRINT@C-68,"(";:
    PRINT@C-6,CHR$(182);
```

```
720 FOR Q=3 TO 5:PRINT@C-Q,C$;:NEXT:
    PRINT@C-2,CHR$(185);:RETURN
730 PRINT@C-134,C$;:PRINT@C-2,C$;:RETURN
740 PRINT@C-68,CHR$(140);:GOSUB 730:RETURN
750 PRINT@C-130,C$;:PRINT@C-6,C$:GOSUB 730:RETURN
760 GOSUB 740:GOSUB 750:RETURN
770 PRINT@C-70,CHR$(140);:PRINT@C-66,CHR$(140);:
    GOSUB 750:RETURN
800 PRINT@52,"GROAN";:RETURN
810 PRINT@820,"GROAN";:RETURN
820 PRINT@434,"-DESPAIR-";:RETURN
830 FOR K=1 TO 800:NEXT:RETURN
840 FOR K=1 TO 2000:NEXT:RETURN
850 PRINT@64,F1$;:G=128:GOSUB 960:
    PRINT@135,"- - S C O R E B O A R D - -";
860 PRINT@192,F3$;:G=256:GOSUB 960:
    PRINT@264,W;"POINTS NEEDED TO WIN";
870 PRINT@320,F3$;:G=384:GOSUB 960
880 PRINT@386,"  POINTS SCORED          YOU     ME";:
    G=448
890 GOSUB 960:PRINT@450,"BEFORE THIS SERIES";:
    PRINT@475,H;
900 PRINT@482,P;:PRINT@512,F3$;:G=576:GOSUB 960
910 PRINT@582,P$;" HAVE";T;"POINTS THIS SERIES";
920 PRINT@640,F2$;:PRINT@768,"";:RETURN
960 PRINT@G,B$;:PRINT@G+41,B$;:RETURN
970 T=0:CLS:GOSUB 850:
    IF P>=W THEN PRINT@768,"SKILL WINS AGAIN"
980 IF H>=W THEN
    PRINT@768,"YOU WIN - IT WAS SHEER LUCK"
990 END
1000 V=P+T:IF V>=W THEN 1100
1010 IF (W-H)<10 THEN 1110
1020 IF P>=H THEN L=T/25:GOTO 1050
1030 IF V<H THEN L=T/35:GOTO 1050
1040 L=T/30
1050 IF RND(0)>L THEN 1110
1100 X=0:RETURN
1110 X=1:RETURN
```

EASY CHANGES

1. If you wish to set the program for a fixed value of the winning score, it can be done by changing line 210 and deleting line 220. Simply set W to the winning score desired. For example:

210 W=100

would make the winning score 100. Don't forget to delete line 220.

2. The rolling dice graphics display before each roll can be eliminated by changing lines 500 and 540 as follows:

500 D=266:R1=RND(6):R2=RND(6):GOTO 540
540 C=D+48:GOSUB 650:C=C+384:GOSUB 650

This has the effect of speeding up the game by showing each dice roll immediately.

3. After you play the game a few times, you may wish to change the delay constants in lines 830 and 840. They control the "pacing" of the game; i.e., the time delays between various messages, etc. To speed up the game try

830 FOR K=1 TO 400:NEXT:RETURN
840 FOR K=1 TO 1000:NEXT:RETURN

Of course, if desired, the constants can be set to larger values to slow down the pacing.

MAIN ROUTINES

120 - 190	Initializes constants.
200 - 270	Initial display. Gets winning score.
300 - 390	Human rolls.
400 - 470	TRS-80 rolls.
500 - 590	Determines dice roll. Drives its display.
600	Delay loop.
700 - 770	Draws die face.
800 - 820	Displays groan messages.
830 - 840	Delay loops.
850 - 960	Displays scoreboard.
970 - 990	Ending messages.
1000 - 1110	Computer's strategy. Sets X=0 to stop rolling or X=1 to continue rolling.

MAIN VARIABLES

W	Amount needed to win.
H	Previous score of human.
P	Previous score of TRS-80.

T	Score of current series of rolls.
X	TRS-80 strategy flag (0=stop rolling; 1=roll again).
L	Cutoff threshold used in computer's built-in strategy.
V	Score TRS-80 would have if it passed the dice.
DL	Delay length.
Q,Q$	Work variable, work string variable.
J,K	Loop indices.
P$	String of name of current roller.
R1,R2	Outcome of roll for die 1, die 2.
R	Outcome of a die roll.
F	Result of roll (0=no frown; 1=one frown; 2=double frown).
C,D,G	Screen printing positions.
NT	Argument for TAB function.
B$ - U$	Strings for graphics displays.

SUGGESTED PROJECTS

1. The computer's built-in strategy is contained from line 1000 on. Remember, after a no frown roll, the TRS-80 must decide whether of not to continue rolling. See if you can improve on the current strategy. You may use, but not modify, the variables P, T, H, W. The variable X must be set before returning. Set X=0 to mean the TRS-80 passes the dice or X=1 to mean the TRS-80 will roll again.
2. Ask the operator for his/her name. Then personalize the messages and scoreboard more.
3. Dig into the workings of the graphics routines connected with the dice rolling. Then modify them to produce new, perhaps more realistic, effects.

JOT

PURPOSE

JOT is a two player word game involving considerable mental deduction. The TRS-80 will play against you. But be careful! You will find your computer quite a formidable opponent.

The rules of JOT are fairly simple. The game is played entirely with three-letter words. All letters of each word must be distinct—no repeats. (See the section on Easy Changes for further criteria used in defining legal words.)

To begin the game, each player chooses a secret word. The remainder of the game involves trying to be the first player to deduce the other's secret word.

The players take turns making guesses at their opponent's word. After each guess, the asker is told how many letters (or hits) his guess had in common with his opponent's secret word. The position of the letters in the word does not matter. For example, if the secret word was "own," a guess of "who" would have 2 hits. The winner is the first person to correctly guess his opponent's secret word.

HOW TO USE IT

The program begins with some introductory messages while asking you to think of your secret word. It then asks whether or not you wish to make the first guess. This is followed by you and the TRS-80 alternating guesses at each other's secret word.

After the TRS-80 guesses, it will immediately ask you how it did. Possible replies are 0, 1, 2, 3, or R. The response of R (for

right) means the TRS-80 has just guessed your word correctly—
a truly humbling experience. The numerical replies indicate that
the word guessed by the TRS-80 had that number of hits in your
secret word. A response of 3 means that all the letters were correct, but they need to be rearranged to form the actual secret
word (e.g. a guess of "EAT" with the secret word being "TEA").

After learning how it did, the computer will take some time
to process its new information. If this time is not trivial, the
TRS-80 will display the message: "I'M THINKING" so you do
not suspect it of idle daydreaming. If it finds an inconsistency
in its information, it will ask you for your secret word and then
analyze what went wrong.

When it is your turn to guess, there are two special replies
you can make. These are the single letters **S** or **Q**. The **S**, for
summary, will display a table of all previous guesses and corresponding hits. This is useful as a concise look at all available
information. It will then prompt you again for your next guess.
The **Q**, for quit, will simply terminate the game.

When not making one of these special replies, you will input
a guess at the computer's secret word. This will be, of course, a
three letter word. If the word used is not legal, the computer
will so inform you. After a legal guess, you will be told how
many hits your guess had. If you correctly guess the computer's
word, you will be duly congratulated. The TRS-80 will then ask
you for your secret word and verify that all is on the "up and
up."

SAMPLE RUN

```
                JOT

JUST A MOMENT PLEASE .....

THANKS, NOW LET'S EACH THINK
OF OUR SECRET WORD
(THIS TAKES ME A WHILE ...)

I'VE ALMOST GOT IT ...

OK, DO YOU WANT TO GO FIRST? NO

MY GUESS IS -- NIP
HOW DID I DO (Ø-3 OR R)? 1
```

I'M THINKING ...

YOUR GUESS (OR S OR Q)? <u>DOG</u>
OF HITS IS 1

MY GUESS IS -- NOR
HOW DID I DO (∅-3 OR R)? <u>∅</u>

I'M THINKING ...
                    .
                    .
        (later in the same game)
                    .
                    .
YOUR GUESS (OR S OR Q)? <u>S</u>

YOUR GUESSES   SUMMARY   MY GUESSES
WORD   HITS   WORD   HITS
 DOG   1   1   NIP   1
 CAT   ∅   2   NOR   ∅
 LIP   ∅   3   DIG   ∅
 SON   ∅   4   PUT   2
                      5   PUB   1

YOUR GUESS (OR S OR Q)? <u>FED</u>
OF HITS IS 2

MY GUESS IS -- PET
HOW DID I DO (∅-3 OR R)? <u>R</u>

IT SURE FEELS GOOD

MY WORD WAS - WED

HOW ABOUT ANOTHER GAME? <u>NO</u>
READY.

PROGRAM LISTING

```
100 REM: JOT
110 REM: COPYRIGHT 1979 BY PHIL FELDMAN AND TOM RUGG
150 CLEAR 200:DEFINT A-Z:RANDOM
160 M=25:N=406
170 DIM A$(N)
```

```
180 DIM G1$(M),G2$(M),H1(M),H2(M)
200 G1=0:G2=0
210 L=N
250 CLS:PRINT TAB(25);"J O T":PRINT
260 PRINT"JUST A MOMENT PLEASE ....":GOSUB 3000:
    PRINT:Q=RND(N)
270 PRINT"THANKS, NOW LET'S EACH THINK OF
    OUR SECRET WORD"
280 PRINT"(THIS TAKES ME A WHILE ...)"
290 GOSUB 2200:M$=A$(Q):PRINT:PRINT"OK, ";
300 INPUT"DO YOU WANT TO GO FIRST";Q$
310 Q$=LEFT$(Q$,1):IF Q$="N" THEN 600
320 IF Q$="Y" THEN 500
330 PRINT:PRINT"YES OR NO PLEASE":PRINT:GOTO 300
500 PRINT:INPUT"YOUR GUESS (OR S OR Q)";P$
510 IF P$="S" THEN GOSUB 1000:GOTO 500
520 IF P$="Q" THEN 1100
530 IF P$=M$ THEN G1=G1+1:G1$(G1)=P$:H1(G1)=9:GOTO 3400
540 GOSUB 1800:
    IF F=0 THEN PRINT"THAT'S NOT A LEGAL WORD";
550 IF F=0 THEN PRINT" -- TRY AGAIN":GOTO 500
560 Q$=M$:GOSUB 2600:Q$=P$:GOSUB 1500:
    PRINT"# OF HITS IS";Q
570 G1=G1+1:G1$(G1)=Q$:H1(G1)=Q:IF G1=M THEN 3600
600 Q$=A$(L):G2=G2+1:G2$(G2)=Q$
610 PRINT:PRINT"MY GUESS IS -- ";Q$
620 INPUT"HOW DID I DO (0-3 OR R)";P$
630 P$=LEFT$(P$,1)
640 IF P$="R" THEN H2(G2)=9:GOTO 3200
650 P=VAL(P$)
660 IF P>3 OR (P=0 AND P$<>"0") THEN PRINT"BAD ANSWER":
    GOTO 610
670 IF L>100 THEN PRINT:PRINT"I'M THINKING ..."
680 H2(G2)=P:GOSUB 800:GOTO 500
800 Q$=G2$(G2):H=H2(G2):J=0:GOSUB 2600:L=L-1:
    IF L<1 THEN 900
810 J=J+1:IF J>L THEN 870
820 Q$=A$(J):GOSUB 1500
830 IF Q=H THEN 810
840 A=J:B=L:GOSUB 2400:L=L-1
850 IF L<1 THEN 900
860 IF L>=J THEN 820
870 RETURN
900 PRINT:PRINT"SOMETHING'S WRONG !!"
910 PRINT:INPUT"WHAT'S YOUR SECRET WORD";P$:GOSUB 1800
```

```
920 IF F<>0 THEN 940
930 PRINT"ILLEGAL WORD - I NEVER HAD A CHANCE":
    GOTO 1100
940 PRINT:PRINT"YOU GAVE A BAD ANSWER SOMEWHERE --"
950 PRINT"HIT ANY KEY TO CHECK THE SUMMARY"
960 Q$=INKEY$:IF Q$="" THEN 960
970 GOSUB 1000:GOTO 1100
1000 PRINT:Q=G1:IF G2>G1 THEN Q=G2
1010 IF Q=0 THEN PRINT"NO GUESSES YET":RETURN
1020 FOR J=1 TO 41:PRINT"-";:NEXT:PRINT"-"
1030 PRINT"YOUR GUESSES      SUMMARY        MY GUESSES"
1040 PRINT"WORD  HITS";TAB(32);"WORD   HITS"
1050 FOR J=1 TO Q:K=1:IF J>9 THEN K=0
1060 IF J>G1 THEN PRINT STRING$(19+K,32);J;
     STRING$(10,32);G2$(J);STRING$(2,32);H2(J):GOTO 1090
1070 IF J>G2 THEN
     PRINT" ";G1$(J);"  ";H1(J);STRING$(10+K,32);J:
     GOTO 1090
1080 PRINT" ";G1$(J);"   ";H1(J);STRING$(10+K,32);J;
     STRING$(10,32);G2$(J);"  ";H2(J)
1090 NEXT:RETURN
1100 PRINT:INPUT"HOW ABOUT ANOTHER GAME";Q$
1110 Q$=LEFT$(Q$,1):IF Q$="Y" THEN 200
1120 IF Q$="N" THEN END
1130 PRINT:PRINT"YES OR NO PLEASE":GOTO 1100
1500 P$=LEFT$(Q$,1):Q=0:GOSUB 1600
1510 P$=MID$(Q$,2,1):GOSUB 1600
1520 P$=RIGHT$(Q$,1):GOSUB 1600:RETURN
1600 IF P$=M1$ OR P$=M2$ OR P$=M3$ THEN Q=Q+1
1610 RETURN
1800 F=0
1810 FOR J=1 TO N
1820 IF A$(J)=P$ THEN F=1:RETURN
1830 NEXT:RETURN
2200 FOR A=N TO 100 STEP -1:B=RND(A):GOSUB 2400
2210 NEXT:PRINT
2220 PRINT"I'VE ALMOST GOT IT ..."
2230 FOR A=99 TO 2 STEP -1:B=RND(A)
2240 GOSUB 2400:NEXT:RETURN
2400 Q$=A$(B):A$(B)=A$(A):A$(A)=Q$:RETURN
2600 M1$=LEFT$(Q$,1):M2$=MID$(Q$,2,1)
2610 M3$=RIGHT$(Q$,1):RETURN
3000 RESTORE:FOR P=1 TO N:READ A$(P):NEXT:RETURN
3200 PRINT:PRINT"IT SURE FEELS GOOD"
3210 PRINT:PRINT"MY WORD WAS - ";M$
```

```
3220 GOTO 1100
3400 PRINT:PRINT"CONGRATULATIONS - THAT WAS IT":PRINT
3410 INPUT"WHAT WAS YOUR WORD";P$:GOSUB 1800:J=1
3420 IF F<>0 THEN 3440
3430 PRINT"ILLEGAL WORD - I HAD NO CHANCE":GOTO 1100
3440 IF A$(J)=P$ THEN PRINT"NICE WORD":GOTO 1100
3450 J=J+1:IF J<=L THEN 3440
3460 PRINT:PRINT"YOU MADE AN ERROR SOMEWHERE --"
3470 PRINT"HIT ANY KEY TO CHECK THE SUMMARY"
3480 Q$=INKEY$:IF Q$="" THEN 3480
3490 GOSUB 1000:GOTO 1100
3600 PRINT"SORRY, I'M OUT OF MEMORY":PRINT
3610 PRINT"MY WORD WAS - ";M$:GOTO 1100
5000 DATA ACE,ACT,ADE,ADO,ADS,AFT,AGE
5010 DATA AGO,AID,AIL,AIM,AIR,ALE,ALP
5020 DATA AND,ANT,ANY,APE,APT,ARC,ARE
5030 DATA ARK,ARM,ART,ASH,ASK,ASP,ATE
5040 DATA AWE,AWL,AXE,AYE,BAD,BAG,BAN
5050 DATA BAR,BAT,BAY,BED,BEG,BET,BID
5060 DATA BIG,BIN,BIT,BOA,BOG,BOW,BOX
5070 DATA BOY,BUD,BUG,BUM,BUN,BUS,BUT
5080 DATA BUY,BYE,CAB,CAD,CAM,CAN,CAP
5090 DATA CAR,CAT,COB,COD,COG,CON,COP
5100 DATA COT,COW,COY,CRY,CUB,CUD,CUE
5110 DATA CUP,CUR,CUT,DAB,DAM,DAY,DEN
5120 DATA DEW,DIE,DIG,DIM,DIN,DIP,DOE
5130 DATA DOG,DON,DOT,DRY,DUB,DUE,DUG
5140 DATA DYE,DUO,EAR,EAT,EGO,ELK,ELM
5150 DATA END,ELF,ERA,FAD,FAG,FAN,FAR
5160 DATA FAT,FED,FEW,FIG,FIN,FIR,FIT
5170 DATA FIX,FLY,FOE,FOG,FOR,FOX,FRY
5180 DATA FUN,FUR,GAP,GAS,GAY,GEM,GET
5190 DATA GIN,GNU,GOB,GOD,GOT,GUM,GUN
5200 DATA GUT,GUY,GYP,HAD,HAG,HAM,HAS
5210 DATA HAT,HAY,HEN,HEX,HID,HIM,HIP
5220 DATA HIS,HIT,HER,HEM,HOE,HOG,HOP
5230 DATA HOT,HOW,HUB,HUE,HUG,HUM,HUT
5240 DATA ICE,ICY,ILK,INK,IMP,ION,IRE
5250 DATA IRK,ITS,IVY,JAB,JAR,JAW,JAY
5260 DATA JOB,JOG,JOT,JOY,JUG,JAG,JAM
5270 DATA JET,JIB,JIG,JUT,KEG,KEY,KID
5280 DATA KIN,KIT,LAB,LAD,LAG,LAP,LAW
5290 DATA LAY,LAX,LED,LEG,LET,LID,LIE
5300 DATA LIP,LIT,LOB,LOG,LOP,LOT,LOW
5310 DATA LYE,MAD,MAN,MAP,MAR,MAT,MAY
```

```
5320 DATA MEN,MET,MID,MOB,MOP,MOW,MUD
5330 DATA MIX,MUG,NAB,NAG,NAP,NAY,NET
5340 DATA NEW,NIL,NIP,NOD,NOT,NOR,NOW
5350 DATA NUT,OAF,OAK,OAR,OAT,ODE,OIL
5360 DATA OLD,ONE,OPT,ORE,OUR,OUT,OVA
5370 DATA OWE,OWL,OWN,PAD,PAL,PAN,PAR
5380 DATA PAT,PAW,PAY,PEA,PEG,PEN,PET
5390 DATA PEW,PIE,PIG,PIT,PLY,POD,POT
5400 DATA POX,PER,PIN,PRO,PRY,PUB,PUN
5410 DATA PUS,PUT,RAG,RAM,RAN,RAP,RAT
5420 DATA RAW,RAY,RED,RIB,RID,REV,RIG
5430 DATA RIM,RIP,ROB,ROD,ROE,ROT,ROW
5440 DATA RUB,RUE,RUG,RUM,RUN,RUT,RYE
5450 DATA SAD,SAG,SAP,SAT,SAW,SAY,SET
5460 DATA SEW,SEX,SHY,SEA,SIN,SHE,SIP
5470 DATA SIR,SIT,SIX,SKI,SKY,SLY,SOB
5480 DATA SOD,SON,SOW,SOY,SPA,SPY,STY
5490 DATA SUE,SUM,SUN,TAB,TAD,TAG,TAN
5500 DATA TAP,TAX,TAR,TEA,TEN,THE,THY
5510 DATA TIC,TIE,TIN,TIP,TOE,TON,TOP
5520 DATA TOW,TOY,TRY,TUB,TUG,TWO,URN
5530 DATA USE,UPS,VAN,VAT,VEX,VIA,VIE
5540 DATA VIM,VOW,YAK,YAM,YEN,YES,YET
5550 DATA YOU,WAD,WAG,WAN,WAR,WAS,WAX
5560 DATA WAY,WEB,WED,WET,WHO,WHY,WIG
5570 DATA WIN,WIT,WOE,WON,WRY,ZIP,FIB
```

EASY CHANGES

1. It is fairly common for players to request a summary before most guesses that they make. If you want the program to automatically provide a summary before each guess, change lines 500 and 510 to read

   500 IF G1>0 OR G2>0 THEN GOSUB 1000
   510 PRINT:INPUT "YOUR GUESS (OR Q)";P$

2. The maximum number of guesses allowed, M, can be changed in line 160. You may wish to increase it in conjunction with Suggested Project 2. You might decrease it to free some memory needed for other program additions. The current value of twenty-five is really somewhat larger than necessary. An actual game almost never goes beyond fifteen guesses. To set M to 15 change line 160 to read

   160 M=15:N=406

3. Modifying the data list of legal words is fairly easy. Our criteria for legal words was as follows: they must have three distinct letters and *not* be

 — capitalized
 — abbreviations
 — interjections (like "ugh", "hey" etc.)
 — specialized words (like "ohm", "sac", "yaw" etc.)

In line 160, N is set to be the total number of words in the data list. The data list itself is from line 5000 on.

To add word(s), do the following. Enter them in data statements after the current data (use line numbers larger than 5570). Then redefine the value of N to be 406 plus the number of new words added. For example, to add the words "ohm" and "yaw" onto the list, change line 160 to read

160 M=25:N=408

and add a new line

5580 DATA OHM,YAW

To delete word(s), the opposite must be done. Remove the words from the appropriate data statement(s) and decrease the value of N accordingly.

MAIN ROUTINES

150 - 180	Dimensions arrays.
200 - 330	Initializes new game.
500 - 570	Human guesses at the computer's word.
600 - 680	TRS-80 guesses.
800 - 870	Evaluates human's possible secret words. Moves them to the front of A$ array.
900 - 970	Processes inconsistency in given information.
1000 - 1090	Displays the current summary table.
1100 - 1130	Inquires about another game.
1500 - 1610	Compares a guess with key word.
1800 - 1830	Checks if input word is legal.
2200 - 2240	Shuffles A$ array randomly.
2400	Swaps elements A and B in the A$ array.
2600 - 2610	Breaks word Q$ into separate letters.
3000	Fill A$ array from data.

MAIN VARIABLES

N	Total number of data words.
M	Maximum number of guesses allowed.
A$	String array holding data words.
G1$,G2$	String arrays of human's, computer's guesses.
H1,H2	Arrays of human's, computer's hits corresponding to G1$, G2$.
G1,G2	Current number of human's, computer's guesses.
M$	Computer's secret word.
M1$,M2$, M3$	First, second, and third letters of a word.
P$,Q$	String temporaries and work variables.
L	Current number of human's possible secret words.
F	Flag for input word legality.
H	Number of hits in last guess.
A,B	A$ array locations to be swapped.
J,P,Q	Temporaries; array and loop indices.

SUGGESTED PROJECTS

1. Additional messages during the course of the game can personify the program even more. After the TRS-80 finds out how its last guess did, you might try an occasional message like one of these:

> JUST AS I THOUGHT . . .
> HMM, I DIDN'T EXPECT THAT . . .
> JUST WHAT I WAS HOPING TO HEAR . . .

The value of L is the number of words to which the computer has narrowed down the human's secret word. You might check its value regularly and when it gets low, come out with something like

> BE CAREFUL, I'M CLOSING IN ON YOU.

2. Incorporate a feature to allow the loser to continue guessing at the other's word. The summary display routine will

already work fine even if G1 and G2 are very different from each other. It will display a value of "9" for the number of hits corresponding to the correct guess of a secret word.

OBSTACLE

PURPOSE

This program allows you and a friend (or enemy) to play the game of OBSTACLE, an arcade-like game that's one of our favorites. A combination of physical skills (reflex speed, hand to eye coordination, etc.) and strategic skills are needed to beat your opponent. Each game generally takes only a minute or two, so you'll want to play a match of several games to determine the better player.

HOW TO USE IT

The object of the game is to keep moving longer than your opponent without bumping into an obstacle. When the program starts, it asks in turn for the name of the player on the left and on the right. Then it displays the playing field, shows the starting point for each player, and tells you to press any key to start.

After a key is pressed, each player begins moving independently in one of four random directions—up, down, left, or right. As each player moves, he or she builds a "wall" inside the playing field. The computer determines the speed of the move; the player can only control his own direction. The player on the left can change direction to up, down, left, or right by pressing the key W, X, A, or D, respectively. The player on the right does the same by using the keys for O (not zero), . (period), K, and ; (semi-colon). Find these keys on the TRS-80 keyboard and you will see the logic behind these choices.

The first time either player bumps into the wall surrounding the playing field or the obstacle wall built by either player, he loses. When this happens, the program indicates the point of impact for a few seconds and displays the name of the winner. Then the game starts over.

The strategic considerations for this game are interesting. Should you attack your opponent, trying to build a wall around him that he must crash into? Or should you stay away from him and try to make efficient moves in an open area until your opponent runs out of room on his own? Try both approaches and see which yields the most success.

When pressing a key to change direction, be sure to press it quickly and release it. *Do not* hold a key down—you might inhibit the computer from recognizing a move your opponent is trying to make. Once in a while, only one key will be recognized when two are hit at once.

SAMPLE RUN

The program starts off by asking for the names of the two players.

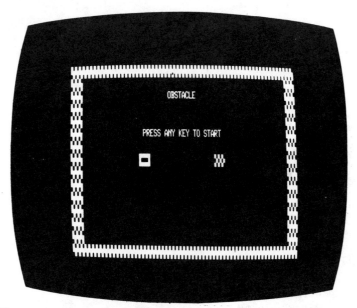

The program draws the playing field and waits for a key to be pressed.

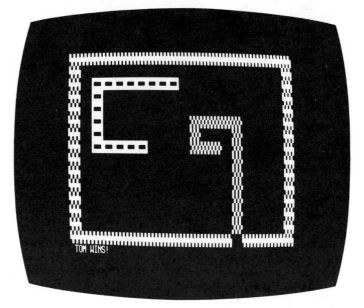

The program redraws the playing field and starts both players moving in a random direction (in this case, both start moving to the left). Phil (on the right) doesn't change directions soon enough and crashes into the wall, making Tom the winner.

PROGRAM LISTING

```
100 REM: OBSTACLE
110 REM: COPYRIGHT 1979 BY TOM RUGG AND PHIL FELDMAN
120 CLEAR 200:DEFINT A-Z:RANDOM:GOSUB 600
125 CLS:PRINT:PRINT
130 PRINT TAB(26);"OBSTACLE"
140 PRINT:PRINT
150 PRINT TAB(19);"PRESS ANY KEY TO START"
155 W=3:Z=191:Z$=STRING$(W,CHR$(Z)):A=466:B=487
160 A$=CHR$(183)+CHR$(179)+CHR$(187):
    B$=STRING$(W,CHR$(153))
165 S=15360:E$=STRING$(W,CHR$(173)):AD=RND(4):BD=RND(4)
170 GOSUB 900:GOSUB 950:FOR J=1 TO 10:R$=INKEY$:NEXT
180 R$=INKEY$:IF R$="" THEN 180
190 CLS
200 GOSUB 950:GOSUB 900:FOR J=1 TO 10:R$=INKEY$:NEXT
210 X=A:D=AD:GOSUB 1000
220 AR=R:A=X
230 X=B:D=BD:GOSUB 1000
240 BR=R:B=X
245 IF AR=1 OR BR=1 THEN 400
250 GOSUB 900
260 FOR J=1 TO 8:R$=INKEY$
270 IF R$="W" THEN AD=1
280 IF R$="X" THEN AD=2
290 IF R$="A" THEN AD=3
300 IF R$="D" THEN AD=4
310 IF R$="O" THEN BD=1
320 IF R$="." THEN BD=2
330 IF R$="K" THEN BD=3
340 IF R$=";" THEN BD=4
350 NEXT
360 GOTO 210
400 GOSUB 700:X=A
410 IF BR=1 THEN X=B
420 FOR J=1 TO 15
430 PRINT@X,Z$;
440 FOR K=1 TO 200:NEXT
450 PRINT@X,"   ";
460 FOR K=1 TO 200:NEXT
470 NEXT
490 GOTO 125
600 CLS:PRINT TAB(20);"OBSTACLE":PRINT
610 INPUT"NAME OF PLAYER ON THE LEFT";AN$
```

```
620 INPUT"PLAYER ON THE RIGHT";BN$
630 RETURN
700 PRINT@960," ";
710 IF AR<>1 OR BR<>1 THEN 730
720 PRINT"YOU BOTH LOSE!";:RETURN
730 R$=AN$:IF AR=1 THEN R$=BN$
740 PRINT R$;" WINS!";
750 RETURN
900 PRINT@A,A$;:PRINT@B,B$;:RETURN
950 FOR X=0 TO 60 STEP 3
960 PRINT@X,E$;:PRINT@X+896,E$;:NEXT
970 FOR X=0 TO 896 STEP 64
980 PRINT@X,E$;:PRINT@X+60,E$;:NEXT
990 RETURN
1000 IF D=1 THEN X=X-64
1010 IF D=2 THEN X=X+64
1020 IF D=3 THEN X=X-3
1030 IF D=4 THEN X=X+3
1040 R=0
1050 IF PEEK(S+X)<>32 THEN R=1
1060 RETURN
```

EASY CHANGES

1. To speed the game up, change the 8 in line 260 to a 5 or so. To slow it down, make it 12 or 15.
2. To make both players always start moving upward at the beginning of each game (instead of in a random direction), insert the following statement:

   168 AD=1:BD=1

   To make the players always start off moving toward each other, use this statement instead:

   168 AD=4:BD=3

3. To change the length of time that the final messages are displayed after each game, modify line 420. Change the 15 to 8 (or so) to shorten it, or to 25 to lengthen it.

MAIN ROUTINES

120 - 170	Initializes variables. Gets players' names. Displays titles, playing field.
180 - 200	Waits for key to be pressed to start game. Re-displays playing field.

210 - 250	Makes move for player A (on left side) and B (on right). Saves results.
260 - 350	Accepts moves from keyboard and translates direction.
400 - 490	Displays winner's name at bottom of screen. Flashes a square where collision occurred. Goes back to start next game.
600 - 630	Subroutine that gets each player's name.
700 - 750	Subroutine that displays winner's name.
900	Subroutine that displays each graphics character of each player's obstacle on the screen.
950 - 990	Subroutine that displays playing field.
1000 - 1060	Subroutine that moves marker and determines if space moved to is empty.

MAIN VARIABLES

A	Player A's current position.
B	Player B's current position.
A$	A's marker.
B$	B's marker.
S	Starting address of CRT memory area.
AD,BD	Current direction that A and B are going (1=up, 2=down, 3=left, 4=right).
E$	Graphics character for edge of playing field.
R$	Character being read from keyboard.
X	Temporary position on screen.
D	Temporary direction.
AR,BR	Result of A's and B's moves (0=okay, 1=loser).
AN$,BN$	Names of players A and B.
Z$	Graphics character displayed when collision is made.
J,K	Loop variables.

SUGGESTED PROJECTS

1. Keep score over a seven game (or so) match. Display the current score after each game. Don't forget to allow for ties.
2. Modify the program to let each player press only two keys—one to turn left from the current direction of travel, and one to turn right.

3. Instead of a game between two people, make it a game of a person against the computer. Develop a computer strategy to keep finding open areas to move to and/or to cut off open areas from the human opponent.

ROADRACE

PURPOSE

Imagine yourself at the wheel of a high-speed race car winding your way along a treacherous course. The road curves unpredictably. To stay on course, you must steer accurately or risk collision. How far can you go in one day? How many days will it take you to race cross-country? Thrills galore without leaving your living room.

The difficulty of the game is completely under your control. By adjusting the road width and visibility conditions, ROADRACE can be made as easy or as challanging as you wish.

HOW TO USE IT

The program begins with a short graphics display. It then asks you for two inputs: road width and visibility. The road width (in characters) can be set anywhere between 4 and 15. The degree of difficulty changes appreciably with different widths. A very narrow setting will be quite difficult and a wide one relatively easy. Visibility can be set to any of four settings, ranging from "terrible" to "good." When visibility is good, the car appears high on the screen. This allows a good view of the twisting road ahead. When visibility is poor, the car appears low on the screen allowing only a brief look at the upcoming road.

Having set road width and visibility, the race is ready to start. The car appears on the road at the starting line. A five-step starting light counts down the start. When the bottom light goes on, the race begins. The road moves continually up the screen. Its twists and turns are controlled randomly. You must steer the car accurately to keep it on track.

The car is controlled with the use of two keys on the keyboard. Pressing the comma (,) will cause the car to move to the left while pressing the period (.) will cause a move to the right. On these keys are the helpful symbols, < and >, respectively. Doing neither will cause the car to continue straight down.

The race proceeds until the car goes "off the road." Each such collision is considered to terminate one day of the race. After each day, you are shown the number of miles achieved that day along with the cumulative miles achieved for consecutive days of the race.

After each collision, you can proceed by pressing either **C**, **R**, or **Q**. Selecting **C** will continue the race for another day with the same road conditions. Cumulative totals will be retained. **R** will restart the race. This allows changing the road conditions and initializing back to day one. **Q** simply quits the race and returns the TRS-80 back to direct Basic. Either of the last two options will produce a display of the average miles travelled per day for the race.

There are several different ways to challenge yourself with the program. You can try to see how far you get in a given number of days. You might see how many days it takes you to go a given number of miles—say 3000 miles for a cross-country trip. As you become proficient at one set of road conditions, make the road narrower and/or the visibility poorer. This will increase the challenge. Different road conditions can also be used as a handicapping aid for two unequally matched opponents.

SAMPLE RUN

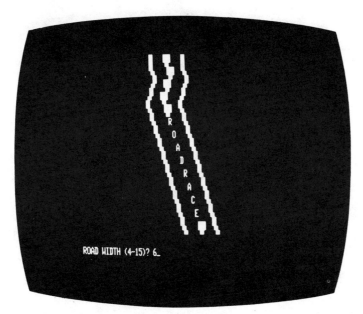

The program displays its logo and begins the short input phase. The operator selects to run a course with a 6 character road width.

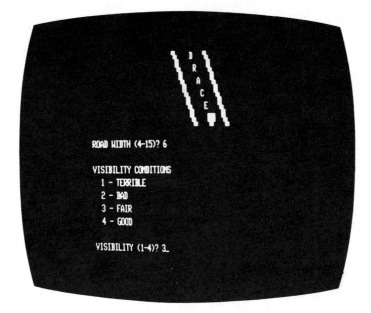

The operator selects fair visibility and the race is ready to begin.

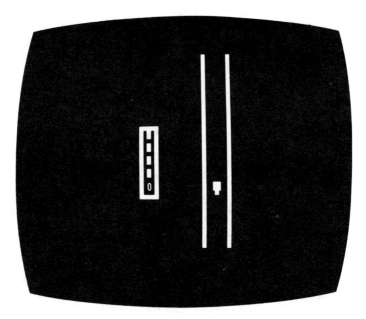

The car is on the starting line. The starting light counts down the beginning of the race. When the last light goes on, the race will be off and running.

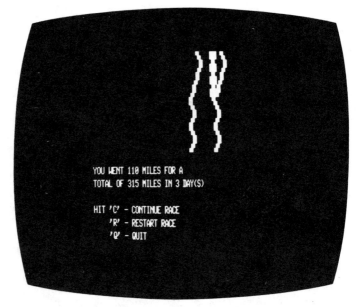

The operator, steering the car from the keyboard, finally crashes. A distance of 110 miles is obtained on this leg for a total of 315 miles in 3 days (legs). The options for continuing are displayed while the program waits for the operator's choice.

PROGRAM LISTING

```
100 REM: ROADRACE
110 REM: COPYRIGHT 1979 BY PHIL FELDMAN AND TOM RUGG
120 CLEAR 200:RANDOM:Q=0:Q$=""
130 LC=.45:RC=1-LC
140 LS$=CHR$(191)+CHR$(32):RS$=CHR$(32)+CHR$(191)
150 L$=",":R$="."
160 LT$=CHR$(184)+CHR$(135):RT$=CHR$(139)+CHR$(180)
170 B=32:EL=2:ER=58:C1=175:C2=159:DEFINT V,W
180 GOSUB 800
200 PRINT:T=0:N=0
210 INPUT"ROAD WIDTH (4-15)";W
220 IF W<4 OR W>15 THEN 200
230 PRINT:PRINT"VISIBILITY CONDITIONS"
240 PRINT"  1 - TERRIBLE"
250 PRINT"  2 - BAD"
260 PRINT"  3 - FAIR"
270 PRINT"  4 - GOOD":PRINT
280 INPUT"VISIBILITY (1-4)";V
290 IF V<1 OR V>4 THEN 280
300 N=N+1:L=24:R=L+W+2:Z=16384-128*V
310 C=INT((L+R)/2):H=0
320 FOR J=1 TO 16:Q$=INKEY$:GOSUB 600:NEXT
330 GOSUB 700
350 H=H+1:Q=RND(0):IF Q>RC AND R<ER THEN GOSUB 640:
    GOTO 400
360 IF Q<LC AND L>EL THEN GOSUB 620:GOTO 400
370 GOSUB 600
400 ZC=Z+C:ZP=ZC+1:Q$=INKEY$:IF Q$=L$ THEN C=C-1
410 IF Q$=R$ THEN C=C+1
420 IF PEEK(ZC)=B AND PEEK(ZP)=B THEN POKE ZC,C1:
    POKE ZP,C2:GOTO 350
430 FOR J=1 TO 8:Q$=INKEY$:POKE ZC,B:POKE ZP,B:
    FOR K=1 TO 50
440 NEXT:POKE ZC,C1:POKE ZP,C2:FOR K=1 TO 50:NEXT:NEXT
450 M=H*5:T=T+M:PRINT:PRINT"YOU WENT";M;"MILES FOR A"
460 PRINT"TOTAL OF";T;"MILES IN";N;"DAY(S)":PRINT
470 PRINT"HIT 'C' - CONTINUE RACE"
480 PRINT"    'R' - RESTART RACE"
490 PRINT"    'Q' - QUIT"
500 Q$=INKEY$:IF Q$="C" THEN 300
510 IF Q$<>"R" AND Q$<>"Q" THEN 500
520 PRINT:PRINT"AVERAGE MILES PER DAY=";T/N
540 IF Q$="R" THEN 200
```

```
550 END
600 PRINT TAB(L);RS$;TAB(R);LS$
610 RETURN
620 PRINT TAB(L);LT$;TAB(R-1);LT$
630 L=L-1:R=R-1:RETURN
640 PRINT TAB(L+1);RT$;TAB(R);RT$
650 L=L+1:R=R+1:RETURN
700 P=Z+C:GOSUB 950:P=Z+C-15360-20
710 Q$=CHR$(191)+CHR$(B)+"O"+CHR$(B)+CHR$(191)
720 P=P-320:PRINT @ P,STRING$(5,176);
730 FOR J=1 TO 5:P=P+64:PRINT @ P,Q$;:NEXT
740 PRINT @ P+64,STRING$(5,131);
750 FOR J=1 TO 600:NEXT
760 FOR J=4 TO 0 STEP -1:FOR K=1 TO 300:NEXT
770 PRINT @ P+2-64*J,CHR$(143);:NEXT:PRINT @896,CHR$(B)
780 RETURN
800 DIM D(9):L=18:R=28:CLS
810 FOR J=1 TO 9:READ D(J):NEXT
820 DATA 82,79,65,68,82,65,67,69,32
830 GOSUB 600
840 GOSUB 640
850 FOR J=1 TO 2:GOSUB 620:NEXT
860 FOR J=1 TO 10:GOSUB 640:NEXT
870 P=15383:POKE P,C1:POKE P+1,C2
880 FOR J=1 TO 500:NEXT
890 P=P+65:GOSUB 950
900 FOR J=1 TO 2:P=P+63:GOSUB 950:NEXT
910 P=P+65:GOSUB 950
920 FOR J=1 TO 9:P=P+65:GOSUB 950
930 POKE P,D(J):POKE P+1,B:NEXT
950 POKE P,C1:POKE P+1,C2:FOR K=1 TO 50:NEXT:RETURN
```

EASY CHANGES

1. The keys which cause the car to move left and right can be easily changed. You may wish to do this if you are left-handed or find that two widely separated keys would be more convenient. The changes are to be made in line 150. Left and right movements are controlled by the two string variables L\$ and R\$. If, for example, you wanted 1 to cause a left move and 9 to cause a right move, change line 150 to read

150 L\$="1":R\$="9"

2. The amount of windiness in the road can be adjusted by changing the value of LC in line 130. Maximum windiness is achieved with a value of 0.5 for LC. To get a straighter road, make LC smaller. A value of 0. will produce a completely straight road. LC should lie between 0. and 0.5 or else the road will drift to one side and linger there. To get a somewhat less winding road, you might change line 130 to read

$$130 \; LC=0.4: RC=1-LC$$

MAIN ROUTINES

120 - 180	Variable initialization.
200 - 290	Gets road conditions from user.
300 - 330	Initializes the road.
350 - 370	Determines the next road condition.
400 - 420	Updates the car position.
430 - 550	Processes end of race day.
600 - 650	Draws next road segment.
700 - 780	Graphics to begin race.
800 - 950	Initial graphics display.

MAIN VARIABLES

W	Road width.
V	Visibility.
M	Miles driven on current day.
N	Number of days of the race.
T	Total miles driven for whole race.
H	Elapsed time during race.
L$,R$	String characters to move car left, right.
L,R	Position of left, right side of road.
LC,RC	Random value cutoff to move road left, right.
EL,ER	Leftmost, rightmost allowable road position.
Q$	User replies.
C	Position of car.
Z,ZC,ZP	POKE arguments for car location.
RS$,LS$	Strings to display road segments.
LT$,RT$	
B	Blank character value.
P	Printing position.
D	Array of POKE arguments for display message.

J,K,Q   Loop indices and work variables.
C1,C2   Graphics characters to display car.

SUGGESTED PROJECTS

1. Write a routine to evaluate a player's performance after each collision. Display a message rating him anywhere from "expert" to "back seat driver." This should involve comparing his actual miles achieved against an expected (or average) number of miles for the given road width and visibility. For starters, you might use

$$\text{Expected miles} = W^3 + (10*V) - 35$$

This formula is crude, at best. The coding can be done between lines 550 and 600.
2. Incorporate provisions for two players racing one at a time. Keep cumulative totals separately. After each collision, display the current leader and how far he is ahead.
3. Add physical obstacles or other hazards onto the road in order to increase the challenge. These can be done with appropriate PRINT or POKE statements before the various RETURNs in lines 600-650. *Warning*: Be sure the address arguments of any POKEs lie between 15360 and 16383. Anything else may result in hanging up your system. The program will recognize a collision if the car moves into any non-blank square.

WARI

PURPOSE

Wari is an old game with roots that are even older. Its origins go back thousands of years to a variety of other similar games, all classified as being members of the Mancala family. Other variations are Awari, Oware, Pallanguli, Kalah, and countless other offshoots.

The program matches you against the computer. You are probably going to lose a few games before you win one—the computer plays a pretty good game. This may hurt your ego a little bit, since Wari is purely a skill game (like chess or checkers). There is no element of luck involved, as would be the case with backgammon, for example. When you lose, it's because you were outplayed.

HOW TO USE IT

When you start the program, the first thing it does is display the Wari board and ask you if you want to go first. The board is made up of twelve squares in two rows of six. Your side is the bottom side, numbered one through six from left to right. The computer's side is on the top, numbered seven through twelve from right to left.

At the start of the game, each square has four "stones" in it. There is no way to differentiate between your stones and the computer's. They all look alike and will move from one side to the other during the course of play.

The first player "picks up" all the stones in one of the squares on his side of the board and drops them, one to a square, starting with the next highest numbered square. The stones continue to be dropped consecutively in each square, continuing over onto the opponent's side if necessary (after square number 12 comes square number 1 again).

If the last stone is dropped onto the opponent's side *and* leaves a total of either two or three stones in that square, these stones are captured by the player who moved, and removed from the board. Also, if the next-to-last square in which a stone was dropped meets the same conditions (on the opponent's side and now with two or three stones), its stones are also captured. This continues backwards until the string of consecutive squares of two or three on the opponent's side is broken.

Regardless of whether any captures are made, play alternates back and forth between the two players.

The object of the game is to be the first player to capture twenty-four or more stones. That's half of the forty-eight stones that are on the board at the beginnning of the game.

There are a few special rules to cover some situations that can come up in the game. It is not legal to capture all the stones on the opponent's side of the board, since this would leave the opponent with no moves on his next turn. By the same token, when your opponent has no stones on his side (because he had to move his last one to your side on his turn), you have to make a move that gives him at least one stone to move on his next turn, if possible. If you cannot make such a move, the game is over and counted as a draw.

During the course of the game, it's possible for a square to accumulate twelve or more stones in it. Moving from such a square causes stones to be distributed all the way around the board. When this happens, the square from which the move was made is skipped over. So, the square moved from is always left empty.

It takes the computer anywhere from five seconds to about forty seconds to make a move, depending on the complexity of the board position. The word THINKING is displayed during this time, and a period is added to it as each possible move is evaluated in sequence (seven through twelve).

SAMPLE RUN

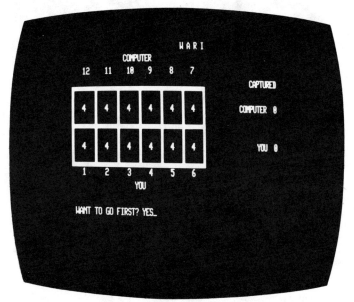

The program starts off by drawing the playing "board" and asking who should move first. The operator decides to go first.

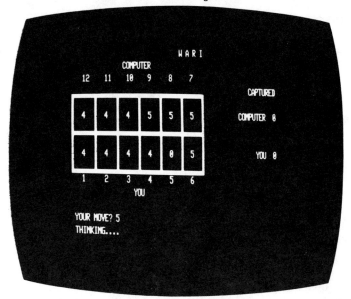

The program asks for the operator's move. He or she decides to move square number 5. The program alters the board accordingly, and begins "thinking" about what move to make.

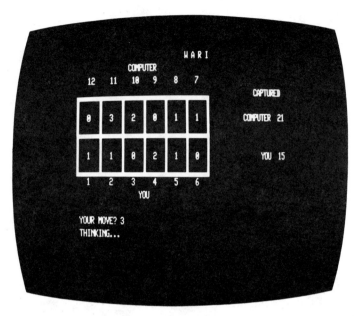

Later is the same game, the computer is about to move square number 11, which will capture four more stones and win the game.

PROGRAM LISTING

```
100 REM: WARI
110 REM: COPYRIGHT 1979 BY TOM RUGG AND PHIL FELDMAN
120 CLEAR 180:DEFINT A-D,J-T,W-Y:J=1:K=1:Q=14:P=13:
    F=50:D=12
130 DIM T(Q),Y(Q),W(Q),V(6),E(6),B(Q)
140 RANDOM:ZB=RND(0):ZB=ZB/Q:ZA=.25+ZB:ZB=.25-ZB:
    GOSUB 750
150 FOR J=1 TO D:B(J)=4:NEXT:B(P)=0:B(Q)=0:MN=0:
    GOSUB 1200:GOSUB 900
160 GOSUB 990:INPUT"WANT TO GO FIRST";R$
170 GOSUB 990:PRINT D$:R$=LEFT$(R$,1):
    IF R$="Y" THEN 250
180 IF R$<>"N" THEN 160
190 GOSUB 1050:PRINT D$;D$;D$;:GOSUB 1050:
    PRINT"THINKING";:GOSUB 510
195 IF M<1 THEN 2000
200 GOSUB 1050:PRINT D$;:GOSUB 1050:PRINT"MY MOVE IS";M
210 FOR J=1 TO Q:T(J)=B(J):NEXT:GOSUB 350
220 FOR J=1 TO Q:B(J)=T(J):NEXT:GOSUB 900
```

```
230 IF B(Q)<24 THEN 250
240 GOSUB 1050:PRINT"I WIN!";D$:GOTO 810
250 GOSUB 990:PRINT D$;D$:GOSUB 990:INPUT"YOUR MOVE";R$
260 M=INT(VAL(R$)):IF M>6 OR M<1 THEN 330
270 FOR J=1 TO Q:T(J)=B(J):NEXT
280 GOSUB 350:IF M<0 THEN 330
290 FOR J=1 TO Q:B(J)=T(J):NEXT
300 MN=MN+1:GOSUB 900
310 IF B(P)<24 THEN 190
320 GOSUB 1050:PRINT"YOU WIN!";D$:GOTO 810
330 PRINT@852," ILLEGAL ";:FOR J=1 TO 3000:NEXT:
    GOTO 250
350 IF T(M)=0 THEN M=-1:RETURN
360 R$="H":IF M>6 THEN R$="C":GOTO 380
370 FOR J=1 TO Q:Y(J)=T(J):NEXT:GOTO 400
380 FOR J=1 TO 6:Y(J)=T(J+6):Y(J+6)=T(J):NEXT
390 Y(P)=T(Q):Y(Q)=T(P):M=M-6
400 C=M:N=Y(C):FOR J=1 TO N:C=C+1
410 IF C=P THEN C=1
420 IF C=M THEN C=C+1:GOTO 410
430 Y(C)=Y(C)+1:NEXT:Y(M)=0:L=C
440 IF L<7 OR Y(L)>3 OR Y(L)<2 THEN 460
450 Y(P)=Y(P)+Y(L):Y(L)=0:L=L-1:GOTO 440
460 S=0:FOR J=7 TO D:S=S+Y(J):NEXT
470 IF S=0 THEN M=-2:RETURN
480 IF R$="H" THEN FOR J=1 TO Q:T(J)=Y(J):NEXT:RETURN
490 FOR J=1 TO 6:T(J)=Y(J+6):T(J+6)=Y(J):NEXT
500 T(Q)=Y(P):T(P)=Y(Q):RETURN
510 FOR A=1 TO 6:M=A+6:IF B(M)=0 THEN E(A)=-F:GOTO 690
530 FOR J=1 TO Q:T(J)=B(J):NEXT:GOSUB 350
540 IF M<0 THEN E(A)=-F:GOTO 690
550 IF T(Q)>23 THEN M=A+6:RETURN
560 FOR J=1 TO Q:W(J)=T(J):NEXT:FOR K=1 TO 6
570 IF T(K)=0 THEN V(K)=F:GOTO 670
580 FOR J=1 TO Q:T(J)=W(J):NEXT:M=K:GOSUB 350
590 IF M<0 THEN V(K)=F:GOTO 670
600 FA=0:FB=0:FC=0:FD=0:FOR J=7 TO D
610 FB=FB+T(J):IF T(J)>0 THEN FA=FA+1
620 IF T(J)<3 THEN FC=FC+1
630 IF T(J)>FD THEN FD=T(J)
640 NEXT:FE=FB:FOR J=1 TO 6:FE=FE+T(J):NEXT
650 FA=FA/6:FD=1-FD/FB:FC=1-FC/6:FB=FB/FE
660 V(K)=ZA*(FA+FB)+ZB*(FC+FD)+T(Q)+B(P)-B(Q)-T(P)
670 NEXT:E(A)=F:FOR J=1 TO 6:IF V(J)<E(A) THEN E(A)=V(J)
680 NEXT
```

```
690 PRINT".";:NEXT:M=0:FA=-F:FOR J=1 TO 6
700 IF E(J)>FA THEN FA=E(J):M=J+6
710 NEXT:RETURN
750 A$="":FOR J=1 TO 36:A$=A$+CHR$(176):NEXT
760 B$=CHR$(170):FOR J=1 TO 6:B$=B$+"      "+CHR$(170):
    NEXT
770 C$=CHR$(170):D$=CHR$(176)+CHR$(176):FOR J=1 TO 6
780 C$=C$+D$+D$+CHR$(176)+CHR$(186)
790 NEXT:D$=" ":FOR J=1 TO 5:D$=D$+D$:NEXT:RETURN
810 PRINT"GOOD GAME!"
840 INPUT"WANT TO PLAY AGAIN";R$
850 R$=LEFT$(R$,1):IF R$="Y" THEN 120
860 IF R$<>"N" THEN 840
870 PRINT:PRINT"SEE YOU LATER"
880 PRINT:END
900 FOR J=0 TO 5
910 PRINT@(322+J*6),B(12-J);
920 IF B(12-J)-0 THEN GOSUB 1100
930 NEXT:PRINT@367,"COMPUTER ";B(Q);
940 FOR J=0 TO 5
950 PRINT@(514+J*6),B(J+1);:IF B(J+1)=0 THEN GOSUB 1100
960 NEXT:PRINT@564,"YOU ";B(P);:RETURN
990 PRINT@832," ";:RETURN
1050 PRINT@896," ";:RETURN
1100 PRINT CHR$(24);" ";:RETURN
1200 CLS:PRINT TAB(30);"W A R I"
1220 PRINT TAB(14);"COMPUTER"
1230 FOR J=0 TO 5:PRINT TAB(6*J+2);12-J;:NEXT
1240 PRINT@192,CHR$(160);:PRINT A$;TAB(50);"CAPTURED"
1250 FOR J=1 TO 2:PRINT B$:PRINT B$:PRINT C$:NEXT
1260 FOR J=0 TO 5:PRINT TAB(6*J+2);J+1;:NEXT
1270 PRINT:PRINT TAB(17);"YOU":RETURN
2000 PRINT"NO LEGAL MOVES.":GOTO 840
```

EASY CHANGES

1. If you have a 4K TRS-80, you'll need to delete lines 100, 110, and 180 to make this program fit in your computer. Line 870 can also be deleted if you need more room to make other changes.

2. Want a faster moving game against an opponent who isn't quite such a good player? Insert the following two lines:

   555 GOTO 600
   665 E(A)=V(K):GOTO 690

In the standard version of the game, the computer looks at each of its possible moves and each of your possible replies when evaluating which move to make. This change causes the computer to only look at each of its moves, without bothering to look at any of your possible replies. As a result, the computer does not play as well, but it takes only a few seconds to make each move.

3. If you are curious about what the computer thinks are the relative merits of each of its possible moves, you can make this change to find out. Change line 690 so it looks like this:

690 PRINT E(A);:NEXT:M=0:FA=−F:FOR J=1 TO 6

This will cause the program to display its evaluation number for each of its moves in turn (starting with square seven). It will select the largest number of the six. A negative value means that it will lose stones if that move is made, assuming that you make the best reply you can. A value of negative 50 indicates an illegal move. A positive value greater than one means that a capture can be made by the computer, which will come out ahead after your best reply.

MAIN ROUTINES

120 - 150	Initializes variables. Displays board.
160 - 180	Asks who goes first. Evaluates answer.
190 - 220	Determines computer's move. Displays new board position.
230 - 240	Determines if computer's move resulted in a win. Displays a message if so.
250 - 300	Gets operator's move. Checks for legality. Displays new board position.
310 - 320	Determines if operator's move resulted in a win.
330	Displays message if illegal move attempted.
350 - 500	Subroutine to make move M in T array.
360 - 390	Copies T array into Y array (inverts if computer is making the move).
400 - 430	Makes move in Y array.
440 - 450	Checks for captures. Removes stones. Checks previous square.
460 - 470	Sees if opponent is left with a legal move.
480 - 500	Copies Y array back into T array.
510 - 710	Subroutine to determine computer's move.

750 - 790	Subroutine to create graphics strings for board display.
810 - 880	Displays ending message. Asks about playing again.
900 - 960	Subroutine to display stones on board and captured.
990	Subroutine to move cursor to "YOUR MOVE" position on screen.
1050	Subroutine to move cursor to "MY MOVE" position on screen.
1100	Subroutine to backspace cursor one space and display one blank character.
1200 - 1270	Subroutine to display Wari board (without stones).
2000	Displays message when computer has no legal move.

MAIN VARIABLES

J,K	Subscript variables.
Q,P,F,D	Constant values of 14, 13, 50 and 12, respectively.
T,Y,W	Arrays with temporary copies of the Wari board.
V	Array with evaluation values of operator's six possible replies to computer's move being considered.
E	Array with evaluation values of computer's six possible moves.
B	Array containing Wari board. Thirteenth element has stones captured by operator. Fourteenth has computer's.
ZA,ZB	Weighting factors for evaluation function.
MN	Move number.
R$	Operator's reply. Also used as switch to indicate whose move it is (C for computer, H for human).
M	Move being made (1 - 6 for operator, 7 - 12 for computer). Set negative if illegal.
C	Subscript used in dropping stones around board.
L	Last square in which a stone was dropped.
S	Stones on opponent's side of the board after a move.
A	Subscript used to indicate which of the six possible computer moves is currently being evaluated.
FA	First evaluation factor used in determining favora-

	bility of board position after a move (indicates computer's number of occupied squares).
FB	Second evaluation factor (total stones on computer's side of the board).
FC	Third evaluation factor (number of squares with two or less stones).
FD	Fourth evaluation factor (number of stones in most populous square on computer's side).
FE	Total stones on board.
A$,B$,C$	Strings of graphics characters used to display the Wari board.
D$	String of thirty-two blanks.

SUGGESTED PROJECTS

1. Modify the program to declare the game a draw if neither player has made a capture in the past thirty moves. Line 300 adds one to the counter of the number of moves made. To make the change, keep track of the move number of the last capture, and compare the difference between it and the current move number with 30.
2. Modify the evaluation function used by the computer strategy to see if you can improve the quality of its play. Lines 600 through 660 examine the position of the board after the move that is being considered. Experiment with the factors and/or the weighting values, or add a new factor of your own.
3. Change the program so it can allow two people to play against each other, instead of just a person against the computer.

Section 4
Graphics Display Programs

INTRODUCTION TO GRAPHICS DISPLAY PROGRAMS

The TRS-80 is an amazing machine. It has very useful graphics capabilities in addition to its other capacities. Programs in the other sections of this book take advantage of these graphics to facilitate and "spice up" their various output. Here we explore the use of the TRS-80's graphic capabilities for sheer fun, amusement, and diversion.

Ever look through a kaleidoscope and enjoy the symmetric changing patterns produced? KALEIDO will create such effects with full eight point symmetry.

Two other programs produce ever changing patterns but with much different effects. SPARKLE will fascinate you with a changing shimmering collage. SQUARES uses geometric shapes to obtain its pleasing displays.

WALLOONS demonstrates a totally different aspect of the TRS-80. This program will keep you entertained with an example of computer animation.

KALEIDO

PURPOSE

If you have ever played with a kaleidoscope, you were probably fascinated by the endless symmetrical patterns you saw displayed. This program creates a series of kaleidoscope-like designs, with each one overlaying the previous one. Some of the designs are symmetrical about eight axes (others about four)—can you find them?

HOW TO USE IT

There is not much to say about how to use this one. Just type RUN, then sit back and watch. Turning down the lights and playing a little music is a good way to add to the effect.

By the way, it is a little misleading to say that the designs you see are symmetrical. It is more accurate to say that the positions occupied by the individual graphics characters are located symmetrically. The overall design is usually not completely symmetrical, since the individual graphics characters are not themselves symmetrical. The characters on the lower half of the design would have to be the upside-down equivalent of the corresponding characters on the upper half for that to be true.

Have a few friends bring their TRS-80s over (all your friends *do* have TRS-80s, don't they?), and get them all going with KALEIDO at once. Let us know if you think you have set a new world's record. Please note that we will not be responsible for any hypnotic trances induced this way.

SAMPLE RUN

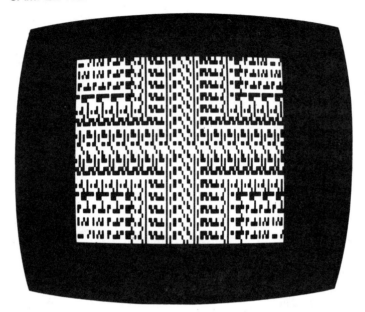

One of the patterns generated by the KALEIDO program.

PROGRAM LISTING

```
100 REM: KALEIDOSCOPE
110 REM: COPYRIGHT 1979 BY TOM RUGG AND PHIL FELDMAN
120 CLEAR 50:RANDOM:CLS:DEFINT A-Z
130 A=477:D=-1
135 W=4:S=7:L=64:M=22:G=169
140 DIM R$(S)
150 FOR J=0 TO S:A$="":FOR K=1 TO W
160 A$=A$+CHR$(RND(M)+G):NEXT
170 R$(J)=A$:NEXT
180 D=-D
190 P=0:Q=S:IF D<0 THEN Q=0:P=S
200 FOR K=P TO Q STEP D
210 FOR J=K TO Q STEP D
220 PRINT@A+J*W+K*L,R$(K);:PRINT@A+K*W+J*L,R$(K);
230 PRINT@A+J*W-K*L,R$(K);:PRINT@A+K*W-J*L,R$(K);
240 PRINT@A-J*W+K*L,R$(K);:PRINT@A-K*W+J*L,R$(K);
250 PRINT@A-J*W-K*L,R$(K);:PRINT@A-K*W-J*L,R$(K);
260 NEXT:NEXT
300 GOTO 150
```

EASY CHANGES

1. To clear the screen before the next pattern about 20% of the time (chosen at random), insert this:

   175 IF RND(100)<=20 THEN CLS

   For 50%, use 50 instead of 20, etc.
2. To randomly select either a square or rectangular pattern, insert:

   176 W=RND(2)+2

   To always get a square pattern, use this instead:

   176 W=3
3. To randomly change the size of the patterns, insert:

   177 S=RND(4)+3
4. To cause only the outward patterns to be displayed, change line 180 to say

   180 D=1

   To cause only inward patterns, change it to say

   180 D=−1
5. To alter the intricacy of the graphics characters used in the patterns, alter the values of M and G in line 135. Be sure both are positive integers, that G is at least 127, and that the sum of M and G does not exceed 191. For example, try M=64 and G=127. Or, try M=16 and G=127. Or, M=4 and G=187.
6. To lengthen the delay after each pattern is drawn, insert this line:

   270 FOR J=1 TO 3000:NEXT

   Use a number larger than 3000 to increase the length of the delay even more.

Note: These changes add a lot of the appeal of the designs. Experiment! Each change can be done by itself or in combination with other changes.

MAIN ROUTINES

120 - 140	Housekeeping. Initializes variables, RND.
150 - 170	Picks S+1 random graphics characters, each W characters wide.
180	Reverses direction of display (inward-outward).

| 190 - 260 | Displays a full screen of the pattern. |
| 300 | Goes back to create next pattern. |

MAIN VARIABLES

A	Pointer to center of design.
D	Direction in which design is drawn (1=outward, −1=inward).
W	Width of each graphics string.
S	Size of one-quarter of the pattern.
L	Length of one line on the screen (64).
M	Multiplier used to determine the range of random graphics characters.
G	Low number in range of random graphics characters.
R$	Array for the S random graphics strings.
J,K	Subscript variables.
P,Q	Inner and outer bounds of design (distance from center).
A$	Temporary string variable used to build graphics strings.

SPARKLE

PURPOSE

This graphics display program provides a continuous series of hypnotic patterns, some of which seem to sparkle at you while they are created. Two types of patterns are used. The first is a set of concentric diamond shapes in the center of the screen. Although the pattern is regular, the sequence in which it is created is random, which results in the "sparkle" effect.

The second type of pattern starts about two seconds after the first has finished. It is a series of "sweeps" across the screen—left to right and top to bottom. Each sweep uses a random graphics character that is spaced equally across the screen. The spacing distance is chosen at random for each sweep. Also, the number of sweeps to be made is chosen at random each time in the range from 11 to 30.

After the second type of pattern is complete, the program goes back to the first type, which begins to overlay the center of the second type.

HOW TO USE IT

Confused by what you just read? Never mind. You have to see it to appreciate it. Just enter the program into your TRS-80, then sit back and watch the results of your labor.

SAMPLE RUN

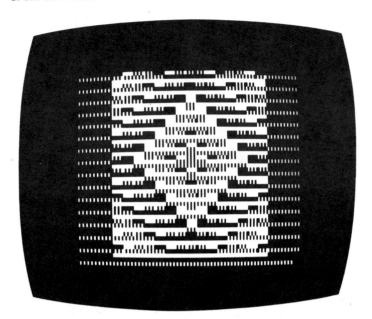

One of the patterns generated by the SPARKLE program.

PROGRAM LISTING

```
100 REM: SPARKLE
110 REM: COPYRIGHT 1979 BY TOM RUGG AND PHIL FELDMAN
120 CLEAR 50:RANDOM:CLS:DEFINT A-Z
130 DIM A(7),B(7):A=10:B=7:S=0
140 T=RND(40)+130
150 FOR J=0 TO 7:A(J)=J:B(J)=J:NEXT
160 FOR J=0 TO 7:R=RND(8)-1:W=A(J):A(J)=A(R)
170 A(R)=W:NEXT
180 FOR J=0 TO 7:R=RND(8)-1:W=B(J):B(J)=B(R)
190 B(R)=W:NEXT
200 FOR J=0 TO 7:FOR K=0 TO 7
210 R=A(J):W=B(K):C=R+W+T
240 X=A+R:Y=B+W:GOSUB 900
250 Y=B-W:GOSUB 900
260 X=A-R:GOSUB 900
270 Y=B+W:GOSUB 900
280 X=A+W:Y=B+R:GOSUB 900
290 Y=B-R:GOSUB 900
300 X=A-W:GOSUB 900
310 Y=B+R:GOSUB 900
```

```
320 NEXT:NEXT
350 FOR J=1 TO 2000:NEXT
400 N=128:M=64
410 FOR J=1 TO RND(20)+10
420 R=RND(17)*2:W=RND(M)
430 T=S:IF RND(0)>.8 THEN T=T+2
440 A$=CHR$(N+W)+CHR$(N+W):PRINT@S,A$;
450 FOR K=T TO S+1021 STEP R
460 PRINT@K,A$;
470 NEXT:NEXT
480 GOTO 140
900 A$=CHR$(C)+CHR$(C)+CHR$(C)
910 PRINT@S+64*Y+3*X,A$;:RETURN
920 PRINT@S+64*Y+3*X+2,CHR$(C);
930 RETURN
```

EASY CHANGES

1. Make the second type of pattern appear first by inserting this line:

   135 GOTO 400

   Or, eliminate the first type of pattern by inserting:

   145 GOTO 400

   Or, eliminate the second type of pattern by inserting:

   360 GOTO 140

2. Increase the delay after the first type of pattern by increasing the 2000 in line 350 to, say, 5000. Remove line 350 to eliminate the delay.

3. Increase the number of sweeps across the screen of the second type of pattern by changing the 10 at the right end of line 410 into a 30 or a 50, for example. Decrease the number of sweeps by changing the 10 to a 1, and also changing the 20 in line 410 to 5 or 10.

4. Watch the effect on the second type of pattern if you change the 17 in line 420 into various integer values between 2 and 100.

5. Change the values of N and M in line 400 to alter the graphics characters used in the second type of pattern. For example, try

   N=128 and M=5
   or, N=142 and M=20

Be sure that N is at least 127, and the sum of N and M is no more than 192.

MAIN ROUTINES

120 - 130	Initializes variables. Clears screen.
140 - 320	Displays square pattern in center of screen.
150 - 190	Shuffles the numbers 0 through 7 in the A and B arrays.
200 - 320	Displays graphics characters on the screen.
350	Delays for about 2 seconds.
400 - 480	Overlays the entire screen with a random graphics string spaced at a fixed interval chosen at random.
900 - 930	Subroutine to display graphics string A$ at location (X,Y). Upper left corner of screen is location (0,0).

MAIN VARIABLES

R	Random integer. Also, work variable.
A,B	Arrays in which shuffled integers from 0 to 7 are stored for use in making first type of pattern.
A,B	Coordinates of center of screen (10 across, 7 down).
S	Address of beginning of screen.
T	Integer from 131 to 170, used in creating random graphics characters. Also, work variable.
J,K	Work and loop variables.
W	Work variable.
X,Y	Coordinates of a position on the screen for a graphics string.
C	Graphics character to be displayed on screen at X,Y.
N	Lowest graphics character to be used in second type of pattern.
M	Multiplier used in getting a random integer to add to N.

SUGGESTED PROJECTS

Make the second type of pattern alternate between "falling from the top" (as it does now) and rising from the bottom of the screen.

SQUARES

PURPOSE

This is another graphics-display program. It draws a series of concentric squares and rectangles, with the graphics character used for each one chosen at random. After a full set of concentric squares is drawn, the next set starts again at the center and overlays the previous one. Each set may be a narrow rectangle, wide rectangle, or square, chosen at random.

HOW TO USE IT

As with most of the other graphics display programs, you just sit back and enjoy watching this one once you get it started.

SAMPLE RUN

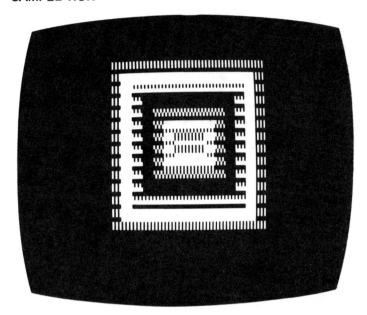

One of the patterns generated by the SQUARES program.

PROGRAM LISTING

```
100 REM: SQUARES
110 REM: COPYRIGHT 1979 BY TOM RUGG AND PHIL FELDMAN
120 CLEAR 50:DEFINT A-Z:RANDOM:CLS
130 N=1:W=RND(4):L=480-W
140 C=RND(64)+127:A$=CHR$(C)
150 C$=STRING$(W,A$)
170 FOR J=1 TO W*N:PRINT@L,A$;:L=L+1:NEXT
180 N=N+1
190 FOR J=1 TO N:PRINT@L,C$;:L=L-64:NEXT:L=L+63
200 FOR J=1 TO W*N:PRINT@L,A$;:L=L-1:NEXT:L=L+65
210 N=N-1
220 FOR J=1 TO N:PRINT@L,C$;:L=L+64:NEXT
230 N=N+2
240 IF N<14 THEN 140
250 FOR J=1 TO 1000:NEXT
260 GOTO 130
```

EASY CHANGES

1. Change the delay after each set of patterns by changing the 1000 in line 250. A bigger number causes a longer delay.
2. To cause the patterns to be only overlaying squares (i.e., no variation in width), change line 130 to say:

130 N=1:W=3:L=480−W

3. To occasionally blank out the screen (about 20% of the time), insert this:

255 IF RND(100)<=20 THEN CLS

MAIN ROUTINES

120	Housekeeping. Clears screen.
130	Initializes counters for the pattern. Points to the center of the screen.
140 - 150	Picks a graphics character and creates a string of W repetitions of it.
170	Draws the bottom side of the square.
190	Draws the right side.
200	Draws the top side.
220	Draws the left side.
240	Tests if the outermost square has been drawn.
250	Delays about one second.
260	Goes back to start at the center again.

MAIN VARIABLES

N	Length of the side currently being drawn.
W	Width of the vertical sides of the square (1 to 4).
L	Location on the screen where characters are currently being displayed.
C	Numeric equivalent of the random graphics character chosen.
A$	String representation of the random graphics character.
C$	String of W consecutive copies of the graphics character.
J	Loop variable.

WALLOONS

PURPOSE

The TRS-80 is quite a versatile machine. This program takes advantage of its powerful graphics capability to produce computer animation. That's right, animation! WALLOONS will entertain you with a presentation from the TRS-80 Theatre.

The TRS-80 Theatre searches the world over to bring you the best in circus acts and other performing artists. Today, direct from their performance before the uncrowned heads of Europe, the Theatre brings you the Flying Walloons.

HOW TO USE IT

Just sit back, relax, and get ready to enjoy the show. Type RUN and the Flying Walloons will be ready to perform. You have a front row center seat and the curtain is about to go up.

Applause might be appropriate if you enjoy their performance. Please note that the Walloons have been working on a big new finish to their act which they haven't yet quite perfected.

SAMPLE RUN

The billboard announces a new presentation of the (in)famous TRS-80 Theatre.

"The Flying Walloons" are to perform!

The Walloons attempt a dangerous trick from their repertoire.

PROGRAM LISTING

```
100 REM: WALLOONS
110 REM:COPYRIGHT 1979 BY PHIL FELDMAN AND TOM RUGG
150 CLEAR 310:D=64:E=128
200 N$=CHR$(32):K$=CHR$(140):K1$=CHR$(131):
    K2$=CHR$(191)
210 B$=K1$+CHR$(171)+K2$+CHR$(151)+K1$:
    T$=K$+CHR$(188)+K$
220 C$=CHR$(184)+CHR$(135)+N$+CHR$(139)+CHR$(180)
230 L$=STRING$(3,176):M$=STRING$(3,140)
240 U$=STRING$(3,131):S$=N$+N$:A$=S$+CHR$(188):
    W$=L$+M$+U$
250 D$=S$+CHR$(188)+STRING$(15,N$)+W$
260 E$=B$+S$+S$+L$+T$+U$:Y$=S$+S$+N$:Y1$=STRING$(8,32)
270 Z$=CHR$(160)+CHR$(190)+K2$+CHR$(189)+CHR$(144)
280 F$=CHR$(184)+CHR$(183)+CHR$(176)+CHR$(143)+K$
290 F$=F$+K$+U$+S$+Z$:G$=STRING$(18,N$)+W$
320 J$=W$+S$+CHR$(160)+CHR$(190)+K2$+CHR$(189)
330 J$=J$+CHR$(144):H$=STRING$(9,N$)+L$+T$+U$
360 D1$=U$+M$+L$+STRING$(15,N$)+CHR$(188)
370 E1$=STRING$(9,N$)+U$+T$+L$+S$+S$+B$
380 F1$=STRING$(11,N$)+Z$+S$+U$+K$+K$
```

```
390 F1$=F1$+CHR$(143)+CHR$(176)+CHR$(187)+CHR$(180)
400 V1$=CHR$(131)+K$+CHR$(176)+CHR$(160)+CHR$(176)
410 V1$=V1$+CHR$(188):V2$=N$+CHR$(176)+K$+CHR$(139)
420 V2$=V2$+CHR$(143)+K2$+K1$+K1$
430 V3$=CHR$(172)+CHR$(144)+N$+CHR$(160)+CHR$(156)
440 V4$=N$+CHR$(171)+CHR$(188)+CHR$(151)
450 V5$=K1$+K1$+K2$+K1$+K1$
470 GOSUB 1300:GOSUB 1400:GOSUB 1800
500 CLS:L=783:GOSUB 900:GOSUB 1800:FOR H=770 TO 782:CLS
510 GOSUB 900:GOSUB 910:NEXT:CLS:GOSUB 920:GOSUB 1800
530 FOR H=298 TO 319:PRINT@H,K1$:NEXT:H=123:GOSUB 910
540 GOSUB 1800:GOSUB 1200:H=101:GOSUB 910
590 FOR J=1 TO 4
600 H=101:FOR K=1 TO 8:GOSUB 940:H=H+D:GOSUB 910
610 NEXT:H=591:CLS:GOSUB 930:GOSUB 910:FOR K=1 TO 8
620 GOSUB 940:H=H-D:GOSUB 910:NEXT:FOR K=1 TO 8:
    GOSUB 940
630 H=H+D:GOSUB 910:NEXT:H=613:CLS:GOSUB 920:GOSUB 910
640 FOR K=1 TO 8:GOSUB 940:H=H-D:GOSUB 910:NEXT:NEXT
700 FOR K=1 TO 3:GOSUB 940:H=H+1:GOSUB 910:NEXT
710 FOR K=1 TO 8:GOSUB 940:H=H+D:GOSUB 910:NEXT
720 GOSUB 940:H=L-37:GOSUB 950:GOSUB 970:H=H+66:
    GOSUB 960
800 GOSUB 1800:CLS:PRINT CHR$(23)
810 PRINT@468,"F I N I S":GOSUB 1800:CLS:END
900 PRINT@L,G$;:PRINT@L+D,H$;:PRINT@L+E,J$;:RETURN
910 PRINT@H,A$;:PRINT@H+D,B$;:PRINT@H+E,C$;:RETURN
920 PRINT@L,D$;:PRINT@L+D,E$;:PRINT@L+E,F$;:RETURN
930 PRINT@L,D1$;:PRINT@L+D,E1$;:PRINT@L+E,F1$;:RETURN
940 PRINT@H,Y$;:PRINT@H+D,Y$;:PRINT@H+E,Y$;:RETURN
950 PRINT@H,V1$;:PRINT@H+D,V2$;:PRINT@H+E,K1$;:RETURN
960 PRINT@H,V3$;:PRINT@H+D,V4$;:PRINT@H+E,V5$;:RETURN
970 PRINT@H,Y1$;:PRINT@H+D,Y1$;:PRINT@H+E,Y1$;:RETURN
1200 FOR H=123 TO 107 STEP -1:GOSUB 910:GOSUB 940:NEXT
1210 GOSUB 910:GOSUB 1800:FOR J=1 TO 3:GOSUB 940:H=H-1
1220 GOSUB 910:NEXT:GOSUB 1800:FOR J=1 TO 6:GOSUB 940:
     H=H+1
1230 GOSUB 910:NEXT:FOR K=1 TO 500:NEXT
1240 FOR J=1 TO 8:PRINT@H,S$+N$;:FOR K=1 TO 50:NEXT
1250 PRINT@H,A$;:FOR K=1 TO 50:NEXT:NEXT:GOSUB 1800
1260 FOR J=1 TO 8:GOSUB 940:H=H-1:GOSUB 910:NEXT:RETURN
1300 CLS:PRINT CHR$(23):H=336:U$=CHR$(143)
1310 PRINT@H,"TRS-80 THEATRE":PRINT@H+E,"   PROUDLY"
1330 PRINT@H+E+E,"   PRESENTS"
1340 FOR J=200 TO 242 STEP 2:PRINT@J,U$:NEXT
```

```
1350 FOR J=200 TO 712 STEP D:PRINT@J,K2$;:NEXT
1360 FOR J=242 TO 754 STEP D:PRINT@J,K2$;:NEXT
1370 FOR J=712 TO 754 STEP 2:PRINT@J,U$;:NEXT
1380 GOSUB 1800:FOR J=0 TO 26:PRINT@H+E+J,"-";
1390 FOR K=1 TO 90:NEXT:NEXT:GOSUB 1800:RETURN
1400 M$="F L Y I N G":U$="W A L L    N S":
     W$=STRING$(16,32)
1410 L$="T H E":CLS:PRINT CHR$(23):
     FOR J=308 TO 260 STEP -2
1420 PRINT@J,W$:GOSUB 1700:PRINT@J,L$:NEXT
1430 FOR J=552 TO 524 STEP -2:PRINT@J,W$:GOSUB 1700:
     PRINT@J,M$
1440 NEXT:FOR J=802 TO 788 STEP -2:PRINT@J,W$:
     GOSUB 1700
1450 PRINT@J,U$:NEXT:GOSUB 1800:FOR J=36 TO 740 STEP D
1460 PRINT@J,"O";:GOSUB 1700:PRINT@J,N$;:NEXT:
     PRINT@804,"O";
1470 FOR J=40 TO 744 STEP D:PRINT@J,"O";:GOSUB 1700
1480 PRINT@J,N$;:NEXT:PRINT@808,"O";:RETURN
1700 FOR K=1 TO 12:NEXT:RETURN
1800 FOR I=1 TO 1400:NEXT:RETURN
```

EASY CHANGES

1. If you wish to have the Walloons perform more (or less) jumps during their performance, change the loop bound value of 4 in line 590 accordingly. To get six jumps, use

   590 FOR J=1 TO 6

2. Timing delays are used often in the program. To change the length of the delay, alter the 1400 in line 1800 to a different value. Values larger than 1400 will lengthen the delays, while values smaller than 1400 will shorten the delays.

3. You might want to personalize the title placard and make yourself the presenter of the Walloons. This can be done by altering the string literal, "TRS-80 THEATRE" in line 1310 to something else. However, you cannot use a string with a length of much more than 16 characters or it will print beyond the end of the placard. To say, for example, that Simon Fenster presents the Walloons, change line 1310 to:

   1310 PRINT @H,"SIMON FENSTER":
        PRINT@H+E,"   PROUDLY"

MAIN ROUTINES

150	Initializes.
200 - 450	Sets string variables.
470	Introduces the Walloons.
500 - 540	The Walloons make their entrance.
590 - 640	Flying Walloons perform.
700 - 720	Concludes Walloon's performance.
800 - 810	Displays final message.
900 - 970	Subroutines to draw (and erase) Walloons and their performing lever.
1200 - 1260	Subroutine for second Walloon's entrance.
1300 - 1390	Subroutine to display placard.
1400 - 1480	Subroutine to announce the performers.
1700 - 1800	Time delaying subroutines.

MAIN VARIABLES

A$-Z$	Various graphics strings.
D,E	Position increments for graphics displays.
L	Location of lever's left end.
H	Location of Walloon's head.
I,J,K	Loop indices.

SUGGESTED PROJECTS

1. There are many possibilities for "spicing up" the Walloons' act with extra tricks or improved ones. Perhaps you would like to change their finish to something less crude. To get you started, here are the changes to produce one alternate ending:

```
650 GOTO 730
730 GOSUB 940:H=H−D:GOSUB 910:GOSUB 940
740 PRINT@H,B$:PRINT@H+D,C$:PRINT@H,Y$
750 PRINT@H+D,Y$:PRINT@H,C$:PRINT@H,Y$
```

2. If you add some alternate tricks or endings as suggested in the previous project, try randomizing if and when they will be done. Thus, the Walloons' performance will be different each time the program is run. At least their ending may be variable.

3. Scour the world yourself for other acts to include in the TRS-80 Theatre. Maybe someday we will have a complete software library of performing artists.

Section 5
Mathematics Programs

INTRODUCTION TO MATHEMATICS PROGRAMS

Since their invention, computers have been used to solve mathematical problems. Their great speed and reliability render solvable many otherwise difficult (or impossible) calculations. Several different numerical techniques lend themselves naturally to computer solution. The following programs explore some of them. They will be of interest mainly to engineers, students, mathematicians, statisticians, and others who encounter such problems in their work.

GRAPH takes advantage of the TRS-80's graphic powers to draw the graph of a function $Y = f(X)$. The function is supplied by you. INTEGRATE calculates the integral, or "area under the curve," for any such function.

Experimental scientific work frequently results in data at discrete values of X and Y. CURVE finds a polynomial algebraic expression to express this data with a formula.

Theoretical scientists (and algebra students) often must find the solution to a set of simultaneous linear algebraic equations. SIMEQN does the trick.

Much modern engineering work requires the solution of differential equations. DIFFEQN will solve any first-order ordinary differential equation that you provide.

STATS will take a list of data and derive standard statistical information describing it. In addition, it will sort the data list into ranking numerical order.

CURVE

PURPOSE AND DISCUSSION

CURVE fits a polynomial function to a set of data. The data must be in the form of pairs of X-Y points. This type of data occurs frequently as the result of some experiment, or perhaps from sampling tabular data in a reference book.

There are many reasons why you might want an analytic formula to express the functional relationship inherent in the data. Often you will have experimental errors in the Y values. A good formula expression tends to smooth out these fluctuations. Perhaps you want to know the value of Y at some X not obtained exactly in the experiment. This may be a point between known X values (interpolation) or one outside the experimental range (extrapolation). If you wish to use the data in a computer program, a good formula is a convenient and efficient way to do it.

This program fits a curve of the form

$$Y = C_0 + C_1 X^1 + C_2 X^2 + \ldots + C_D X^D$$

to your data. You may select D, the degree (or power) of the highest term, to be as large as 9. The constant coefficients, $C_0 - C_D$, are the main output of the program. Also calculated is the goodness of fit, a guide to the accuracy of the fit. You may fit different degree polynomials to the same data and also ask to have Y calculated for specific values of X.

The numerical technique involved in the computation is known as least squares curve fitting. It minimizes the sum of the squares of the errors. The least squares method reduces the problem to a set of simultaneous algebraic equations. Thus these equations could be solved by the algorithm used in SIMEQN. In fact, once the proper equations are set up, CURVE uses the identical subroutine found in SIMEQN to solve the equations. For more information, the bibliography contains references to descriptions of the numerical technique.

HOW TO USE IT

The first thing you must do, of course, is enter the data into the program. This consists of typing in the pairs of numbers. Each pair represents an X value and its corresponding Y value. The two numbers (of each pair) are separated by a comma. A question mark will prompt you for each data pair. After you have entered them all, type

$$999,999$$

to signal the end of the data. When you do this, the program will respond by indicating how many data pairs have been entered. A maximum of 30 data pairs is allowed.

Next, you must input the degree of the polynomial to be fitted. This can be any non-negative integer subject to certain constraints. The maximum allowed is 4. Also, D must be less than the number of data pairs.

A few notes regarding the selection of D may be of interest. If D=0, the program will output the mean value of Y as the coefficient C_0. If D=1, the program will be calculating the best straight line through the data. This special case is known as "linear regression." If D is one less than the number of data pairs, the program will find an exact fit to the data (barring round-off and other numerical errors). This is a solution which passes exactly through each data point.

Once you have entered the desired degree, the program will begin calculating the results. There will be a pause while this calculation is performed. The time involved depends on the number of data pairs and the degree selected. For twenty data pairs and a second degree fit, the pause will be about fifteen seconds. Thirty data pairs and a fourth degree fit will take about forty-five seconds.

The results are displayed in a table. It gives the values of the coefficients for each power of X from 0 to D. That is, the values of C_0 - C_D are output. Also shown in the percent goodness of fit. This is a measure of how accurately the program was able to fit the given case. A value of 100 percent means perfect fit, lesser values indicate correspondingly poorer fits. It is hard to say what value denotes *satisfactory* fit since much depends on the accuracy of data and the purpose at hand. But as a rule of thumb, anything in the high nineties is quite good. For those interested, the formula to calculate the percent goodness of fit is

$$P.G.F = 100 * \sqrt{1 - \frac{\sum_i (Y_i - \hat{Y}_i)^2}{\sum_i (Y_i - \bar{Y})^2}}$$

where Y_i are the actual Y data values, $\hat{Y}_i$ are the calculated Y values (through the polynomial expression), and $\bar{Y}$ is the mean value of Y.

To continue the run, hit any key when requested to do so. Next, you are presented with three options for continuing the run. These are 1) determining specific points, 2) fitting another degree, 3) ending the program. Simply type 1, 2, or 3 to make your selection. A description of each choice now follows.

Option 1 allows you to see the value of Y that the current fit will produce for a given value of X. In this mode you are continually prompted to supply any value of X. The program then shows what the polynomial expression produces as the value for Y. Input 999 for an X value to leave this mode.

Option 2 allows you to fit another degree polynomial to the same data. Frequently, you will want to try successively higher values of D to improve the goodness of fit. Unless round-off errors occur, this will cause the percent goodness of fit to increase.

Option 3 simply terminates the program and with that we will terminate this explanation of how to use CURVE.

SAMPLE PROBLEM AND RUN

Problem: An art investor is considering the purchase of Primo's masterpiece, "Frosted Fantasy." Since 1940, the painting has been for sale at auction seven times. Here is the painting's sales record from these auctions.

Year	Price
1940	$ 8000.
1948	$13000.
1951	$16000.
1956	$20000.
1962	$28000.
1968	$39000.
1975	$53000.

The painting is going to be sold at auction in 1979. What price should the investor expect to have to pay to purchase the painting? If he resold it in 1983, how much profit should he expect to make?

Solution: The investor will try to get a polynomial function that expresses the value of the painting as a function of the year. This is suitable for CURVE. The year will be represented by the variable X, and the price is shown by the variable Y. To keep the magnitude of the numbers small, the years will be expressed as elapsed years since 1900, and the price will be in units of $1000. (Thus a year of 40 represents 1940, a price of 8 represents $8000.)

SAMPLE RUN

```
    - LEAST SQUARES CURVE FITTING -

ENTER A DATA PAIR IN RESPONSE TO EACH
QUESTION MARK. EACH PAIR IS AN X VALUE
AND A Y VALUE SEPARATED BY A COMMA.

AFTER ALL DATA IS ENTERED, TYPE
 999 , 999
IN RESPONSE TO THE LAST QUESTION MARK.

THE PROGRAM IS CURRENTLY SET TO ACCEPT
A MAXIMUM OF 3Ø DATA PAIRS.

X,Y=? 4Ø,8
X,Y=? 48,13
X,Y=? 51,16
X,Y=? 56,2Ø
X,Y=? 62,28
X,Y=? 68,39
```

```
X,Y=? 75,53
X,Y=? 999,999
 7 DATA PAIRS ENTERED
DEGREE OF POLYNOMIAL TO BE FITTED? 1

X POWER      COEFFICIENT
   0         -48.2707
   1          1.28724

PERCENT GOODNESS OF FIT= 97.5302
HIT ANY KEY TO CONTINUE

CONTINUATION OPTIONS

   1 - DETERMINE SPECIFIC POINTS
   2 - FIT ANOTHER DEGREE TO SAME DATA
   3 - END PROGRAM

WHAT NEXT? 2

DEGREE OF POLYNOMIAL TO BE FITTED? 2

X POWER      COEFFICIENT
   0          38.5297
   1         -1.83686
   2          .0270514

PERCENT GOODNESS OF FIT= 99.9486
               :
   (continuation options displayed again)
               :
WHAT NEXT? 1

ENTER 999 TO LEAVE THIS MODE

X=? 79
Y= 62.2451

X=? 83
Y= 72.427

X=? 999
                    :
   (continuation options displayed again)
                    :
WHAT NEXT? 3
READY.
```

Initially, a first degree fit was tried and a goodness of fit of about 97.5% was obtained. The investor wanted to do better, so he tried a second degree fit next. This had a very high goodness of fit. He then asked for the extrapolation of his data to the years 1979 and 1983. He found that he should expect to pay about $62250 to buy the painting in 1979. Around a $10000 profit could be expected upon resale in 1983.

Of course, the investor did not make his decision solely on the basis of this program. He used it only as one guide to his decision. There is never any guarantee that financial data will perform in the future as it has done in the past. Though CURVE is probably as good a way as any, extrapolation of data can never be a totally reliable process.

PROGRAM LISTING

```
100 REM: CURVE
110 REM: COPYRIGHT 1979 BY PHIL FELDMAN AND TOM RUGG
120 CLEAR 50
140 DEFINT I-L
150 MX=30
160 EF=999
170 MD=4
200 DIM X(MX),Y(MX)
210 Q=MD+1:DIM A(Q,Q),R(Q),V(Q)
220 Q=MD*2:DIM P(Q)
300 CLS:PRINT"   - LEAST SQUARES CURVE FITTING -":PRINT
310 PRINT"ENTER A DATA PAIR IN RESPONSE TO EACH"
320 PRINT"QUESTION MARK.  EACH PAIR IS AN X VALUE"
330 PRINT"AND A Y VALUE SEPARATED BY A COMMA.":PRINT
340 PRINT"AFTER ALL DATA IS ENTERED, TYPE"
350 PRINT EF;",";EF
360 PRINT"IN RESPONSE TO THE LAST QUESTION MARK.":PRINT
370 PRINT"THE PROGRAM IS CURRENTLY SET TO ACCEPT"
380 PRINT"A MAXIMUM OF";MX;"DATA PAIRS."
400 PRINT:J=0
410 J=J+1:INPUT"X,Y=";X(J),Y(J)
420 IF X(J)=EF AND Y(J)=EF THEN J=J-1:GOTO 450
430 IF J=MX THEN PRINT"** NO MORE DATA ALLOWED **":
    GOTO 450
440 GOTO 410
450 NP=J:PRINT
460 IF NP=0
    PRINT"** FATAL ERROR! ** -- NO DATA ENTERED":STOP
470 PRINT NP;"DATA PAIRS ENTERED"
```

```
500 PRINT:INPUT"DEGREE OF POLYNOMIAL TO BE FITTED";D:
    PRINT
510 IF D<0 PRINT"** ERROR! ** -- DEGREE MUST BE >= 0":
    GOTO 500
520 D=INT(D):IF D<NP THEN 540
530 PRINT"** ERROR! ** -- NOT ENOUGH DATA":GOTO 500
540 D2=2*D
550 IF D>MD PRINT"** ERROR! ** -- DEGREE TOO HIGH":
    GOTO 500
560 N=D+1
600 FOR J=1 TO D2:P(J)=0:FOR K=1 TO NP
610 P(J)=P(J)+X(K)^J:NEXT:NEXT::P(0)=NP
620 R(1)=0:FOR J=1 TO NP:R(1)=R(1)+Y(J)
630 NEXT:IF N=1 THEN 660
640 FOR J=2 TO N:R(J)=0:FOR K=1 TO NP
650 R(J)=R(J)+Y(K)*X(K)^(J-1):NEXT:NEXT
660 FOR J=1 TO N:FOR K=1 TO N:A(J,K)=P(J+K-2):NEXT:NEXT
670 GOSUB 2000
700 PRINT:PRINT"X POWER            COEFFICIENT"
710 FOR J=1 TO N:PRINT"  ";J-1,V(J):NEXT
720 Q=0:FOR J=1 TO NP:Q=Q+Y(J):NEXT:M=Q/NP:T=0:G=0
730 FOR J=1 TO NP:Q=0:FOR K=1 TO N:Q=Q+V(K)*X(J)^(K-1):
    NEXT
740 T=T+(Y(J)-Q)^2:G=G+(Y(J)-M)^2:NEXT
750 IF G=0 THEN T=100:GOTO 770
760 T=100*SQR(1-T/G)
770 PRINT:PRINT"PERCENT GOODNESS OF FIT=";T
780 PRINT:PRINT"HIT ANY KEY TO CONTINUE"
790 Q$=INKEY$:IF Q$="" THEN 790
800 PRINT:PRINT"CONTINUATION OPTIONS"
810 PRINT"  1 - DETERMINE SPECIFIC POINTS"
820 PRINT"  2 - FIT ANOTHER DEGREE TO SAME DATA"
830 PRINT"  3 - END PROGRAM"
840 INPUT"WHAT NEXT";Q:Q=INT(Q):IF Q=3 THEN END
850 IF Q=2 THEN 500
860 IF Q<>1 THEN 800
900 PRINT:PRINT"ENTER";EF;"TO LEAVE THIS MODE"
910 PRINT:INPUT"X=";XV:IF XV=EF THEN 800
920 YV=0:FOR K=1 TO N
930 YV=YV+V(K)*XV^(K-1):NEXT:PRINT"Y=";YV
940 GOTO 910
2000 IF N=1 THEN V(1)=R(1)/A(1,1):RETURN
2010 FOR K=1 TO N-1
2020 I=K+1
2030 L=K
```

```
2040 IF ABS(A(I,K))>ABS(A(L,K)) THEN L=I
2050 IF I<N THEN I=I+1:GOTO 2040
2060 IF L=K THEN 2100
2070 FOR J=K TO N:Q=A(K,J):A(K,J)=A(L,J)
2080 A(L,J)=Q:NEXT
2090 Q=R(K):R(K)=R(L):R(L)=Q
2100 I=K+1
2110 Q=A(I,K)/A(K,K):A(I,K)=0
2120 FOR J=K+1 TO N:A(I,J)=A(I,J)-Q*A(K,J):NEXT
2130 R(I)=R(I)-Q*R(K):IF I<N THEN I=I+1:GOTO 2110
2140 NEXT
2150 V(N)=R(N)/A(N,N):FOR I=N-1 TO 1 STEP -1
2160 Q=0:FOR J=I+1 TO N:Q=Q+A(I,J)*V(J)
2170 V(I)=(R(I)-Q)/A(I,I):NEXT:NEXT
2180 RETURN
```

EASY CHANGES

1. The program uses 999 as the flag number to terminate various input modes. This may cause a problem if your data include 999. You can easily change the flag number by modifying the value of EF in line 160 to any value not needed in your data. To use 10101, for example, make this change:

   160 EF=10101

2. The current dimensioning is set to accomodate a TRS-80 with 4K of RAM memory. If you have a 16K machine, you can handle well over 500 data pairs. To use up to 500 pairs, set the value of MX in line 150 appropriately:

   150 MX=500

3. A 16K machine will also allow you to use higher degree fits. To achieve up to tenth degree fits, set the value of MD appropriately:

   170 MD=10

   However, it must be stressed that it can be unreliable to attempt high degree fits. Unless your data is well behaved (X and Y values close to 1), the program will often not produce accurate results if D is greater than 5 or so. This is because sums of powers of X and Y are calculated up to powers of 2*D. These various sums are several orders of magnitude different than each other. Errors result because of the numerous truncation and round-off operations involved in doing arithmetic with them. A practical limit for MD is 7.

4. For some applications, significantly improved accuracy can be attained by using "double-precision" computation. This can be achieved by simply inserting the following line:

130 DEFDBL A-Z

MAIN ROUTINES

120 - 170	Initializes constants.
200 - 220	Dimensions arrays.
300 - 380	Displays introductory messages.
400 - 470	Gets X-Y input data from the user.
500 - 560	Gets degree of polynomial from the user, determines if it is acceptable.
600 - 670	Sets up equations for the simultaneous equation solver and calls it.
700 - 790	Calculates percent goodness of fit, displays all results.
800 - 860	Gets user's continuation option and branches to it.
900 - 940	Determines Y value corresponding to any X value.
2000 - 2180	Subroutine to solve simultaneous linear algebraic equations.

MAIN VARIABLES

MX	Maximum number of data pairs allowed.
MD	Maximum degree allowed to fit.
EF	Ending flag value for data input and X point mode.
X,Y	Arrays of X and Y data points.
NP	Number of data pairs entered.
D	Degree of polynomial to fit.
D2	2*D, the maximum power sum to compute.
N	D+1, number of simultaneous equations to solve.
A,R,V	Arrays for simultaneous linear equation solver.
P	Array for holding sums of various powers of X.
I,J,K,L	Loop indices.
Q,G	Work variables.
M	Mean value of Y.
T	Percent goodness of fit.

XV	Specific X point to calculate Y for.
YV	Y value corresponding to XV.
Q$	User input string.

SUGGESTED PROJECTS

1. No provision for modifying the data is incorporated into the program. Often it would be nice to add, subtract, or modify parts of the data after some results are seen. Build in a capability to do this.
2. You may desire other forms of output. A useful table for many applications might include the actual X values, calculated Y values, and/or percentage errors in Y.
3. Sometimes certain points (or certain regions of points) are known to be more accurate than others. Then you would like to weight these points as being more important than others to be fit correctly. The least squares method can be modified to include such a weighting parameter with each data pair. Research this technique and incorporate it into the program. (Note: you can achieve some weighting with the current program by entering important points two or more times. There is a certain danger in this, however, You must only ask for a solution with D less than the number of *unique* data points. A division by zero error may result otherwise.)
4. Often you wish to try successively higher degree polynomials until a certain minimum percent goodness of fit is obtained. Modify the program to accept a minimally satisfactory percent goodness of fit from the user. Then have the program automatically try various polynomial fits until it finds the lowest degree fit, if any, with a satisfactory goodness of fit.

DIFFEQN

PURPOSE

Differential equations express functions by giving the rate of change of one variable with respect to another. This type of relation occurs regularly in almost all the physical sciences. The solution of these equations is necessary in many practical engineering problems.

For many such equations, a closed form (or exact analytical expression) solution can be obtained. However, for just as many, no such "simple" solution exists. The equation must then be solved numerically, usually by a computer program such as this.

There are many types and classes of differential equations. This program solves those of a simple type; namely, first order, ordinary differential equations. This means the equation to be solved can be written in the form

$$\frac{dY}{dX} = \text{(any function of X,Y)}$$

Here, X is the independent variable and Y is the dependent variable. The equation expresses the derivative (or rate of change) of Y with respect to X. The right-hand-side is an expression which may involve X and/or Y.

To use the program, you must supply it with the differential equation to be solved. The procedure to do this is explained in the "How To Use It" section.

A technique known as the "fourth-order, Runge-Kutta" method is used to solve the equation. Space limitations prevent

any detailed explanation of it here. However, it is discussed well
in the numerical analysis books referenced in the bibliography.

The program allows two forms of output. You can have the
answers tabulated in columns or plotted graphically.

HOW TO USE IT

The first thing you must do is enter the differential equation
into the program. This must be done at line 3000. Currently
this line contains a GOTO statement. This GOTO will cause an
error message to be displayed if the program is run before you
have changed line 3000. The form of line 3000 should be:

3000 D = (your function of X,Y)

D represents dY/dX. GOSUBs are made to line 3000 with X and
Y set to their current values. Thus, when each RETURN is
made, D will be set to the appropriate value of dY/dX for that
given X and Y. If necessary, you may use the lines between
3000 and 3999 to complete the definition of D. Line 3999 already contains a RETURN statement so you do not need to add
another one.

The program begins by warning you that you should have
already entered the equation at line 3000. You acknowledge
that this has been done by hitting the C key to continue.

Now the various initial conditions are input. You are prompted
for them one at a time. They consist of: the initial values of X
and Y, the stepsize interval in X at which to display the output,
and the final value of X.

You now have a choice between two types of output. Enter a
T for tabular output or a G for graphical output. The tabular
form is simply a two column display of the corresponding values
of X and Y.

The graphical output plots the values of Y along a horizontal
axis as each corresponding X value is displayed on successive
lines of the screen. This graphical display requires you to input
the minimum and maximum values of Y that will be used on
the Y axis. You will be prompted for them if this output form
is chosen. An open circle is used to plot the value of Y. If, however, the value of Y is "off–scale," an asterisk is plotted at the
appropriate edge of the graph.

With the input phase completed, the program initializes things
to begin the output. A question mark will be displayed in the

lower left of the screen, telling you the program is waiting for you to hit any key to begin the output.

The output is displayed at each interval of the stepsize until the final value of X is reached. Output may temporarily be halted at any time by simply hitting any key. This will stop the display until you hit any key to resume the output. The output may be started and stopped as often as desired, thus enabling you to leisurely view intermediate results before they scroll off the screen. It is applicable to both the tabular and graphical forms of output.

SAMPLE PROBLEM AND RUN

Problem: A body, originally at rest, is subjected to a force of 2000 dynes. Its initial mass is 200 grams. However, while it moves, it loses mass at the rate of 1 gram/sec. There is also an air resistance equal to twice its velocity retarding its movement. The differential equation expressing this motion is:

$$\frac{dY}{dX} = \frac{(2000 - 2Y)}{(200 - X)} \quad \text{where Y=velocity (cm./sec.)}$$
$$\text{X=time (sec.)}$$

Find the velocity of the body every 10 seconds up through two minutes. Also, plot this velocity as a function of time.

Solution and Sample Run: The solution and sample run are illustrated in the accompanying photographs.

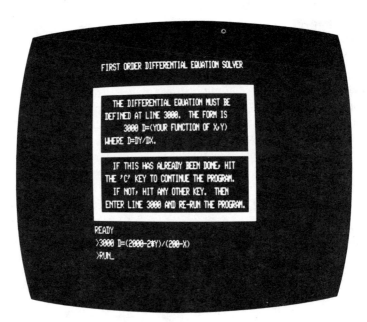

The operator hits a key to exit from the program. Then he enters the differential equation into line 3000. He types RUN to restart the program.

The operator has hit the "C" key. The program responds by beginning the input phase.

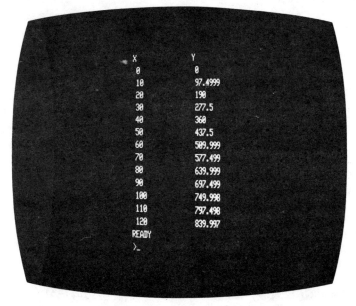

```
INITIAL VALUE OF X? 0
INITIAL VALUE OF Y? 0
STEPSIZE IN X? 10
FINAL VALUE OF X? 120
OUTPUT FORM (T=TABLE, G=GRAPH)? T
```

```
    THE FOLLOWING OUTPUT CAN BE HALTED BY HITTING
ANY KEY.  IT CAN THEN BE RESUMED BY HITTING ANY
KEY.  THIS MAY BE DONE AS OFTEN AS DESIRED.

    WHEN THE QUESTION MARK (?) APPEARS, HIT ANY
KEY TO BEGIN THE OUTPUT.
```

```
X              Y
?
```

The operator has completed the input and requested tabular output. The program signals with a question mark that it is waiting for him to hit any key. It will not continue the run until he does so.

```
     X              Y
     0              0
     10             97.4999
     20             190
     30             277.5
     40             360
     50             437.5
     60             509.999
     70             577.499
     80             639.999
     90             697.499
     100            749.998
     110            797.498
     120            839.997
     READY
     >_
```

The operator hits a key and the program responds with the tabulated output. X is time in seconds and Y is velocity in cm./sec.

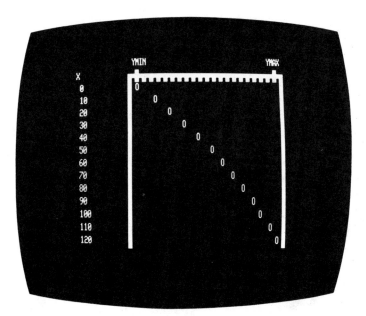

The program is rerun requesting graphical output. Before this photo, the program requested a minimum and maximum value of Y to use on the Y axis. Values of 0 and 850 respectively were entered. The program displays the desired graph.

PROGRAM LISTING

```
100 REM: DIFFEQN
110 REM: COPYRIGHT 1979 BY PHIL FELDMAN AND TOM RUGG
150 CLEAR 150
200 CLS:FOR J=1 TO 10:R$=INKEY$:NEXT
210 PRINT" FIRST ORDER DIFFERENTIAL EQUATION SOLVER"
220 PRINT@197,"THE DIFFERENTIAL EQUATION MUST BE"
230 PRINT@259,"DEFINED AT LINE 3000.  THE FORM IS"
240 PRINT@328,"3000 D=(YOUR FUNCTION OF X,Y)"
250 PRINT@387,"WHERE D=DY/DX."
260 PRINT@517,"IF THIS HAS ALREADY BEEN DONE, HIT"
270 PRINT@579,"THE ´C´ KEY TO CONTINUE THE PROGRAM."
280 PRINT@645,"IF NOT, HIT ANY OTHER KEY.  THEN"
290 PRINT@707,"ENTER LINE 3000 AND RE-RUN THE PROGRAM."
300 PRINT@130,STRING$(41,143);:B$=STRING$(2,191)
310 FOR J=128 TO 768 STEP 64:PRINT@J,B$;:NEXT
320 PRINT@450,STRING$(41,140);:FOR J=171 TO 747 STEP 64
330 PRINT@J,B$;:NEXT:PRINT@768,STRING$(45,143)
400 R$=INKEY$:IF R$="" THEN 400
410 IF R$<>"C" THEN END
```

```
420 INPUT"INITIAL VALUE OF X";XX
430 INPUT"INITIAL VALUE OF Y";YY:Y=YY:X=XX:GOSUB 3000
440 INPUT"STEPSIZE IN X";DX:INPUT"FINAL VALUE OF X";XF
450 INPUT"OUTPUT FORM (T=TABLE, G=GRAPH)";F$
460 F$=LEFT$(F$,1):IF F$<>"T" AND F$<>"G" THEN 450
470 IF F$="T" THEN 600
480 INPUT"MINIMUM Y FOR THE GRAPH AXIS";YL
490 INPUT"MAXIMUM Y FOR THE GRAPH AXIS";YH
500 IF YH>YL THEN 600
510 PRINT"*** ERROR! -- MAX Y MUST BE > MIN Y ***"
520 GOTO 480
600 PRINT:PRINT STRING$(50,45)
610 PRINT"    THE FOLLOWING OUTPUT CAN
    BE HALTED BY HITTING"
620 PRINT"ANY KEY.  IT CAN THEN BE RESUMED BY
    HITTING ANY"
630 PRINT"KEY.  THIS MAY BE DONE AS OFTEN AS DESIRED.":
    PRINT
640 PRINT"    WHEN THE
    QUESTION MARK (?) APPEARS, HIT ANY"
650 PRINT"KEY TO BEGIN THE OUTPUT.":
    PRINT STRING$(50,45)
700 IF F$="T" THEN PRINT "X","Y":GOTO 800
710 PRINT TAB(14);"YMIN=";YL;TAB(45);"YMAX=";YH
720 PRINT:PRINT TAB(15);"YMIN";TAB(54);"YMAX"
730 B$=CHR$(188):C$=CHR$(140):D$=CHR$(191):E$=B$+C$+D$
740 FOR J=1 TO 19:E$=E$+C$+B$:NEXT:E$=E$+C$+D$+C$+B$
750 PRINT "X";TAB(14);E$
800 PRINT"?";
810 R$=INKEY$:IF R$="" THEN 810
820 PRINT CHR$(24);CHR$(32);CHR$(24);
830 GOSUB 1500
900 Q=XX+DX:IF Q>XF+1.E-5 THEN END
910 X=XX:Y=YY:GOSUB 3000:K0=D:X=XX+DX/2:Y=YY+K0*DX/2
920 GOSUB 3000:K1=D:Y=YY+K1*DX/2:GOSUB 3000:K2=D
930 X=XX+DX:Y=YY+K2*DX:GOSUB 3000:K3=D
940 DY=DX*(K0+2*K1+2*K2+K3)/6
950 YY=YY+DY:XX=XX+DX:GOSUB 1500
960 GOTO 900
1000 PRINT:
     PRINT"*** ERROR! -- YOU HAVE NOT DEFINED THE"
1010 PRINT"    DIFFERENTIAL EQUATION IN LINE 3000."
1020 PRINT
1030 END
1500 IF F$="T" THEN PRINT XX,YY:GOSUB 1600:RETURN
```

```
1510 F=(YY-YL)/(YH-YL):V=INT(16+40*F+0.5)
1520 C=79:IF V<16 THEN V=16:C=42
1530 IF V>56 THEN V=56:C=42
1540 PRINT XX;TAB(14);D$;TAB(V);CHR$(C);TAB(58);D$
1550 GOSUB 1600:RETURN
1600 R$=INKEY$:IF R$="" THEN RETURN
1610 R$=INKEY$:IF R$="" THEN 1610
1620 RETURN
2900 REM
2910 REM ****************************************************
2920 REM * THE DIFFERENTIAL EQUATION MUST BE DEFINED *
2930 REM * BETWEEN LINES 3000 AND 3999.              *
2940 REM *                                           *
2950 REM * LINE 3000 MUST BE OVERWRITTEN, MAKING IT  *
2960 REM * THE FIRST LINE OF THE EQUATION.           *
2970 REM ****************************************************
2980 REM
3000 GOTO 1000:
     REM MAKE THIS LINE D=(YOUR FUNCTION OF X,Y)
3999 RETURN
```

EASY CHANGES

1. If you have already entered the differential equation and
   wish to skip the introductory output, add this line:

                    205 GOTO 420

   This will immediately begin the input dialog.
2. If you wish to use negative stepsizes, line 900 must be
   changed to:

         900 Q=XX+DX:IF Q<XF−1.E−5 THEN END

MAIN ROUTINES

200 - 330	Displays initial messages.
400 - 520	Gets user's inputs.
600 - 650	Displays additional messages.
700 - 750	Initializes output display.
800 - 830	Waits for user to hit a key to start the output.
900 - 960	Computes each step.
1000 - 1030	Error message.
1500 - 1550	Plots graphical output.
1600 - 1620	Stops and starts output.
3000 - 3999	User supplied routine to define D.

MAIN VARIABLES

D	Value of dY/dX.
X,Y	Values of X,Y on current step.
XX,YY	Values of X,Y on last step.
DX	Stepsize in X.
XF	Final value of X.
F$	Output flag string (T=table, G=graph).
YL,YH	Minimum, maximum values of Y plot axis.
F	Fractional distance of graphical point along Y axis.
V	Tab position for graphical output.
C	CHR$ argument for graphical output.
K0,K1,	Runge-Kutta coefficients.
K2,K3	
R$	User entered string.
Q	Work variable.
J	Loop index.
B$,C$	Graphical format strings.
D$,E$	

SUGGESTED PROJECTS

1. Modify the program to display the tabular output followed by the graphical output. During the tabular phase, the minimum and maximum values of Y can be saved and automatically used as the plot limits for the graphical output.
2. The value of dY/dX as a function of X is often a useful quantity to know. Modify the program to add it to the columnar display and/or the graphical display.
3. The inherent error in the calculation depends on the stepsize chosen. Most cases should be run with different stepsizes to insure the errors are not large. If the answers do not change much, you can be reasonably certain that your solutions are accurate. Better yet, techniques exist to vary the stepsize during the calculation to insure the error is sufficiently small during each step. Research these methods and incorporate them into the program.
4. The program can be easily broadened to solve a set of coupled, first order, differential equations simultaneously. This would greatly increase the types of problems that could be solved. Research this procedure and expand the program to handle it.

GRAPH

PURPOSE

Is a picture worth a thousand words? In the case of mathematical functions, the answer is often "yes." A picture, i.e. a graph, enables you to see the important behavior of a function quickly and accurately. Trends, minima, maxima, etc. become easy and convenient to determine.

GRAPH produces a two-dimensional plot of a function that you supply. The function must be in the form Y = (any function of X). The independent variable X will be plotted along the abscissa (horizontal axis). The dependent variable Y will be plotted along the ordinate (vertical axis). You have complete control over the scaling that is used on the X and Y axes.

HOW TO USE IT

Before running the program, you must enter into it the function to be plotted. This is done as a subroutine beginning at line 5000. It must define Y as a function of X. The subroutine will be called with X set to various values. It must then set the variable Y to the correct corresponding value. The subroutine may be as simple or as complex as necessary to define the function. It can take one line or several hundred lines. Line 5999 is already set as a RETURN statement, so you need not add another one.

Having entered this subroutine, you are ready to run the program. The program begins by warning you that it assumes the function has already been entered at line 5000. It will then ask you for the domain of X, i.e. the lowest and highest values of X that you wish to have plotted. Values can be positive or negative as long as the highest value is actually larger than the lowest one.

Now you must choose the scale for Y. To do this intelligently, you probably need to know the minimum and maximum values of Y over the domain of X selected. The program finds these values and displays them for you. You must then choose the minimum and maximum values you wish to have on the Y scale. Again, any two values are acceptable as long as the maximum scale value of Y is larger than the minimum scale value of Y.

The program will now display the plot of your function. Each axis is forty characters long, with the origin defined as the minimum scale values of both X and Y. Twenty tick marks appear on each axis. The minimum, middle, and maximum values on each scale are displayed appropriately.

If a value for Y should be off-scale, an asterisk will be displayed at the appropriate value of X. If the actual value of Y is too large, it will be plotted at the maximum Y value. Similarly, it will be drawn at the minimum Y value if it is too low.

Some plots have open circles plotted along the X axis. These correspond to points whose Y values are equal to the value of Y along the X axis.

After the plot is drawn, the program will tell you to hit any key to continue. When you do so, information about the plot scaling is provided. For both X and Y, you are given the minimum, mid, and maximum values on each axis.

You now have the option of hitting G to draw the graph again or any other key to terminate the program.

GRAPH   207

SAMPLE RUN

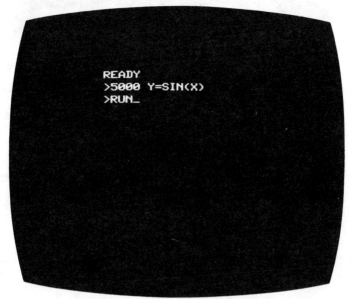

After loading the program, the operator enters line 5000 to request the graph Y=SIN(X). RUN is typed to begin the program.

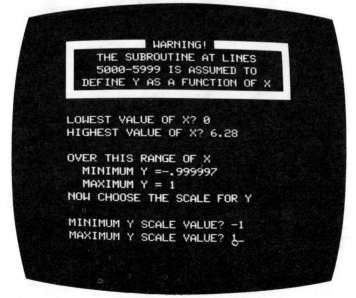

The input dialog transpires. The operator asks that the domain of X be 0-6.28. The program responds by showing the maximum and minimum value of Y over this domain. The operator chooses an appropriate scale for the Y axis.

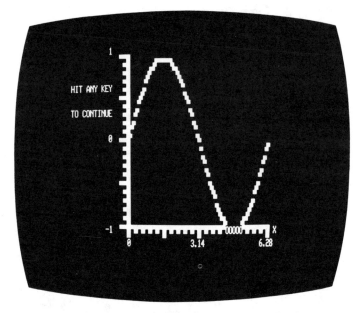

The graph is displayed as requested. The program waits for the operator to hit any key to continue.

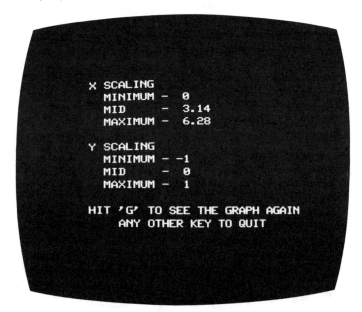

Relevant scaling information is shown. By pressing "G", the operator can see the graph again.

GRAPH 209

PROGRAM LISTING

```
100 REM: GRAPH
110 REM: COPYRIGHT 1979 BY PHIL FELDMAN AND TOM RUGG
120 CLEAR 50:A$=CHR$(191):B$=CHR$(143):C$=CHR$(179)
130 H$=CHR$(131):M$=CHR$(140):L$=CHR$(176):F$="*":
    X$="0"
200 CLS:PRINT CHR$(23);TAB(11);"G R A P H":PRINT
210 GOSUB 1000:PRINT
220 PRINT:INPUT"LOWEST VALUE OF X";XL
230 INPUT"HIGHEST VALUE OF X";XU
240 IF XU<=XL THEN PRINT:PRINT"   -- BAD X RANGE --":
    GOTO 220
250 GOSUB 800:GOSUB 300:GOSUB 500
260 GOSUB 900:CLS:END
300 CLS:FOR J=80 TO 912 STEP 64:PRINT@J,A$;:NEXT
310 FOR J=913 TO 952:PRINT@J,H$;:NEXT:
    PRINT@14,L$;L$;L$;
320 FOR J=79 TO 719 STEP 128:PRINT@J,M$;:PRINT@J+64,C$;
330 NEXT:PRINT@847,M$;:PRINT@270,H$;:PRINT@462,M$;
340 PRINT@654,L$;:PRINT@910,H$;H$;:
    FOR J=914 TO 952 STEP 2
350 PRINT@J,B$;:NEXT:FOR J=922 TO 952 STEP 10:
    PRINT@J,A$;:NEXT
360 PRINT@12,"Y";:PRINT@954,"X";
370 XM=(XL+XU)/2:YM=(YL+YU)/2:Q=LEN(STR$(YU))
380 PRINT@12-Q,YU;:Q=LEN(STR$(YM)):PRINT@460-Q,YM;
390 Q=LEN(STR$(YL)):PRINT@908-Q,YL;:Q=LEN(STR$(XL))/2
400 PRINT@976-Q,XL;:Q=LEN(STR$(XM))/2:PRINT@996-Q,XM;
410 Q=LEN(STR$(XU))/2:PRINT@1016-Q,XU;:RETURN
500 DX=(XU-XL)/80:DY=(YU-YL)/40:FOR J=0 TO 80
510 X=XL+DX*(J):XP=32+J:GOSUB 700
520 IF F=1 THEN PRINT@912+J/2,F$;:GOTO 560
530 IF F=2 THEN PRINT@16+J/2,F$;:GOTO 560
540 IF F=3 THEN PRINT@912+J/2,X$;:GOTO 560
550 SET(XP,YP):SET(XP+1,YP)
560 NEXT
570 PRINT@193,"HIT ANY KEY";:PRINT@321,"TO CONTINUE";
580 Q$=INKEY$:IF Q$="" THEN 580
590 RETURN
700 GOSUB 5000:V=(Y-YL)/DY:D=INT(V)
710 IF Y<YL THEN F=1:RETURN
720 IF Y>YU THEN F=2:RETURN
730 IF D=0 THEN F=3:RETURN
740 F=0:YP=42-D:RETURN
```

```
800 DX=(XU-XL)/80:X=XL:GOSUB 5000:MN=Y:MX=Y:
    FOR J=1 TO 80
810 X=XL+DX*J:GOSUB 5000:IF Y>MX THEN MX=Y
820 IF Y<MN THEN MN=Y
830 NEXT
840 PRINT:PRINT"OVER THIS RANGE OF X":
    PRINT" MINIMUM Y =";MN
850 PRINT" MAXIMUM Y =";MX:
    PRINT"NOW CHOOSE THE SCALE FOR Y"
860 PRINT:INPUT"MINIMUM Y SCALE VALUE";YL
870 INPUT"MAXIMUM Y SCALE VALUE";YU:
    IF YU>YL THEN RETURN
880 PRINT:PRINT" -- BAD Y SCALING --":GOTO 840
900 CLS:PRINT CHR$(23);"X SCALING":
    PRINT" MINIMUM - ";XL
910 PRINT" MID     - ";XM:PRINT" MAXIMUM - ";XU:
    PRINT
920 PRINT"Y SCALING":PRINT" MINIMUM - ";YL
930 PRINT" MID     - ";YM:PRINT" MAXIMUM - ";YU:
    PRINT
940 PRINT"HIT 'G' TO SEE THE GRAPH AGAIN"
950 PRINT"    ANY OTHER KEY TO QUIT"
960 Q$=INKEY$:IF Q$="" THEN 960
970 IF Q$="G" THEN GOSUB 300:GOSUB 500
980 RETURN
1000 PRINT@128,A$;:FOR J=130 TO 148:PRINT@J,B$;:NEXT
1010 PRINT@152,"WARNING!";:FOR J=170 TO 188:
     PRINT@J,B$:NEXT
1020 PRINT@190,A$;:PRINT@200,"THE SUBROUTINE AT LINES";
1030 PRINT@264,"5000-5999 IS ASSUMED TO";
1040 PRINT@324,"DEFINE Y AS A FUNCTION OF X";
1050 FOR J=192 TO 320 STEP 64:PRINT@J,A$;:K=J+62:
     PRINT@K,A$;
1060 NEXT:PRINT@384,B$;:PRINT@446,B$;:FOR J=386 TO 444
1070 PRINT@J,B$;:NEXT:RETURN
4950 REM
4960 REM ***********************************************
4970 REM *    SUBROUTINE AT LINE 5000 MUST BE SET    *
4980 REM ***********************************************
4990 REM
5000 REM *** Y=F(X) GOES HERE  ***
5999 RETURN
```

GRAPH

211

EASY CHANGES

1. You may want the program to self-scale the Y axis for you. That is, you want it to use the minimum and maximum Y values that it finds as the limits on the Y axis. This can be accomplished by adding the following line:

> 833 IF MX<=MN THEN 840
> 835 YU=MX:YL=MN:RETURN

2. Do you sometimes forget to enter the subroutine at line 5000 despite the introductory warning? As is, the program will plot the straight line Y=0 if you do this. If you want a more drastic reaction to prevent this, change line 5000 to read

> 5000 Y=1/0

Now, if you don't enter the actual subroutine desired, the program will stop and print the following message after you enter the X scaling values.

> ?/0 ERROR IN 5000

MAIN ROUTINES

120 - 130	Initializes constants.
200 - 210	Displays introductory warning.
220 - 260	Mainline routine–gets X scaling from user and calls various subroutines.
300 - 410	Subroutines to draw graph axes and scale labeling.
500 - 590	Subroutine to plot the function.
700 - 740	Subroutine to determine the plotting position for Y.
800 - 880	Subroutine which determines the minimum, maximum Y values; gets Y scale from user.
900 - 980	Subroutine which displays the scaling parameters, asks user if he wants the graph re-plotted.
1000 - 1070	Subroutines to display the introductory warning.
5000 - 5999	User supplied subroutine to evaluate Y as a function of X.

MAIN VARIABLES

XL,XM, XU	Lower, middle, upper scale values of X.
YL,YM, YU	Lower, middle, upper scale values of Y.

DX,DY	Scale increments of X,Y.
X,Y	Current values of X,Y.
XP,YP	Plot position of X,Y point.
A$,B$,C$,	Strings used in messages, graph axes, and scale
H$,M$,L$	labeling.
F$	Off-axis character string.
X$	X-axis character string.
Q	Axis number string length.
F	Special plot character flag (1=Y too high, 2=Y too low, 3=Y on X axis).
V	Value of X or Y in scale units.
D	Integer value of V.
MN,MX	Minimum, maximum values of Y.
Q$	User reply string.
J	Loop index.

SUGGESTED PROJECTS

1. Determine and display the values of X at which the minimum and maximum values of Y occur.
2. After the graph is plotted, allow the user to obtain the exact value of Y for any given X.
3. Expand the graph to a 30 character width in the X direction.

INTEGRATE

PURPOSE AND DEFINITION

The need to evaluate integrals occurs frequently in much scientific and mathematical work. This program will numerically integrate a function that you supply using a technique known as Simpson's rule. It will continue to grind out successive approximations of the integral until you are satisfied with the accuracy of the solution.

Mathmetical integration will probably be a familiar term to those who have studied some higher mathematics. It is a fundamental subject of second-year calculus. The integral of a function between the limits $x=\ell$ (lower limit) and $x=u$ (upper limit) represents the area under its curve; i.e. the shaded area in Figure 1.

We may approximate the integral by first dividing up the area into rectangular strips or segments. We can get a good estimate of the total integral by summing the areas of these segments by using a parabolic fit across the top. For those who understand some mathematical theory, Simpson's rule may be expressed as

$$\int_{x=\ell}^{x=u} f(x)\, dx \cong \frac{\Delta}{3} \left\{ f(\ell) + f(u) \right.$$

$$\left. + 4 \sum_{j=1}^{N/2} f[\ell + \Delta(2j-1)] + 2 \sum_{j=1}^{(N-2)/2} f[\ell + 2\Delta j] \right\}$$

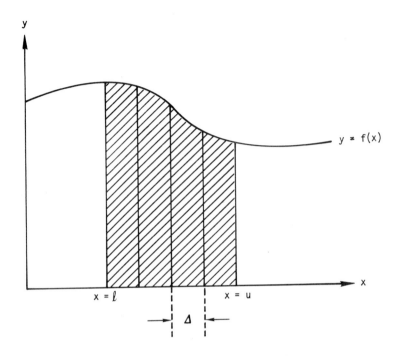

Figure 1. The Integral of f(x)

Here N is the number of segments into which the total interval is divided. N is 4 in the diagram.

For a good discussion of the numerical evaluation of integrals see: McCracken, Dorn, *Numerical Methods and Fortran Programming*, New York, Wiley, 1964,pp.160. Don't let the word "Fortran" scare you away. The discussions in the book are independent of programming language with only some program examples written in Fortran.

HOW TO USE IT

The program begins with a warning! This is to remind you that you should have already entered the subroutine to evaluate Y as a function of X. This subroutine must start at line 5000. More about it shortly.

You will then be asked to provide the lower and upper limits of the integration domain. Any numerical values are acceptable.

It is not even necessary that the lower limit of X be smaller than the upper one.

The program will now begin displaying its numerical evaluations of the integral. The number of segments used in the calculation continually doubles. This causes the accuracy of the integral to increase at the expense of additional computation time. For most functions, you should see the value of the integral converging quickly to a constant (or near constant) value. This, of course, will be the best numerical evaluation of the integral at hand.

When you are satisfied with the accuracy of the solution, you must hit the **BREAK** key to terminate the program. If not, the program will run forever (assuming you can pay the electric bills). The amount of computation is approximately doubled each step. This means it will take the computer about the same amount of time to compute the next step that it took to compute *all* the previous steps. Thus, it will soon be taking the TRS-80 hours, days, and weeks to compute steps. Eventually, round-off errors begin degrading the results, causing a nice, constant, converged solution to change. However, the high precision of the computer's floating point arithmetic will postpone this for quite a while. You will probably lose patience before seeing it.

The function to be integrated can be as simple or as complicated as you desire. It may take one line or a few hundred lines of code. In any case, the subroutine to express it must start at line 5000. This subroutine will be continually called with the variable X set. When it returns, it should have set the variable Y to the corresponding value of the function for the given X. The subroutine must be able to evaluate the function at any value of X between the lower and upper bounds of the integration domain.

If your function consists of experimental data at discrete values of X, you must do something to enable the subroutine to evaluate the function at intermediate values of X. We recommend one of two approaches. First, you could write the subroutine to linearly interpolate the value of Y between the appropriate values of X. This will involve searching your data table for the pair of experimental X values that bound the value of X where the function is to be evaluated. Secondly, the program CURVE presented elsewhere in this section can produce an approximate polynomial expression to fit your experimental data. This expression can then be easily entered as the subroutine at line 5000.

By the way, Simpson's rule is *exact* for any polynomial of degree 3 or less. This means that if the function can be written in the form

$$Y = A*X\uparrow3 + B*X\uparrow2 + C*X + D$$

where A, B, C, D are constants, the program will calculate the integral exactly even with only two segments.

SAMPLE RUN

The sample run illustrates the following integration

$$\int_{x=0}^{x=1} \frac{4}{1+x^2} \, dx$$

This integral has the theoretical value of π (pi) as the correct answer! Pi, as you may know, has the value 3.1415926535. . . Before the run in started, the above function is entered at line 5000.

```
5000  Y=4/(1+X*X)
RUN
```

```
        INTEGRAL BY SIMPSON'S RULE

  ┌──────────── WARNING! ────────────┐
  │                                   │
  │   THE  SUBROUTINE  AT  LINES      │
  │                                   │
  │   5000-5999  IS  ASSUMED  TO  DEFINE │
  │                                   │
  │       Y  AS  A  FUNCTION  OF  X   │
  └───────────────────────────────────┘

LOWER  LIMIT  OF  X?  0

UPPER  LIMIT  OF  X?  1
```

# SEGMENTS	INTEGRAL
2	3.13333
4	3.14157
8	3.14159
16	3.14159
32	3.14159
64	3.14159
128	3.14159

(BREAK key pressed)

PROGRAM LISTING

```
100 REM: INTEGRATE
110 REM: COPYRIGHT 1979 BY PHIL FELDMAN AND TOM RUGG
150 CLEAR 200:DEFINT J,M,N
160 N=2
200 V$=STRING$(11,131)
210 L$=CHR$(149)
220 R$=CHR$(170)
230 CLS
240 PRINT CHR$(196);"INTEGRAL BY SIMPSON'S RULE":PRINT
250 PRINT CHR$(151)+V$+" WARNING! "+V$+CHR$(171)
260 PRINT L$+"      THE SUBROUTINE AT LINES     "+R$
270 PRINT L$+" 5000-5999 IS ASSUMED TO DEFINE "+R$
280 PRINT L$+"      Y AS A FUNCTION OF X       "+R$
290 PRINT CHR$(141)+STRING$(32,140)+CHR$(142)
300 INPUT"LOWER LIMIT OF X";L
310 INPUT"UPPER LIMIT OF X";U
360 PRINT
380 PRINT"# SEGMENTS","INTEGRAL"
400 DX=(U-L)/N:T=0
410 X=L:GOSUB 5000:T=T+Y
420 X=U:GOSUB 5000:T=T+Y
450 M=N/2:Z=0
460 FOR J=1 TO M
470 X=L+DX*(2*J-1):GOSUB 5000:Z=Z+Y
480 NEXT:T=T+4*Z
500 M=M-1:IF M=0 THEN 600
510 Z=0:FOR J=1 TO M
520 X=L+DX*2*J:GOSUB 5000:Z=Z+Y
530 NEXT:T=T+2*Z
600 A=DX*T/3
610 PRINT N,A
```

```
620 N=N*2
630 GOTO 400
4970 REM
4980 REM *** ENTER SUBROUTINE AT LINE 5000 ***
4990 REM
5000 REM ***** Y=F(X) GOES HERE *****
5999 RETURN
```

EASY CHANGES

1. You might want the program to stop calculation after the integral has been evaluated for a given number of segments. Adding the following line will cause the program to stop after the integral is evaluated for a number of segments greater than or equal to 100.

615 IF N>=100 THEN END

Of course, you may use any value you wish instead of 100.

2. Perhaps you would like to see the number of segments change at a different rate during the course of the calculation. This can be done by modifying line 620. To increase the rate of change, try

620 N=N*4

To change it at a constant (and slower) rate, try

620 N=N+50

Be sure, however, that the value of N is always even.

3. Take advantage of TRS-80 Basic's double-precision to compute the results to a high degree of accuracy. Simply change line 150 to:

150 CLEAR 200:DEFDBL A-Z:DEFINT J,M,N

How long does it take to compute Pi to 15 correct decimal digits?

MAIN ROUTINES

150 - 160	Initializes constants.
200 - 290	Displays introductory messages and warning.
300 - 310	Gets integration limits from operator.
360 - 380	Displays column headings.

400 - 420	Computes integral contribution from end points.
450 - 480	Adds contribution from one summation.
500 - 530	Adds contribution from other summation.
600 - 630	Completes integral calculation and displays it. Increases number of segments and restarts calculation.
5000 - 5999	Operator supplied subroutine to evaluate f(x).

MAIN VARIABLES

N	Number of segments.
J	Loop index.
L,U	Lower, Upper integration limit of x.
DX	Width of one segment.
T	Partial result of integral.
M	Number of summations.
Z	Subtotal of summations.
A	Value of integral.
X	Current value of x.
Y	Current value of the function y=f(x).
V\$,L\$,R\$	Strings used in messages.

SUGGESTED PROJECTS

1. Research other similar techniques for numerical integration such as the simpler trapezoid rule. Then add a column of output computing the integral with this new method. Compare how the two methods converge toward the (hopefully) correct answer.

SIMEQN

PURPOSE

This program solves a set of simultaneous linear algebraic equations. This type of problem often arises in scientific and numerical work. Algebra students encounter them regularly —many "word" problems can be solved by constructing the proper set of simultaneous equations.

A TRS-80 with 4K of memory can handle upwards of fifteen equations in fifteen unknowns. This should prove more than sufficient for any practical application. A 16K system can handle many more if, somehow, this should ever be necessary.

The equations to be solved can be written mathematically as follows:

$$A_{11}X_1 + A_{12}X_2 + \ldots + A_{1N}X_N = R_1$$
$$A_{21}X_1 + A_{22}X_2 + \ldots + A_{2N}X_N = R_2$$
$$\vdots \qquad \vdots \qquad \qquad \vdots \qquad \vdots$$
$$A_{N1}X_1 + A_{N2}X_2 + \ldots + A_{NN}X_N = R_N$$

N is the number of equations and thus the number of unknowns also. The unknowns are denoted X_1 through X_N.

Each equation contains a coefficient multiplier for each unknown and a right-hand-side term. These coefficients (the A matrix) and the right-hand-sides (R_1 through R_N) must be constants—positive, negative, or zero. The A matrix is denoted with double subscripts. The first subscript is the equation number and the second one is the unknown that the coefficient multiplies.

HOW TO USE IT

The program will prompt you for all necessary inputs. First, it asks how many equations (and thus how many unknowns) comprise your set. This number must be at least 1. If it is too large, a OM or BS error will immediately result.

Next, you must enter the coefficients and right-handsides for each equation. The program will request these one at a time, continually indicating which term it is expecting next.

Once it has all your inputs, the program begins calculating the solution. This may take a little while if the value of N is high. The program ends by displaying the answers. These, of course, are the values of each of the unknowns, X_1 through X_N.

If you are interested, the numerical technique used to solve the equations is known as Gaussian elimination. Row interchange to achieve pivotal condensation is employed. (This keeps maximum significance in the numbers.) Then back substitution is used to arrive at the final results. This technique is much simpler than it sounds and is described well in the numerical analysis books referenced in the bibliography.

SAMPLE PROBLEM AND RUN

Problem: A painter has a large supply of three different colors of paint: dark green, light green, and pure blue. The dark green is 30% blue pigment, 20% yellow pigment, and the rest base. The light green is 10% blue pigment, 35% yellow pigment, and the rest base. The pure blue is 90% blue pigment, no yellow pigment, and the rest base. The painter, however, needs a medium green to be composed of 25% blue pigment, 25% yellow pigment, and the rest base. In what percentages should he mix his three paints to achieve this mixture?

Solution: Let X_1 = percent of dark green to use,

X_2 = percent of light green to use,

X_3 = percent of pure blue to use.

The problem leads to these three simultaneous equations to solve:

$$0.3 X_1 + 0.1\ X_2 + 0.9 X_3 = 0.25$$
$$0.2 X_1 + 0.35 X_2 \qquad\quad = 0.25$$
$$X_1 + \qquad X_2 + \qquad X_3 = 1.0$$

The first equation expresses the amount of blue pigment in the mixture. The second equation is for the yellow pigment. The third equation states that the mixture is composed entirely of the three given paints. (Note that all percentages are expressed as numbers from 0-1.) The problem leads to the following use of SIMEQN.

SAMPLE RUN

```
A SIMULTANEOUS LINEAR EQUATION SOLVER
HOW MANY EQUATIONS IN THE SET? 3
THE 3   UNKNOWNS WILL BE DENOTED
X1 THROUGH X3
-----------------------------------
ENTER THE PARAMETERS FOR EQUATION 1

COEFFICIENT OF X1? .3
COEFFICIENT OF X2? .1
COEFFICIENT OF X3? .9
RIGHT HAND SIDE? .25
-----------------------------------
ENTER THE PARAMETERS FOR EQUATION 2

COEFFICIENT OF X1? .2
COEFFICIENT OF X2? .35
COEFFICIENT OF X3? 0
RIGHT HAND SIDE? .25
-----------------------------------
ENTER THE PARAMETERS FOR EQUATION 3

COEFFICIENT OF X1? 1
COEFFICIENT OF X2? 1
COEFFICIENT OF X3? 1
RIGHT HAND SIDE? 1
-----------------------------------
THE SOLUTION IS
  X1= .55
  X2= .4
  X3= .05

READY.
```

Thus, the painter should use a mixture of 55% dark green, 40% light green, and 5% pure blue.

PROGRAM LISTING

```
100 REM: SIMEQN
110 REM: COPYRIGHT 1979 BY PHIL FELDMAN AND TOM RUGG
150 CLEAR 50:DEFINT I,J,K,L,N
200 CLS
210 PRINT"A SIMULTANEOUS LINEAR EQUATION SOLVER"
220 PRINT
300 INPUT"HOW MANY EQUATIONS IN THE SET";N
310 IF N>0 THEN 330
320 PRINT"** ERROR! ** THERE MUST BE AT LEAST 1":
    GOTO 300
330 DIM A(N,N),R(N),V(N)
340 PRINT"THE";N;"UNKNOWNS WILL BE DENOTED"
350 PRINT"X1 THROUGH X"MID$(STR$(N),2,10)
360 GOSUB 900:FOR J=1 TO N
370 PRINT"ENTER THE PARAMETERS FOR EQUATION";J
380 PRINT:FOR K=1 TO N
390 PRINT"COEFFICIENT OF X";MID$(STR$(K),2,10);
400 INPUT A(J,K):NEXT
410 INPUT"RIGHT HAND SIDE";R(J)
420 GOSUB 900:NEXT
430 GOSUB 2000
500 PRINT"THE SOLUTION IS":PRINT
510 FOR J=1 TO N
520 PRINT"  X";MID$(STR$(J),2,10);"=";V(J)
530 NEXT:END
900 PRINT STRING$(35,"-")
910 RETURN
2000 IF N=1 THEN V(1)=R(1)/A(1,1):RETURN
2010 FOR K=1 TO N-1
2020 I=K+1
2030 L=K
2040 IF ABS(A(I,K))>ABS(A(L,K)) THEN L=I
2050 IF I<N THEN I=I+1:GOTO 2040
2060 IF L=K THEN 2100
2070 FOR J=K TO N:Q=A(K,J):A(K,J)=A(L,J)
2080 A(L,J)=Q:NEXT
2090 Q=R(K):R(K)=R(L):R(L)=Q
2100 I=K+1
2110 Q=A(I,K)/A(K,K):A(I,K)=0
2120 FOR J=K+1 TO N:A(I,J)=A(I,J)-Q*A(K,J):NEXT
2130 R(I)=R(I)-Q*R(K):IF I<N THEN I=I+1:GOTO 2110
2140 NEXT
2150 V(N)=R(N)/A(N,N):FOR I=N-1 TO 1 STEP -1
```

```
2160 Q=0:FOR J=I+1 TO N:Q=Q+A(I,J)*V(J)
2170 V(I)=(R(I)-Q)/A(I,I):NEXT:NEXT
2180 RETURN
```

EASY CHANGES

You may be surprised sometime to see the program fail completely and display this message:

?/0 ERROR IN 2150

This means your input coefficients (the A array) were ill-conditioned and no solution was possible. This can arise from a variety of causes; e.g. if one equation is an exact multiple of another, or if *every* coefficient of one particular unknown is zero. If you would like the program to print a diagnostic message in these cases, add this line.

2145 IF A(N,N)=0 THEN PRINT"ILL-CONDITIONED
INPUT":STOP

MAIN ROUTINES

200 - 220	Clears screen and displays program title.
300 - 430	Gets input from user and calculates the solution.
500 - 530	Displays the solution.
900 - 910	Subroutine to space and separate the output.
2000 - 2180	Subroutine to calculate the solution; consisting of the following parts:
2000	Forms solution if N=1.
2010 - 2140	Gaussian elimination.
2030 - 2100	Interchanges rows to achieve pivotal condensation.
2150 - 2180	Back substitution.

MAIN VARIABLES

I,J,K,L	Loop indices and subscripts.
N	Number of equations (thus number of unknowns also).
A	Doubly dimensioned array of the coefficients.
R	Array of right-hand-sides.
V	Array of the solution.
Q	Work variable.

SUGGESTED PROJECTS

1. The program modifies the A and R arrays while computing the answer. This means the original input cannot be displayed after it is input. Modify the program to save the information and enable the user to retrieve it after the solution is given.
2. Currently, a mistake in typing input cannot be corrected once the **ENTER** key is pressed after typing a number. Modify the program to allow correcting previous input.

STATS

PURPOSE

Ever think of yourself as a statistic? Many times we lament at how we have become just numbers in various computer memories, or we simply moan at our insurance premiums. To most people, the word "statistics" carries a negative connotation. To invoke statistics is almost to be deceitful, or at least de-humanizing. But really, we all use statistical ideas regularly. When we speak of things like "she was average height" or the "hottest weather in years," we are making observations in statistical terms. It is difficult not to encounter statistics in our lives, and this book is no exception.

Of course, when used properly, statistics can be a powerful, analytical tool. STATS analyzes a set of numerical data that you provide. It will compile your list, order it sequentially, and/or determine several statistical parameters which describe it.

This should prove useful in a wide variety of applications. Teachers might determine grades by analyzing a set of test scores. A businessman might determine marketing strategy by studying a list of sales to clients. Little leaguers always like to pore over the current batting and pitching averages. You can probably think of many other applications.

HOW TO USE IT

Before entering the data, the program will ask whether or not you wish to use identifiers with the data values. These identifiers can be anything associated with the data: e.g. names accompanying test scores, cities accompanying population values, corporations accompanying sales figures, etc. Hit the **Y** or **N** key to indicate yes or no regarding the use of identifiers. You do not need to hit the **ENTER** key.

Next, your data list must be entered. The program will prompt you for each value with a question mark. If identifiers are being used, you will be prompted for them before being asked for the associated data value. You may use any length character strings you desire for identifiers. However, if you limit them to a maximum of forty characters, the formatting of later output will be "cleaner."

Two special inputs, *END and *BACK, may be used at any time during this data input phase. They are applicable whether or not identifiers are being used. To signal the end of data, input the four character string, *END, in response to the (last) question mark. You must, of course, enter at least one data value.

If you discover that you have made a mistake, the five character string, *BACK, can be used to back up the input process. This will cause the program to re-prompt you for the previous entry. By successive uses of *BACK you can return to any previous position.

With the input completed, the program enters a command mode. You have four options to continue the run:

1) List the data in the order input
2) List the data in ranking order
3) Display statistical parameters
4) End the program

Simply input the number 1, 2, 3, or 4 to indicate your choice. If one of the first three is selected, the program will perform the selected function and return to this command mode to allow another choice. This will continue until you choose 4 to terminate the run. A description of the various options now follows.

Options 1 and 2 provide lists of the data. Option 1 does it in the original input order while option 2 sorts the data from highest value to lowest. In either case the identifiers, if used, will be shown alongside their associated values.

The lists are started by hitting any key when told to do so. Either list may be temporarily halted by hitting any key while the list is being displayed. This allows you to leisurely view data that might otherwise start scrolling off the screen. Simply hit any key to resume the display. This starting and stopping can be repeated as often as desired. When the display is completed, you must again hit a key to re-enter the command mode.

Option 3 produces a statistical analysis of your data. Various statistical parameters are calculated and displayed. The following is an explanation of some that may not be familiar to you.

Three measures of location, or central tendency, are provided. These are indicators of an "average" value. The *mean* is the sum of the values divided by the number of values. If the values are arranged in order from highest to lowest, the *median* is the middle value if the number of values is odd. If it is even, the median is the number halfway between the two middle values. The *midrange* is the number halfway between the largest and smallest values.

These measures of location give information about the average value of the data. However, they give no idea of how the data is dispersed or spread out around this "average." For that we need "measures of dispersion" or as they are sometimes called, "measures of variation." The simplest of these is the *range* which is just the difference between the highest and lowest data values. Two other closely related measures of dispersion are given: the *variance* and the *standard deviation*. The variance is defined as:

$$VA = \frac{\sum_{i=1}^{N} (V_i - M)^2}{N - 1}$$

Here N is the number of values, V_i is value i, M is the mean value. The standard deviation is simply the square root of the variance. We do not have space to detail a lengthy discussion of their theoretical use. For this refer to the bibliography. Basically, however, the smaller the standard deviation, the more all the data tends to be clustered close to the mean value.

One word of warning—the first time option 2 or 3 is selected, the program must take some time to sort the data into numerical order. The time this requires depends upon how many items are on the list and how badly they are out of sequence. Average times are twenty-five seconds for twenty-five items, almost two minutes for fifty items, about seven minutes for a hundred items. The TRS-80 will pause while this is occurring, so don't think it has hung up or fallen asleep! If you have several items on your list, this is the perfect chance to rob your refrigerator, make a quick phone call, or whatever.

SAMPLE RUN

The program describes its wares. It asks whether or not the operator wishes to use identifiers with his or her input data. The operator replies yes.

```
+++++++++++++++++++++++++++++++++++++++++++++++++++++++++++++++++++++++
   THE DATA MUST NOW BE ENTERED.

   FOR EACH DATA ITEM, ENTER ITS IDENTIFIER
(ABBREVIATED I.D.) AND ITS VALUE IN RESPONSE
TO THE SEPARATE QUESTION MARKS.

   IF YOU MAKE A MISTAKE, TYPE
#BACK  TO RE-ENTER THE LAST DATUM.

   WHEN THE LIST IS COMPLETED, TYPE
#END  TO TERMINATE THE LIST.
+++++++++++++++++++++++++++++++++++++++++++++++++++++++++++++++++++++++

DATA ITEM # 1
I.D.? _
```

```
          VALUE? 76

          DATA ITEM # 3
          I.D.? O'FURTH
          VALUE? 81.5

          DATA ITEM # 4
          I.D.? RUGG
          VALUE? 97.5

          DATA ITEM # 5
          I.D.? SAVAGE
          VALUE? 69

          DATA ITEM # 6
          I.D.? #END_
```

The operator completes entering the names and scores of those who took a programming aptitude test. The actual test was given to many people, but for demonstration purposes, only five names are used here. The special string, *END, is used to signal the end of the data.

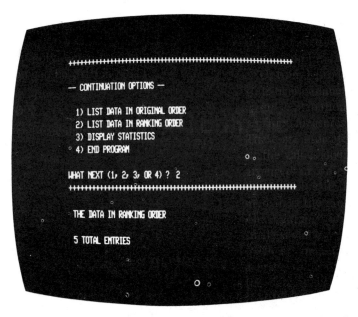

The operator requests that the list be sorted into numerical order. The program first shows the total number of entries.

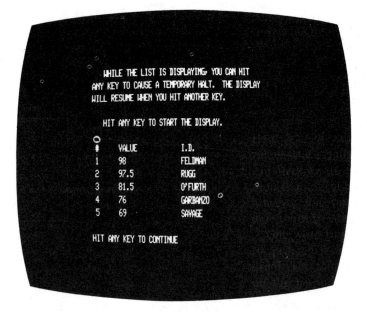

The operator hits a key to start the display and is then shown the data list in ranking order. The program waits for the pressing of a key to continue.

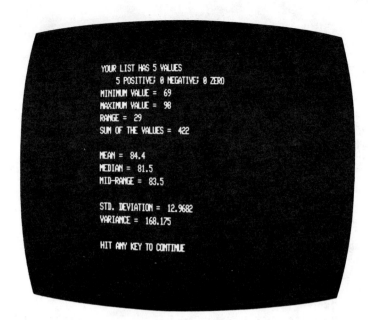

```
YOUR LIST HAS 5 VALUES
     5 POSITIVE; 0 NEGATIVE; 0 ZERO
MINIMUM VALUE =  69
MAXIMUM VALUE =  98
RANGE =  29
SUM OF THE VALUES =  422

MEAN =  84.4
MEDIAN =  81.5
MID-RANGE =  83.5

STD. DEVIATION =  12.9682
VARIANCE =  168.175

HIT ANY KEY TO CONTINUE
```

Later in the run, the operator selects continuation option 3. This calculates and displays the various statistical quantities.

PROGRAM LISTING

```
100 REM: STATS
110 REM: COPYRIGHT 1979 BY PHIL FELDMAN AND TOM RUGG
130 CLEAR 500
150 B$="*BACK":E$="*END"
160 MX=100
170 DIM D$(MX),V(MX),Z(MX)
180 Z(0)=0:N$=CHR$(32)
200 CLS:PRINT TAB(24);"S T A T S":PRINT
210 PRINT"    THIS PROGRAM DOES A
    STATISTICAL ANALYSIS ON A"
220 PRINT"LIST OF DATA VALUES.  IT WILL ORDER THE
    LIST AND"
230 PRINT"FIND SEVERAL STATISTICAL QUANTITIES
    DESCRIBING"
240 PRINT"THE DATA.":PRINT
250 PRINT"    THE DATA MAY BE ENTERED IN EITHER OF
    TWO FORMS:"
260 PRINT"    1) AS A SIMPLE LIST OF VALUES, OR"
270 PRINT"    2) WITH AN IDENTIFIER ACCOMPANYING EACH
    VALUE."
```

```
280 PRINT
290 PRINT"   WOULD YOU LIKE TO USE IDENTIFIERS WITH"
300 PRINT"YOUR INPUT (Y OR N) ? ";
310 R$=INKEY$:IF R$="" THEN 310
320 IF R$="Y" THEN PRINT"YES":F=1:GOTO 400
330 IF R$="N" THEN PRINT"NO":F=0:GOTO 400
340 GOTO 310
400 FOR J=1 TO 300:NEXT:GOSUB 2100
410 PRINT"   THE DATA MUST NOW BE ENTERED.":PRINT
420 IF F=1 THEN 450
430 PRINT"   ENTER EACH VALUE SEPARATELY IN RESPONSE TO"
440 PRINT"THE QUESTION MARK.":GOSUB 2000:GOTO 500
450 PRINT"   FOR EACH DATA ITEM, ENTER ITS IDENTIFIER"
460 PRINT"(ABBREVIATED I.D.) AND ITS VALUE IN RESPONSE"
470 PRINT"TO THE SEPARATE QUESTION MARKS.":GOSUB 2000
500 GOSUB 2100:FOR J=1 TO 9:R$=INKEY$:NEXT:N=1
510 IF N<1 THEN N=1
520 PRINT:PRINT"DATA ITEM #";N
530 IF F=0 THEN D$(N)=N$:GOTO 570
540 INPUT"I.D.";R$:IF R$=E$ THEN 700
550 IF R$=B$ THEN N=N-1:GOTO 510
560 D$(N)=R$
570 INPUT"VALUE";R$:IF R$=E$ THEN 700
580 IF R$=B$ AND F=1 THEN 520
590 IF R$=B$ THEN N=N-1:GOTO 510
600 V(N)=VAL(R$)
610 IF N=MX THEN PRINT ELSE 630
620 PRINT"** NO MORE DATA ALLOWED! **":N=N+1:GOTO 700
630 N=N+1:GOTO 510
700 N=N-1:IF N=0 THEN PRINT ELSE 720
710 PRINT"** NO DATA -- RUN ABORTED **":END
720 GOSUB 2100
730 PRINT:PRINT"-- CONTINUATION OPTIONS --":PRINT
740 PRINT"   1) LIST DATA IN ORIGINAL ORDER"
750 PRINT"   2) LIST DATA IN RANKING ORDER"
760 PRINT"   3) DISPLAY STATISTICS"
770 PRINT"   4) END PROGRAM
780 PRINT:PRINT"WHAT NEXT (1, 2, 3, OR 4) ? ";
790 R$=INKEY$:IF R$="" THEN 790
800 R=VAL(R$):IF R<1 OR R>4 THEN 790
810 PRINT R:IF R=4 THEN END
820 ON R GOSUB 1000,1200,1500
830 GOTO 720
1000 GOSUB 2100:PRINT
1010 PRINT"   THE ORIGINAL DATA ORDER":PRINT
```

```
1020 PRINT N;"TOTAL ENTRIES":GOSUB 2300
1030 PRINT:PRINT" #      VALUE";
1040 IF F=0 THEN PRINT
1050 IF F=1 THEN PRINT STRING$(12,32);"I.D."
1060 FOR J=1 TO N:FOR K=1 TO 100:NEXT
1070 PRINT J;TAB(6);V(J);TAB(24);D$(J)
1080 GOSUB 2500
1090 NEXT:GOSUB 2900:RETURN
1200 GOSUB 2100:PRINT
1210 PRINT" THE DATA IN RANKING ORDER":PRINT
1220 PRINT N;"TOTAL ENTRIES"
1230 GOSUB 2700
1280 GOSUB 2300:PRINT:PRINT" #      VALUE";
1290 IF F=0 THEN PRINT
1300 IF F=1 THEN PRINT STRING$(12,32);"I.D."
1310 FOR J=1 TO N:FOR K=1 TO 100:NEXT
1320 PRINT J;TAB(6);V(Z(J));TAB(24);D$(Z(J))
1330 GOSUB 2500
1340 NEXT:GOSUB 2900:RETURN
1500 GOSUB 2100:PRINT
1510 PRINT TAB(8);"STATISTICAL ANALYSIS":PRINT
1520 FOR J=1 TO 800:NEXT:PRINT"YOUR LIST HAS";N;"VALUES"
1530 NP=0:NN=0:NZ=0:SQ=0:W=0
1540 FOR J=1 TO N:W=W+V(J):SQ=SQ+V(J)*V(J)
1550 IF V(J)>0 THEN NP=NP+1:GOTO 1590
1560 IF V(J)<0 THEN NN=NN+1:GOTO 1590
1570 NZ=NZ+1
1590 NEXT:M=W/N:VA=0:IF N=1 THEN 1610
1600 VA=(SQ-N*M*M)/(N-1)
1610 SD=SQR(VA)
1620 PRINT "   ";NP;"POSITIVE;";NN;"NEGATIVE;";NZ;"ZERO"
1630 GOSUB 2700:PRINT"MINIMUM VALUE = ";V(Z(N))
1640 PRINT"MAXIMUM VALUE = ";V(Z(1))
1650 PRINT"RANGE = ";V(Z(1))-V(Z(N))
1660 PRINT"SUM OF THE VALUES = ";W:PRINT
1670 PRINT"MEAN = ";M
1680 Q=INT(N/2)+1:MD=V(Z(Q)):IF N/2>INT(N/2) THEN 1700
1690 MD=(V(Z(Q))+V(Z(Q-1)))/2
1700 PRINT"MEDIAN = ";MD
1710 PRINT"MID-RANGE = ";(V(Z(1))+V(Z(N)))/2
1720 PRINT:PRINT"STD. DEVIATION = ";SD
1730 PRINT"VARIANCE = ";VA
1740 GOSUB 2900:RETURN
2000 PRINT:PRINT"    IF YOU MAKE A MISTAKE, TYPE"
2010 PRINT B$;"   TO RE-ENTER THE LAST DATUM."
```

```
2020 PRINT:PRINT"   WHEN THE LIST IS COMPLETED, TYPE"
2030 PRINT E$;"   TO TERMINATE THE LIST.":RETURN
2100 FOR J=1 TO 64:PRINT"+";:NEXT:RETURN
2300 PRINT:PRINT"   WHILE THE LIST IS
     DISPLAYING, YOU CAN HIT"
2310 PRINT"ANY KEY TO CAUSE A TEMPORARY HALT.   THE
     DISPLAY"
2320 PRINT"WILL RESUME WHEN YOU HIT ANOTHER KEY."
2330 PRINT:PRINT"   HIT ANY KEY TO START THE DISPLAY."
2340 R$=INKEY$:IF R$="" THEN 2340
2350 RETURN
2500 R$=INKEY$:IF R$="" THEN RETURN
2510 R$=INKEY$:IF R$="" THEN 2510
2520 RETURN
2700 IF Z(0)=1 THEN RETURN
2710 FOR J=1 TO N:Z(J)=J:NEXT:IF N=1 THEN RETURN
2720 NM=N-1:FOR K=1 TO N:FOR J=1 TO NM:N1=Z(J)
2730 N2=Z(J+1):IF V(N1)>V(N2) THEN 2750
2740 Z(J+1)=N1:Z(J)=N2
2750 NEXT:NEXT:Z(0)=1:RETURN
2900 PRINT:PRINT"HIT ANY KEY TO CONTINUE"
2910 R$=INKEY$:IF R$="" THEN 2910
2920 RETURN
```

EASY CHANGES

1. The program arrays are currently dimensioned to allow a maximum of 100 data items. The total storage required for the program depends on the maximum dimension parameter, MX; whether or not identifiers are being used; and if so, on the length of a typical identifier. A 16K TRS-80 has enough storage for 500 data items with associated identifiers of 10 character length. If no identifiers are being used, over 900 data values can be accommodated. If there are more than 100 items in your application, you will need to adjust the value of MX in line 160 and change the argument of the CLEAR function in line 130. To achieve up to 900 data items with no identifiers, make these changes:

> 130 CLEAR 1000
> 160 MX=900

To achieve up to 500 data items with 10 character identifiers, make these changes:

$$130 \text{ CLEAR } 5000$$
$$160 \text{ MX}=500$$

Note that the argument of the CLEAR function should be greater than or equal to the value of MX times the average identifier length. Even with no identifiers, this argument must be at least the value of MX. Should an OS error (out of string space) occur when running the program, try increasing the argument of the CLEAR function and/or lowering the value of MX, if possible.

2. Because of possible conflicts with identifiers in your list, you may wish to change the special strings that signal termination of data input and/or the backing up of data input. These are controlled by the variables E$ and B$, respectively. They are set in line 150. If you wish to terminate the data with /DONE/ and to back up with /LAST/ for example, line 150 should be:

$$150 \text{ B\$}=\text{"/LAST/"}:\text{E\$}=\text{"/DONE/"}$$

3. You may wish to see your lists sorted from smallest value to largest value instead of the other way around, as done now. This can be accomplished by changing the "greater than" sign ($>$) in line 2730 to a "less than" sign ($<$). Thus:

$$2730 \text{ N2}=\text{Z}(\text{J}+1):\text{IF } \text{V}(\text{N1})<\text{V}(\text{N2}) \text{ THEN } 2750$$

This will, however, cause a few funny things to happen to the statistics. The real minimum value will be displayed under the heading "maximum" and vice-versa. Also, the range will have its correct magnitude but with an erroneous minus sign in front. To cure these afflictions, make these changes also:

```
1630 GOSUB 2700:PRINT"MINIMUM VALUE = ";V(Z(1))
1640 PRINT"MAXIMUM VALUE = ";V(Z(N))
1650 PRINT"RANGE = ";V(Z(N))-V(Z(1))
```

MAIN ROUTINES

130 - 180	Initializes constants and dimensioning.
200 - 340	Displays messages, determines if identifiers will be used.
400 - 630	Gets data from the user.
700 - 710	Checks that input contains at least one value.
720 - 830	Command mode - gets user's next option and does a GOSUB to it.

MAIN VARIABLES

MX	Maximum number of data values allowed.
D$(MX)	String array of identifiers.
V(MX)	Array of the data values.
Z(MX)	Array of the sorting order.
N	Number of data values in current application.
F	Flag on identifier usage (1=yes, 0=no).
B$	Flag string to back up the input.
E$	Flag string to signal end of the input.
N$	String for a null identifier.
R$	User input string.
NM	N−1.
R	Continuation option.
NP	Number of positive values.
NN	Number of negative values.
NZ	Number of zero values.
W	Sum of the values.
SQ	Sum of the squares of the values.
M	Mean value.
MD	Median of the values.
VA	Variance.
SD	Standard deviation.
J,K	Loop indices.
N1,N2	Possible data locations to interchange during sorting.
Q	Work variable.

SUGGESTED PROJECTS

1. The sorting algorithm used in the program is efficient only when the number of list items is fairly small—less than

twenty-five or so. This is because it does not do checking along the way to see when the list becomes fully sorted. If your lists tend to be longer than twenty-five items, you might wish to use another sorting algorithm more appropriate for longer lists. Try researching other sorts and incorporating them into the program. To get you started, try these changes:

```
2720 Q=0:FOR J=1 TO N−1:N1=Z(J)
2730 N2=Z(J+1):IF V(N1)>=V(N2) THEN 2750
2745 Q=1
2750 NEXT:IF Q=1 THEN 2720
2760 Z(0)=1:RETURN
```

If your lists are short, this routine will probably be a little slower than the current one. However, for longer lists it will save proportionately more and more time.

2. Because the INPUT statement is used when entering identifiers, commas cannot be used inside identifier names. Basic will ignore anything entered past the comma. This can be circumvented if you use quotes around the identifier name, but you may forget to do this. By modifying the input routine to use a series of INKEY$ commands, you can build up the identifier strings piecemeal and allow imbedded commas. Modify the appropriate routine to do this.

3. Many other statistical parameters exist to describe this kind of data. Research them and add some that might be useful to you. One such idea is classifying the data. This consists of dividing the range into a number of equal classes and then counting how many values fall into each class.

Section 6
Miscellaneous Programs

INTRODUCTION TO MISCELLANEOUS PROGRAMS

These programs show how simple programs can do interesting things. All of them have a mathematical flavor. They are short and, as such, would be useful for study for those just learning BASIC in particular or programming in general.

Monte Carlo simulation involves programming the computer to conduct an experiment. (It doesn't involve high-stakes gambling!) PI shows how this technique can be used to calculate an approximation to the famous mathematical constant pi.

PYTHAG will find all right triangles with integral side lengths. A clever algorithm is utilized to do this.

Have you ever looked around your classroom or club meeting and wondered if any two people had the same birthdate? BIRTHDAY will show you what the surprising odds are.

Very high precision arithmetic can be done on the TRS-80 with the proper "know-how." POWERS will calculate the values of integers raised to various powers; not to the TRS-80's "normal" six or sixteen digit precision, but up to 250 full digits of precision.

BIRTHDAY

PURPOSE

Suppose you are in a room full of people. What is the probability that two or more of these people have the same birthday? How many people have to be in the room before the probability becomes greater than 50 per cent? We are talking only about the month and day of birth, not the year.

This is a fairly simple problem to solve, even without a computer. With a computer to help with the calculations, it becomes very easy. What makes the problem interesting is that the correct answer is nowhere near what most people immediately guess. Before reading further, what do you think? How many people have to be in a room before there is better than a 50-50 chance of birthday duplication? 50? 100? 200?

HOW TO USE IT

When you RUN the program, it starts by displaying headings over two columns of numbers that will be shown. The left column is the number of people in the room, starting with one. The right column is the probability of birthday duplication.

For one person, of course, the probability is zero, since there is no one else with a possible duplicate birthday. For two people, the probability is simply the decimal equivalent of 1/365 (note that we assume a 365 day year, and an equal likelihood that each person could have been born on any day of the year).

What is the probability of duplication when there are three people in the room? No, not just 2/365. It's actually

$$1 - (364/365 \text{ times } 363/365)$$

This is simply one minus the probability of *no* duplicate birthdays.

The probability for four people is

$$1 - (364/365 \text{ times } 363/365 \text{ times } 362/365)$$

The calculation continues like this, adding a new term for each additional person in the room. You will find that the result (probability of duplication) exceeds .50 surprisingly fast.

The program continues with the calculation until there are 60 people in the room. You will have to BREAK the program long before that to see the point where the probability first exceeds 50 per cent.

SAMPLE RUN

```
NO. OF        PROB. OF 2 OR MORE
PEOPLE        WITH SAME BIRTHDAY
  1               0
  2               2.73973E-03
  3               8.2041E-03
  4               .0163558
  5               .0271355
  6               .0404624
  .
  .
  .
(etc.)
```

PROGRAM LISTING

```
100 REM: COINCIDENT BIRTHDAY PROBABILITY PROBLEM
110 REM: COPYRIGHT 1979 BY TOM RUGG AND PHIL FELDMAN
120 CLS
130 PRINT"NO. OF      PROB. OF 2 OR MORE"
140 PRINT"PEOPLE      WITH SAME BIRTHDAY"
150 Q=1
160 FOR N=1 TO 60
170 PRINT N,1-Q
180 Q=Q*(365-N)/365
190 NEXT N
200 END
```

EASY CHANGES

1. Change the constant value of 60 in line 160 to alter the range of the number of people in the calculation. For example, change it to 100 and watch how fast the probability approaches 1.
2. Insert this line to make double precision calculations:

125 DEFDBL Q

MAIN ROUTINES

120 - 140	Displays headings.
150	Initializes Q to 1.
160 - 190	Calculates probability of no duplication, then displays probability of duplication.

MAIN VARIABLES

N	Number of people in the room.
Q	Probability of no duplication of birthdays.

SUGGESTED PROJECTS

Modify the program to allow for leap years in the calculation, instead of assuming 365 days per year.

PI

PURPOSE AND DISCUSSION

The Greek letter pi, π represents probably the most famous constant in mathematical history. It occurs regularly in many different areas of mathematics. It is best known as the constant appearing in several geometric relationships involving the circle. The circumference of a circle of radius r is $2\pi r$, while the area enlosed by the circle is πr^2.

Being a transcendental number, pi cannot be expressed exactly by any number of decimal digits. To nine significant digits, its value is 3.14159265. Over many centuries, man has devised many different methods to calculate pi.

This program uses a valuable, modern technique known as computer simulation. The name "simulation" is rather self-explanatory; the computer performs an experiment for us. This is often desirable for many different reasons. The experiment may be cheaper, less dangerous, or more accurate to run on a computer. It may even be impossible to do in "real life." Usually, however, the reason is that the speed of the computer allows the simulation to be performed many times faster than actually conducting the real experiment.

This program simulates the results of throwing darts at a specially constructed dartboard. Consider Figure 1 which shows the peculiar square dartboard involved. The curved arc, outlining the shaded area, is that of a circle with the center in the lower left hand corner. The sides of the square, and thus the radius of the circle, are considered to have a length of 1.

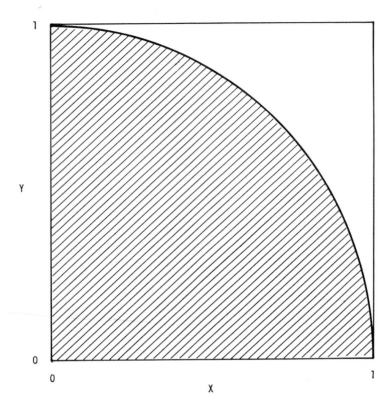

Figure 1. The PI Dartboard

Suppose we were able to throw darts at this square target in such a way that each dart had an equal chance of landing anywhere within the square. A certain percentage of darts would result in "hits," i.e. land in the shaded area. The expected value of this percentage is simply the area of the shaded part divided by the area of the entire square.

The area of the shaded part is one fourth of the area the entire circle would enclose if the arc were continued to completely form the circle. Recall the area of a circle is πr^2 where r is the radius. In our case, r=1, and the area of the entire circle would simply be π. The shaded area of the dartboard is one fourth of this entire circle and thus has an area of $\pi/4$. The area of the square is s^2, where s is the length of a side. On our dartboard, s=1, and the area of the whole dartboard is 1.

Now the expected ratio of "hits" to darts thrown can be expressed

$$RATIO = \frac{\#hits}{\# \ thrown} = \frac{shaded \ area}{entire \ area} = \frac{\pi/4}{1} = \frac{\pi}{4}$$

So we now have an experimental way to approximate the value of π. We perform the experiment and compute the ratio of "hits" observed. We then multiply this number by 4 and we have calculated π experimentally.

But instead of actually constructing the required dartboard and throwing real darts, we will let the TRS-80 do the job. The program "throws" each dart by selecting a separate random number between 0 and 1 for the X and Y coordinates of each dart. This is accomplished by using the built-in RND function of Basic. A "dart" is in the shaded area if $X^2 + Y^2 < 1$ for it.

So the program grinds away, continually throwing darts and determining the ratio of "hits." This ratio is multiplied by 4 to arrive at an empirical approximation to π.

HOW TO USE IT

The program requires only one input from you. This is the "sample size for printing," i.e. how many darts it should throw before printing its current results. Any value of one or higher is acceptable.

After you input this number, the program will commence the simulation and display its results. A cumulative total of "hits," darts thrown, and the current approximation to π will be displayed for each multiple of the sample size.

This will continue until you press the **BREAK** key. When you are satisfied with the total number of darts thrown, press the **BREAK** key to terminate the program execution.

SAMPLE RUN

```
           A DARTBOARD PI CALCULATOR

SAMPLE SIZE FOR PRINTING? 150
```

A DARTBOARD PI CALCULATOR

# HITS	# THROWN	PI
116	150	3.09333
230	300	3.06667
337	450	2.99556
462	600	3.08
584	750	3.11467
697	900	3.09778
818	1050	3.11619
940	1200	3.13333
1060	1350	3.14074
1179	1500	3.144

(BREAK key pressed)

PROGRAM LISTING

```
100 REM: PI
110 REM: COPYRIGHT 1979 BY PHIL FELDMAN AND TOM RUGG
150 RANDOM:CLEAR 50:DEFINT J
160 T=0:TH=0
300 GOSUB 600
310 INPUT"SAMPLE SIZE FOR PRINTING";NP
320 NP=INT(NP):IF NP<1 THEN 300
330 GOSUB 600
340 PRINT"# HITS       # THROWN";TAB(36);"PI"
400 GOSUB 500:TH=TH+NH:T=T+NP:P=4*TH/T
410 PRINT TH,T,P
420 GOTO 400
500 NH=0:FOR J=1 TO NP
510 X=RND(0):Y=RND(0)
520 IF (X*X+Y*Y)<1 THEN NH=NH+1
530 NEXT:RETURN
600 CLS:PRINT TAB(6);
610 PRINT"A DARTBOARD PI CALCULATOR"
620 PRINT:RETURN
```

EASY CHANGES

1. If you want the program to always use a fixed sample size, change line 310 to read

    310 NP=150

    Of course, the value of 150 given here may be changed to whatever you wish. With this change, line 320 is not needed and may be deleted.

2. If you want the program to stop by itself after a certain number of darts have been thrown, add the following two lines:

    315 INPUT"TOTAL # DARTS TO THROW";ND
    415 IF T>=ND THEN END

    This will ask the operator how many total darts should be thrown, and then terminate the program when they have been thrown.

3. The calculated values of pi will be shown with six digits of precision as is standard for single precision variables in Level II Basic. This is sufficient for the degree of accuracy possible in this simulation. However, you might want to try the following change to see the effects of computing pi to double precision:

    155 DEFDBL P-Z

MAIN ROUTINES

150 - 160	Initializes constants.
300 - 340	Gets operator input, displays column headings.
400 - 420	Calculates and displays results.
500 - 530	Throws NP darts and records number of "hits."
600 - 620	Clears screen and displays program title.

MAIN VARIABLES

T	Total darts thrown.
TH	Total "hits."
NP	Sample size for printing.
NH	Number of hits in one group of NP darts.
P	Calculated value of pi.

X,Y   Random-valued coordinates of a dart.

J   Loop index.

SUGGESTED PROJECTS

1. Calculate the percentage error in the program's calculation of pi and display it with the other results. You will need to define a variable, say PI, which is set to the value of pi. Then the percentage error, PE, can be calculated as:

$$PE = 100*ABS(P - PI)/PI$$

2. The accuracy of this simulation is highly dependent on the quality of the computer's random number generator. Try researching different algorithms for pseudo random number generation. Then try incorporating them into the program. Change line 510 to use the new algorithm(s). This can actually be used as a test of the various random number generators. Gruenberger's book, referenced in the bibliography, contains good material on various pseudo random number generators.

POWERS

PURPOSE

By now you have probably learned that the TRS-80 keeps track of six significant digits when dealing with numbers. For integers less than one million (1,000,000), the TRS-80 can retain the precise value of the number. But for larger integers the TRS-80 only keeps track of the most significant (leftmost) six digits, plus the exponent. This means, of course, that there is no way you can use the TRS-80 to deal with precise integers greater than one million, right?

Wrong.

Of course, you say. You can use double precision variables to get precise results up to 16 digits. So, undoubtedly, the absolute limit on the TRS-80 is 16 digit integers, right?

Wrong again.

This program calculates either factorials or successive powers of an integer, and can display precise results that are up to 250 digits long. By using a "multiple-precision arithmetic" technique, this program can tell you *exactly* what 973 to the 47th power is, for example.

HOW TO USE IT

The program first asks you how many digits long you want the largest number to be. This can be any integer from 1 to 250. So, for example, if you enter 40, you will get answers up to forty digits long.

Next you are asked for the value of N. If you respond with a value of 1, you are requesting to be shown all the factorials that will fit in the number of digits you specified. First you will get one factorial, then two factorial, and so on. In case you have forgotten, three factorial is 3 times 2 times 1, or 6. Four factorial is 4 times 3 times 2 times 1, or 24.

If you enter an N in the range from 2 through 100,000, you are requesting the successive powers of that number up to the limit of digits you specified. So, if you provide an N of 23, you will get 23 to the first power, then 23 squared, then 23 cubed, and so on.

Finally, after it has displayed the largest number that will fit within the number of digits you entered, the program starts over. The larger the number of digits you ask for, the longer it will take the program to calculate each number.

SAMPLE RUN

The operator wants answers up to 40 digits long in the calculations of the powers of 98789. The program calculates numbers up to 98789^8 and then asks for the number of digits again (in preparation for the next calculation the operator requests).

PROGRAM LISTING

```
100 REM: POWERS AND FACTORIALS
110 REM: COPYRIGHT 1979 BY TOM RUGG AND PHIL FELDMAN
120 CLS:CLEAR 50:DEFINT J,D
130 PRINT TAB(10);"POWERS AND FACTORIALS"
140 PRINT
160 DIM N(255)
170 INPUT"NUMBER OF DIGITS";M
180 M=INT(M):IF M>250 OR M<1 THEN 170
190 INPUT"N";N
200 N=INT(N)
210 IF N<1 OR N>100000 THEN 190
220 PRINT
230 F=0:IF N=1 THEN F=1:PRINT"FACTORIALS"
240 IF F=0 THEN PRINT"POWERS OF";N
250 T=10:K=1:N(0)=N
260 FOR J=0 TO M
270 IF N(J)<T THEN 300
280 Q=INT(N(J)/T):W=N(J)-Q*T
290 N(J)=W:N(J+1)=N(J+1)+Q
300 NEXT
310 J=M+1
320 IF N(J)=0 THEN J=J-1:GOTO 320
330 IF J>=M THEN 500
340 D=0:PRINT K;TAB(7);
350 N$=STR$(N(J)):N$=RIGHT$(N$,1)
360 D=D+1:IF D>50 THEN D=1:PRINT:PRINT TAB(7);
370 PRINT N$;:J=J-1:IF J>=0 THEN 350
380 IF F=1 THEN N=N+1
390 K=K+1:PRINT
400 FOR J=0 TO M:N(J)=N(J)*N:NEXT
410 GOTO 260
500 FOR J=1 TO 255:N(J)=0:NEXT
510 M=0:N=0:PRINT:GOTO 170
```

EASY CHANGES

1. To change the program so that it always uses, say, fifty digit numbers, remove lines 170 and 180, and insert this line:

   170 M=50

2. To clear the screen before the output begins being displayed, change line 220 to say:

   220 CLS

3. If 250 digits isn't enough for you, you can go higher. For 500 digits, make these changes:

    a. In line 160, change the 255 into 505.
    b. In line 180, change the 250 into 500.
    c. In line 500, change the 255 into 505.

MAIN ROUTINES

120 - 160	Displays title. Sets up array for calculations.
170 - 240	Asks for number of digits and N. Checks validity of responses. Displays heading.
250	Initializes variables for calculations.
260 - 300	Performs "carrying" in N array so each element has a value no larger than 9.
310 - 320	Scans backwards through N array for first non-zero element.
330	Checks to see if this value would be larger than the number of digits requested.
340 - 370	Displays counter and number. Goes to second line if necessary.
380 - 390	Prepares to multiply by N to get next number.
400 - 410	Multiplies each digit in N array by N. Goes back to line 260.
500 - 510	Zeroes out N array in preparation for next request. Goes back to 170.

MAIN VARIABLES

N	Array in which calculations are made.
M	Number of digits of precision requested by operator.
N	Starting value. If 1, factorials. If greater than 1, powers of N.
F	Set to zero if powers, 1 if factorials.
T	Constant value of 10.
K	Counter of current power or factorial.
J	Subscript variable.
Q,W	Temporary variables used in reducing each integer position in the N array to a value from 0 to 9.

D   Number of digits displayed so far on the current line (maximum is 50).

N$ String variable used to convert each digit into displayable format.

SUGGESTED PROJECTS

1. Determine the largest N that could be used without errors entering into the calculation (because of intermediate results exceeding one million), then modify line 210 to permit values that large to be entered. Then declare the necessary variables to be double prcision, and determine how large N can be.

2. Create a series of subroutines that can add, subtract, multiply, divide, and exchange numbers in two arrays, using a technique like the one used here. Then you can perform high precision calculations by means of a series of GOSUB statements.

PYTHAG

PURPOSE

Remember the Pythagorean Theorem? It says that the sum of the squares of the two legs of a right triangle is equal to the square of the hypotenuse. Expressed as a formula, it is $a^2 + b^2 = c^2$. The most commonly remembered example of this is the 3-4-5 right triangle ($3^2 + 4^2 = 5^2$). Of course, there are an infinite number of other right triangles.

This program displays integer values of a, b, and c that result in right triangles.

HOW TO USE IT

To use this program, all you need to do is RUN it and watch the "Pythagorean triplets" (sets of values for a, b, and c) come out. The program displays thirteen sets of values on each screen, and then waits for you to press any key (except **BREAK**) before it continues with the next thirteen. It will go on indefinitely until you press the **BREAK** key.

The left-hand column shows the count of the number of sets of triplets produced, and the other three columns are the values of a, b, and c.

The sequence is which the triplets are produced is not too obvious, so we will explain how the numbers are generated.

It has been proved that the following technique will generate all *primitive* Pythagorean triplets. ("Primitive" means that no set is an exact multiple of another.) If you have two positive integers called R and S such that:

1. R is greater than S,
2. R and S are of opposite parity (one is odd and the other is even), and
3. R and S are relatively prime (they have no common integer divisors except 1),

then a, b, and c can be found as follows:

$a = R^2 - S^2$
$b = 2RS$
$c = R^2 + S^2$

The program starts with a value of 2 for R. It generates all possible S values for that R (starting at R−1 and then decreasing) and then adds one to R and continues. So, the first set of triplets is created when R is 2 and S is 1, the second set when R is 3 and S is 2, and so on.

SAMPLE RUN

```
                   **** PYTHAGOREAN TRIPLETS ****
      COUNT              --A--              --B--              --C--
        1                  3                  4                  5
        2                  5                 12                 13
        3                  7                 24                 25
        4                 15                  8                 17
        5                  9                 40                 41
        6                 21                 20                 29
        7                 11                 60                 61
        8                 35                 12                 37
        9                 13                 84                 85
       10                 33                 56                 65
       11                 45                 28                 53
       12                 15                112                113
       13                 39                 80                 89
      PRESS ANY KEY TO CONTINUE
```

PROGRAM LISTING

```
100 REM: PYTHAGOREAN TRIPLETS
110 REM: COPYRIGHT 1979 BY TOM RUGG AND PHIL FELDMAN
120 CLEAR 50:DEFDBL A-Z
130 R=2:K=1:D=0
150 GOSUB 350
180 S=R-1
190 A=R*R-S*S
200 B=2*R*S
210 C=R*R+S*S
220 PRINT K,A,B,C
230 K=K+1:D=D+1:GOTO 400
240 S=S-2:IF S<=0 THEN R=R+1:GOTO 180
250 S1=S
255 B1=R
260 N=INT(B1/S1)
270 R1=B1-(S1*N)
280 IF R1<>0 THEN B1=S1:S1=R1:GOTO 260
300 IF S1<>1 THEN 240
320 GOTO 190
350 CLS
360 PRINT TAB(10);"**** PYTHAGOREAN TRIPLETS ****"
380 PRINT"COUNT","--A--","--B--","--C--"
390 RETURN
400 IF D<13 THEN 240
420 PRINT"PRESS ANY KEY TO CONTINUE";
430 IF INKEY$="" THEN 430
440 GOSUB 350
450 D=0
460 GOTO 240
```

EASY CHANGES

1. Alter the starting value of R in line 130. Instead of 2, try 50 or 100.
2. If you want, you can change the number of sets of triplets displayed on each screen. Change the 13 in line 400 to a 10, for example. You probably won't want to try a value greater than 13, since that would cause the column headings to roll off the screen.
3. To make the program continue without requiring you to press a key for the next screen of values, insert either of these lines:

405 GOTO 440

or

405 GOTO 450

The first will display headings for each screen. The second
will only display the headings at the beginning of the run.

MAIN ROUTINES

130	Initializes variables.
150	Displays the title and column headings.
180	Calculates first value of S for current R value.
190 - 210	Calculates A, B, and C.
220 - 230	Displays one line of values. Adds to counters.
240	Calculates next S value. If no more, calculates next R value.
250 - 300	Determines if R and S are relatively prime.
350 - 390	Subroutine to display title and column headings.
400 - 460	Checks if screen is full yet. If so, waits for key to be pressed.

MAIN VARIABLES

R,S	See explanation in "How To Use It."
K	Count of total number of sets displayed.
D	Count of number of sets displayed on one screen.
A,B,C	Lengths of the three sides of the triangle.
S1,B1, R1,N	Used in determining if R and S are relatively prime.

SUGGESTED PROJECTS

1. In addition to displaying K, A, B, and C on each line, display
   R and S. You will have to squeeze the columns closer together.
2. Because this program uses integer values that get increasingly
   large, eventually some will exceed the TRS-80's double precision integer capacity and produce incorrect results. Can you
   determine when this will be? Modify the program to stop
   when this occurs.

Appendix I
Memory Usage

Each of the programs in this book will fit in a Radio Shack TRS-80 Level II computer that has 16K or more of user memory. If your TRS-80 has only 4K of user memory, you'll find that the great majority of the programs will still fit in your computer with no changes. A few other programs will require minor changes that are discussed in the text of the corresponding chapters.

Based on our estimates, here are the programs that will *not* fit in a 4K TRS-80:

Programs that will probably fit in a 4K TRS-80 if you make fairly extensive changes:
(for example, eliminating unnecessary spaces from program statements, reducing the length of text literals where possible, deleting REM statements, removing unneeded options, reducing array sizes where possible, etc.)

CHECKBOOK

Programs that are too large to be compressed into 4K:

DECIDE, JOT, STATS

Bibliography

BOOKS

Bell, R. C., *Board and Table Games From Many Civilizations*, Oxford University Press, London, 1969. (WARI)

Brown, Jerald R., *Instant BASIC*, Dymax, Menlo Park, Calif., 1977. (Self-teaching text on the BASIC language)

Cohen, Daniel, *Biorhythms in Your Life*, Fawcett Publications, Greenwich, Connecticut, 1976. (BIORHYTHM)

Crow, E. L., David, F. A., and Maxfield, M. W., *Statistics Manual*, Dover Publications, New York, 1960. (STATS)

Croxton, F. E., Crowden, D. J., and Klein, S., *Applied General Statistics* (Third Edition), Prentice-Hall, Englewood Cliffs, N. J., 1967. (STATS)

Gruenberger, Fred J., and Jaffray, George, *Problems for Computer Solution*, John Wiley and Sons, New York, 1965. (BIRTHDAY, PI)

Gruenberger, Fred J., and McCracken, Daniel D., *Introduction to Electronic Computers*, John Wiley and Sons, New York, 1961. (MILEAGE, PI, PYTHAG, WARI as Oware)

Hildebrand, F. B., *Introduction to Numerical Analysis*, McGraw-Hill, New York, 1956. (CURVE, DIFFEQN, INTEGRATE, SIMEQN)

Kuo, S. S., *Computer Applications of Numerical Methods*, Addison-Wesley, Reading, Massachusetts, 1972. (CURVE, DIFFEQN, INTEGRATE, SIMEQN)

McCracken, Daniel D., and Dorn, W. S., *Numerical Methods And FORTRAN Programming*, John Wiley and Sons, New York, 1964. (CURVE, DIFFEQN, INTEGRATE, SIMEQN)

Shefter, Harry, *Faster Reading Self-Taught*, Washington Square Press, New York, 1960. (TACHIST)

PERIODICALS

Feldman, Phil, and Rugg, Tom, "Pass the Buck", *Kilobaud*, July 1977, pp. 90-96. (DECIDE)

Fliegel, H. F., and Van Flandern, T. C., "A Machine Algorithm for Processing Calendar Dates", *Communications of the ACM*, October, 1968, p. 657. (BIORHYTHM)

All of the programs in this book have been tested carefully and are working correctly to the best of our knowledge. However, we take no responsibility for any losses which may be suffered as a result of errors or misuse. You must bear the responsibility of verifying each program's accuracy and applicability for your purposes.

If you want to get a copy of an errata sheet that lists corrections for any errors or ambiguities we have found to date, send one dollar ($1.00) and a self addressed stamped envelope (SASE) to the address below. Ask for errata for this book (by name). In addition to any errors we can tell you about, we'll send you an entertaining new program for the TRS-80.

If you think you've found an error, please let us know. If you want an answer, include a SASE.

Tom Rugg and Phil Feldman
Errata—32 Programs for the TRS-80
P.O. Box 24815
Los Angeles, CA 90024